She's a Tale in My Story

A Memoir

by

Jody Unrau

Copyright © 2025 by Jody Unrau

All rights reserved.

No part of this publication may be reproduced, stored in a retrieval system, or transmitted in any form or by any means—electronic, mechanical, photocopying, recording, or otherwise—without the prior written permission of the author, except in the case of brief quotations used in reviews or critical articles.

This is a work of nonfiction based on the author's personal memories and experiences. Some names and identifying details have been changed to protect privacy.

For information, speaking inquiries, or workshop requests, please visit:

www.embraceyourreflection.com

Cover design by Casey Lanxon-Whitford

First edition, 2025

Printed in Canada

ISBN: 9798289155191

This book is protected under the Canadian Copyright Act. All rights reserved by the author

For the girl I once was.

The younger version of me who carried silent battles, wore a smile as armor, and kept going despite the storms she faced.

You were resilient long before you had the words for it. You endured what tried to break you, and now, you speak. Not just for yourself, but for anyone who's ever felt broken.

This is for you.

Thank you for surviving.

Thank you for staying.

Thank you for becoming the reason I am who I am today.

Disclaimer

This memoir contains content that may be triggering to some readers, including references to eating disorders, body dysmorphia, trauma, and sexual assault. While these experiences are shared with honesty and care, they may evoke strong emotional responses.

This book is not intended to provide medical, therapeutic, legal, or psychological advice. It reflects the author's personal experiences and opinions. While it may resonate with others, each path to healing is unique, and readers are encouraged to seek professional support tailored to their individual needs.

Names and identifying details have been changed in some cases to protect privacy.

Please take care of yourself while reading. If you are in crisis or need support, consider reaching out to a trusted mental health professional or crisis resource in your area.

Table of Contents

Chapter 1: The Girl on the Bathroom Floor 1
Chapter 2: Butterflies, Bruises & Backyard Dreams 13
Chapter 3: Here, Yet Somehow Gone 26
Chapter 4: The Letter 39
Chapter 5: First Bell, New Beginning 52
Chapter 6: The Moment That Broke Me 60
Chapter 7: The Rumor 77
Chapter 8: Dysfunctional Relationships 95
Chapter 9: Beautiful Chaos: Transition Into Adulthood 106
Chapter 10: The Trigger 114
Chapter 11: Slippery Slope 127
Chapter 12: Downhill Spiral 140
Chapter 13: Living in Denial 160
Chapter 14: Rock Bottom 179
Chapter 15: Where Recovery Took Roots 203
Chapter 16: The Courage to Continue 229
Chapter 17: He Saw Me For Me 239
Chapter 18: The Girl in the Mirror: Who Is She? 259
Chapter 19: Pencils, Passion, Purpose 268
Chapter 20: Motherhood: No Manual, Just Love 277
Chapter 21: Stretch Marks & Strength: Postpartum Body 294
Chapter 22: War with My Reflection 313
Chapter 23: Resurrecting the Darkness 326
Chapter 24: Not My Shame 358
Chapter 25: Becoming Whole: My Healing Journey 371
Chapter 26: Perfectly Imperfect 384
Chapter 27: The Ending, That Feels Like the Beginning 396
Acknowledgement 410
Resources & Support 411
About the Author 412
A Note to You 415

Introduction

Before you begin, there's something you should know.

This book isn't just about who I am or what happened to me.

It's about the resilience I carry, loudly and proudly, in the face of what tried to break me.

It's about a girl who smiled through storms, laughed through pain, and tried to outrun trauma by being everything for everyone. The girl who never felt good enough. The one who carried silence like armor. Who wore shame like a second skin and fought like hell to reclaim her voice.

She's a Tale in My Story isn't just a memoir.

It's a reckoning.

A peeling back of layers.

A coming home to truth.

Within these pages, you'll find the raw reality of living with an eating disorder and the long shadow cast by sexual assault. These are wounds that left their mark, but they're not where my story ends.

Some of the stories here are hard to read.

They were even harder to live.

But they matter, because I know I'm not alone.

I share them to break the silence.

To illuminate experiences too often hidden or misunderstood.

To remind you that your story is valid, your healing is yours to define, and you are worthy of care, understanding, and truth.

My eating disorder nearly killed me.

It wasn't just about food or control. It was a war inside my mind. A relentless battle between appearance and worth, survival and self-destruction.

I'm sharing the unfiltered truth so others can understand what it really feels like to live inside this illness. To feel stuck, scared, exhausted, and still find a way to show up. This memoir offers insight and lived experience. It holds the coping tools and strategies I've learned over the past twenty years. Each one came from walking through recovery, one day at a time.

Eating disorders are still deeply misunderstood. They are not a choice. Not a diet gone too far. They are complex psychological illnesses that strip away identity, joy, connection, and self-worth.

They hollow you out until you barely recognize yourself.

And yet, recovery is possible.

Not perfect.

Not linear.

But real.

It's not a finish line where everything magically gets better. It's an ongoing process. A daily decision to keep going. To rebuild a life that feels like your own.

There will be mornings when you wake up not as your disorder, but as yourself. Not every day will be easy. But with time, healing begins to take root. And moments of joy become possible, even in the midst of it all.

This story is not just about what I've survived.

It's also about who I've always been.

Even in my hardest chapters, I've held onto something deeper: a desire to bring light into the world.

To offer hope.

To bring sunshine to someone's grey.

To make someone smile, even for a moment.

Spreading kindness isn't just what I do.

It's who I am.

Ever since I was a little girl, I've believed in making a positive difference in this world. For as long as I can remember, I've wanted to help people feel less alone. And maybe, in telling my story, I can do just that.

When I chose to write about my sexual assault, it wasn't for shock value. And it wasn't just to share my experience. I wrote it because silence no longer felt survivable.

That moment changed me. It fractured something. And for years, I carried the weight of that pain. Shame settled deep inside me. But it was never mine to hold.

Sexual assault isn't just an event. It's a fracture. A scar that may fade from sight, but never from the soul. I'm healing not only from what happened, but from the silence that followed. It will always be part of my story, but it no longer defines my worth.

To every survivor who stayed quiet, and to those who found their voice through the darkness…

This is for you.

This is for us.

You are not alone.

You are not broken.

Your story matters, even if you've never spoken it aloud.

I wrote this part of my story so someone else might feel less invisible. So that one more survivor might feel seen.

Not exposed.

Not judged.

Just seen.

Because sexual assault doesn't always look the way the world imagines. It isn't always dark alleys and strangers. It's often familiar places and familiar faces.

Consent is not a grey area. It is a line that should never be crossed. And speaking the truth is not what breaks us. Staying silent does.

So, if you've ever battled your reflection.
If you've ever felt broken by things you couldn't name.
If you've ever wondered if healing is possible…

This book is for you.

This isn't a story tied up with a bow.
It's raw.
It's messy.
It's real.
But it's also proof that light can be found in even the darkest corners. And sometimes, the most powerful thing you can do is stay.

Stay alive, even when the weight of the world sits heavy on your chest.
Stay true to your essence, even as life tries to sculpt you into something smaller, quieter, more acceptable.
Stay inside the fire of healing, even when every step burns with memory.
Stay open to wonder, to laughter, to the golden flickers of joy that still find their way in. Even when your past tells you to close the door and disappear, let the light in anyway.

Welcome to my story.
Welcome to yours.

CHAPTER 1

The Girl on the Bathroom Floor

"And one day, you will tell your story of how you overcame what you went through, and it will be someone else's survival guide."

— Brené Brown

I hit the floor with force, my body slamming against the cold tiles like a fallen star, stripped of its light, plummeting into the abyss.

It felt like gravity had turned against me, morphing into a living darkness, latching onto my limbs, dragging me down... deeper into a place I couldn't escape.

The shadow gripped tighter, wrapping around me like suffocating vines. Twisting, squeezing, trapping me in the endless void of rock bottom.

I wasn't just falling.

I was disappearing.

The room blurred, mirroring the haze clouding my mind.

Swirling steam crept through the air, thick and choking, curling around me until it swallowed me whole.

Each breath made the walls close in. The space shrank, pressing in on all sides, erasing the line between reality and the relentless torment of my thoughts.

The thick veil of steam wrapped around my body, tightening like a vice, coiling itself into my lungs, making every shallow breath feel like a battle I was destined to lose.

It whispered in the faint hiss of air, a voice so quiet, yet so certain.

"Just let go."

It brought me eye to eye with death, promising I had nothing left.

No fight.

No strength.

This... was the end.

The final urge to resist had been ripped from my bones, leaving behind nothing but an empty vessel, a body fading, a soul on the brink of surrender.

That was the first shower I'd taken on my own in a long time.

For months, my mom, Molly, had been the one gently washing my hair. Her fingers threaded through my coarse strands with a tenderness I no longer knew how to give myself. She would quietly remove the loose ones, disguising the loss with soft, deliberate motions. Each strand slipping away like a whisper of something that once had life.

As warm water poured over me, I curled into a tight ball in the tub, knees pulled to my chest, as if I could fold myself small enough to disappear. Small enough to slip away unnoticed, like the strands of hair washing down the drain.

Afterward, she would help me rise, steadying me as my brittle legs wobbled beneath me.

They felt like twigs.

Fragile, hollow, threatening to snap with each uncertain step.

I moved like a newborn fawn, limbs twisting beneath me, desperate to find balance... to remember how to stand.

But like that fawn, I was determined.

Even as my body betrayed me.

Even as I trembled.

Once I found my footing, she'd wrap an arm around me, guiding me out of the bathroom and toward the long, narrow staircase. Step by step, we climbed, each movement a quiet battle against the weight of exhaustion. By the time we reached my room, I was shaking, completely drained by the simple act of going upstairs.

To think, I once ran laps on those same steps, energy boundless and unstoppable.

And now...

Just one slow lap upward was enough to bring me to my knees.

After layering my shivering body with thick, warm clothing, my mom would gently pull back the blankets. Their fabric soft and inviting, as if they could wrap me in safety for the long night ahead. She tucked the covers in tight, folding them snugly around me, creating a cocoon meant to protect.

Except there was no comfort in my cocoon.

There was no warmth.

There was no transformation.

Every inch of my body throbbed.

Every muscle ached.

This wasn't a place of becoming.

There was no promise of wings, no dream of flight.

Only stillness.

Not the stillness of rest, but of disappearance.

I was trapped.

A prisoner in dark, suffocating agony.

No light slipped through the cracks.

No air.

No hope.

There was no future where I soar.

No return to that girl who once ran wild and laughed freely.

The only thing my cocoon offered was silence.

I lay there, wrapped in that silence, its weight pressing down like the blankets my mom had so lovingly arranged, clinging in the quiet.

She didn't sing me lullabies; no melody could soften the pain or coax me to sleep. Instead, she held my trembling hand. Her fingers warm, steady, and grounding. Her touch was gentle, an anchor pulling me back from the edge, grounding me just enough to distract me from the relentless ache.

And in that stillness, she'd whisper…

"I love you."

Just three words.

But in her voice, they flickered like light piercing through the darkness.

Brief, but enough.

Sleep became my only escape, the only place where my body wasn't a prison. Knowing this, she stayed. Perched at the edge of my bed, never rushing, never wavering, just waiting. Waiting with slow, soothing motions. She would rub my back, tracing gentle circles, over and over. Her touch was quiet reassurance.

Gradually, the tremors would fade. My breath would even out. My heavy eyelids would finally surrender. As I slipped into sleep, I found a sliver of peace.

A dream of life beyond the pain.

A life where my body wasn't my enemy.

A life beyond this curse, where I was free.

She was taking care of her daughter, just as she always had.

Just like when I was a bright-eyed little girl chasing butterflies in the backyard.

But this time was different.

This time, her daughter wasn't running wild with wonder.

She was twenty-one years old, fading right before her eyes.

Instead of stepping into a world of endless possibilities, like most girls do in their early twenties, her daughter was slipping away.

She was losing me to a dark, relentless disorder.

One that wrapped itself around me, pulling tighter and tighter, threatening to consume me whole.

There were evenings when my mom couldn't be there. She was a single, working mother, doing everything she could to keep us afloat.

On those nights, when responsibility pulled her away, my older brother, Michael, stepped in without hesitation.

I don't know many older brothers who would have cared for their fragile younger sister the way he did. He never made me feel like a burden. He just showed up, doing the best he could, in the only ways he knew how.

He didn't untangle my hair in the bath or gently wash it like my mom did. Instead, he waited just outside the bathroom door, a silent presence that made me feel safe, a quiet reminder that I wasn't alone.

Perched on the narrow staircase, he'd tell me jokes. The worst jokes. Some were old, some didn't make sense, and some were so absurd they made me roll my eyes.

But that was never the point. His jokes weren't meant to be funny. They were meant to distract me from my agony. And they did.

He could hear my tearful laughter echoing from behind the door, and in that moment, he knew, in his own way he was helping me to hold on.

Laughter is good for the soul.

And in those rare flickers of joy, I caught glimpses of something I hadn't felt in a long time.

Hope.

Hope that one day, things might get better.

He never rushed me. His patience wrapped around me like a steady force. Calm, stable, and grounding. Even when I felt like I was falling apart.

When I finally emerged from the bathroom, weak and unsteady, he'd silently extend his arm, waiting for me to take hold. With his firm but gentle grip, he'd support me. My arm draped over his as we made our way up the stairs. Step by step, he matched my pace.

Never pushing, never pulling.

Just walking beside me.

And when we finally reached the top, when I was safe in my bed, he would tuck me in with quiet reassurance.

He didn't wrap me in a cocoon of blankets like my mom did.

He gave me something else.

He gave me his unwavering kindness.
His steady, unspoken patience.
His silent way of saying… I love you. I'm here.
He stood by me in the unpredictable battle for my life.
Never asking for thanks.
Never expecting praise.
He didn't need it.
His only goal was to make sure I felt safe before he quietly stepped away.
Unaware of the depth of his impact.
Unaware of how much I needed him.
Unaware of how deeply I cherished the way he stepped in, took the lead, and cared for his little sister when she needed him most.

Back to the moment my body came crashing down.
The impact was violent and unforgiving like fragile glass shattering against concrete.
The cold tile struck with merciless force, jolting through my bones, leaving me breathless and weightless all at once.
A sharp, ringing silence pulsed through my skull, deafening and endless, as if the world itself had gone mute.
I felt detached.
Just a spectator watching the fall unfold, watching myself vanish.
Everything was blurred, distant, and unreachable.
I hadn't just hit the floor.
I had plummeted into my void, sinking into an abyss that stretched endlessly below.
Invisible chains wrapped around me, binding me to the darkness.
Helpless.
Trapped.
Like I would never break free.
Like I would be stuck there forever.
I was alone.
No one to gently wash my hair.

No warm hands threading through coarse strands, concealing the lost ones. No one waiting outside the door with terrible jokes and soft reassurances. No one to catch me as my body collapsed beneath the weight of itself.

My hands shot out, desperate to grab hold of something, anything.

Rock bottom had already called my name, and nothing was strong enough to stop the fall.

Maybe I fell because the water was scalding. I wouldn't have known; I couldn't feel it. I'd been frozen for so long, numb from the inside out, untouched by heat, no matter how high I turned the dial.

My body was vanishing piece by piece.

The essence of me was slipping away like sand through open fingers.

It was performing its final act.

Desperately and instinctively redirecting every last drop of energy inward.

Fighting to keep my heart beating, my organs alive.

Just barely.

But there wasn't enough left.

No spark to generate warmth.

No fuel to keep the fire alive.

I was losing the battle.

I don't remember the fall hurting. It was as if my body had already surrendered, given up before it hit the ground. The sensation felt less like collapsing and more like floating.

Weightless.

Detached.

There was nothing to break the fall.

No cushion, no resistance.

Just skin and sharp, protruding bones slamming into cold, unforgiving tile.

But the pain never came.

My body was always aching with every movement, every breath.

So, what was one more crash?

It didn't register.

Instead, a heavy stillness swept over me like a rising tide in the dark, pulling me under.

It didn't sting, it didn't burn.

It just consumed me.

When I realized where I was, panic surged through me like electricity, snapping me back into my body. I tried to call out, to yell for help, but the sound barely escaped. A broken whisper, swallowed by the fog. Even my voice had surrendered, drowned by stillness and exhaustion.

My eyes darted across the empty room, searching and hoping.

But there was nothing.

No warmth, no movement.

No one to pull me out of the darkness.

I was alone.

My feeble attempts to speak dissolved into silent tears, but even they didn't last long. I had no strength left. No energy to express my despair.

The walls felt like they were closing in, pressing against me inch by inch, amplifying the silence.

I wanted to fight but even that will was slipping away.

All I could do was lie there, alone in the stillness, inhaling the thick suffocating air of that evil cloud surrounding me.

It clung to my lungs like poison, refusing to let go.

Each exhale brought sharp fleeting jolts of pain, and bursts of false relief that vanished before they could save me.

The pain was stitched into my bones.

Into my soul.

My pale cheeks, once full of warmth, were now pressed against the cold floor.

A small puddle of tears formed beneath me, each drop echoing the hurt that refused to leave. My face, once familiar, now felt foreign, sunken and hollow. Cheekbones jutting beneath thin skin like they were trying to break free. Dark shadows circled my eyes, proof of countless sleepless nights and endless wars within.

My body trembled. My lips, tinged blue, quivered with every breath. My teeth chattered, breaking the silence with their desperate rhythm. The chill crawled through my veins like ice, consuming me from the inside out. I looked like a ghost, a reflection of sorrow, lying still and broken.

My instinct was to reach for a towel, to find warmth, to do something.

But I couldn't move.

My limbs were unresponsive.

The tile clung to my skin like glue.

I could not get up.

My body, pale and brittle, was fading.

I felt paralyzed, as if all the life inside me were being siphoned away, leaving nothing but a hollow shell. Veins pierced through my flesh, forming an intricate web of survival across my frame.

And this...

This was where I was meant to stay.

Rock bottom.

Face down on that cold, damp floor.

Lost in the void that had been calling my name for far too long.

Then the realization hit me like a blow to the chest.

I was trapped, powerless, and sinking deeper into the stillness that claimed me as its own.

I stayed there for hours.

Though each hour felt like an eternity.

The silence should have been absolute, but I could hear my heart pounding. A desperate rhythm, echoing through my body. Each thud rattled my bones, shook my trembling limbs, forced them to stay alive. It beat against my ribcage like a drum, like a distant battle cry.

In that moment, I thought about the heart.

How it keeps us alive, how every beat sends life through the body.

How, despite everything, despite the stillness, despite my weakness, it refused to stop.

I wished it would.

Every thud felt like a cruel reminder that I was still here.

Still trapped in this agony.

The thought of my heart skipping just one beat, just one, felt like a step closer to peace.

Closer to escape.

If it all just stopped...

The voices in my head, the ache in my chest, the chills running down my spine.

Maybe then I could finally rest.

Maybe then I could disappear.

No longer shackled to a body that didn't feel like mine.

No longer drowning in a world that felt like a prison with no key.

The only way to break free of the pain... was death.

As long as I was alive, the pain would always find me.

It would always win.

I was a victim, trapped inside my own skin, merely along for the ride.

A passenger in my own existence, staring out the window as life passed me by.

Ready to close my eyes.

Ready to say goodbye.

I thought about doing it.

It was a whisper, soft, yet insistent, curling through my mind.

I thought about reaching for the blade, the one perched on the edge of the bathtub, glinting beneath the dim light.

I thought about taking matters into my own hands.

About ending it.

About escaping.

The idea felt like release.

Like a door cracking open to a world where pain no longer followed me.

Where the ache inside finally faded into silence.

But I couldn't do it.

Not because my body was too weak, though it was, trembling and unresponsive.

But because something deeper held me back.

Something beyond the emptiness.

Because pressing that blade to my skin, choosing to leave, would mean that, for once, I had control.

But that was the cruelest lie of all, I had no control.

My disorder had taken the wheel long ago, steering me straight into the dark.

It didn't want me to die quickly.

That would be too easy, too merciful.

No…

It wanted me to suffer.

To break slowly, piece by piece.

To feel every drop of self-hatred, every ounce of helplessness.

It wanted to watch me wither away, trapped inside a body that didn't feel like mine.

Because this wasn't just destruction.

This was punishment.

And once again, I was defeated.

An empty shell, too tired to try, too weak to resist.

So, I stayed there, pressed against the cold, unforgiving floor, cradled by the weight of my own rock bottom.

Wishing I could close my eyes and slip into a sleep so deep, so peaceful, I'd never have to wake up again.

No more pain.

No more disorder.

Maybe, just maybe a miracle would happen, and I'd get my wish.

Miracles happen.

So why couldn't one happen for me?

The girl I once was, the one who laughed, who dreamed, who felt alive.

She was already gone.

She faded long before this moment, leaving behind only a hollow version of what once was.

So why couldn't I go too?

Why was I still here, trapped in a body that no longer felt like mine?

In a life that no longer felt worth living.

What cruel force kept me tethered to this pain, forcing me to endure a suffering that had already erased me?
Why won't it let me go?

There I am… broken, naked, shivering.
Nothing but skin and bones, a fragile frame barely holding itself together.
The cold bathroom floor pressed into my spine, my ribs, my hips.
A cruel reminder of how little of me was left.
I am alone.
Motionless.
My body too weak to move.
My mind too exhausted to care.
The disorder had sunk its claws in deep, wrapping around my bones like a parasite.
It wasn't just part of me anymore…
It was me.
And there was no escape.

You're probably wondering…
How did I get here?

Well, we all have a story to tell.
And this one?
It's mine.

CHAPTER 2

Butterflies, Bruises & Backyard Dreams

"Sometimes you will never know the value of a moment until it becomes a memory."

— Dr. Seuss

I'm sure you're wondering about that girl on the bathroom floor. The one with trembling hands, knees to chest, clutching at cold tiles as her tears sank into the floor.

We'll get there.

But first, let's step back.

Let's talk about who she was before her world caved in.

She was the girl who laughed loud enough to turn heads, joy rippling through rooms like sunlight breaking clouds. The girl who danced barefoot in summer rain, twirling as warm droplets kissed her skin.

She felt deeply and carried others' pain like it was her own. Trusted so easily, she missed the cracks forming beneath her.

She was radiant.

Untamed.

Alive.

Until the darkness found her.

It didn't ask permission.

It didn't knock.

It seeped in through unseen fractures, coiling around her ribs, threading into her mind.

One minute, she lit up a room.

The next, she was drowning in a shadow so thick that it smothered the light inside her.

So, where do I begin?

I suppose I have to start at the beginning with the woman who shaped me.

My childhood is a mosaic of memories, and at the center of each one is my mom, Molly.

Yes, she gave me life, but she was so much more than that. She was the rhythm of my days, the hum of comfort in the background of my world, and the steady heartbeat in every moment.

She cheered the loudest, hugged the tightest, and somehow made everything feel okay, even when it wasn't.

Mom smelled like vanilla and fabric softener. Her hands were soft but strong. Wiped away many tears and smoothed my hair like she was ironing out the weight of the world.

She wasn't just my mother.

She was my first home.

Every ounce of kindness I carry, every thread of resilience stitched into my bones, is because of her.

She worked tirelessly as a single mom, giving everything she had without ever asking for anything in return.

No rest.

No breaks.

Just love on repeat.

Think of the most caring, thoughtful, selfless person you know. The one who gives without hesitation and puts others first simply because that's who they are.

For me, that's my mom.

She is love in its purest form, a quiet strength that never wavers.

We didn't grow up with much.

No fancy furniture or shiny gadgets. Just second-hand everything and walls that held stories instead of artwork. But none of that mattered, because what we had was love.

Not the pretty, filtered kind. The real kind, the kind that welcomes everyone, no questions asked. It wraps around you like a warm blanket and says, "You belong here." Our home was patched together with care and compromise. We didn't need perfect, we just needed each other.

And then there was the smell, familiar and comforting, like a warm embrace. It didn't smell like store-bought candles. It smelled like life. Homemade cookies from grandma's recipe, Sunday pancakes, fresh laundry warmed by the sun, and the lingering spices of last night's dinner.

Our house wasn't grand, the wallpaper peeled, the floors creaked, and the dark red sofa had seen better days. But that sofa held everything. Our movie nights, whispered secrets, exhausted tears, and belly-deep laughter.

We'd curl up in blankets, Disney movies on loop, our laughter flickering with the TV screen. The Lion King made my mom and me cry every time. My brother pretended not to care, but we saw him blinking a little too fast.

The Little Mermaid was my favorite. Ariel enchanted me. She was curious, brave, and wild-hearted. She wasn't just dreaming; she was chasing something more.

I wanted to be like that.

Sometimes, we watched movies just suspenseful enough to make our hearts race. Afterward, my brother and I would tiptoe into my mom's room, scared of the closet monsters we swore didn't exist. But in her bed, we were safe. Her breath, steady and soft, was all we needed to fall asleep.

Our house wasn't a showroom, it wasn't meant to be. It was a place full of life, where laughter mattered more than spotless counters and where love was measured in memories, not in how organized the shelves were.

Our Christmas tree wasn't fancy. Just an artificial one that barely fit in the corner. But it was spectacular in its own way.

Chaotic, colorful, and full of love. Rainbow lights tangled like vines. Tinsel everywhere. Ornaments that didn't match, but each held a special memory.

It wasn't a Pinterest tree. It was a Molly tree.

Now that I think about it... maybe it was a me tree too.

My mom will deny it, but she's a bit of a hoarder, not the kind who clutters for no reason, but the kind who keeps stories. Every photo album, every chipped mug, every random keepsake held a piece of her heart.

She didn't just love people. She collected them. Friends, neighbors, strangers in need. If you entered her orbit, you became family.

That kind of love stretched beyond blood, beyond walls.

She wasn't just my mom; she was everyone's mom.

The kind who listened without judgment. The one who reminded you, even in your darkest moments, that everything would be okay.

My friends came over not just to see me, but to see her.

To talk.

To feel seen.

To be reminded they mattered.

One of my closest friends, Carrie, struggled with depression so heavy it led to suicidal thoughts. She couldn't turn to her own parents, but she felt safe confiding in my mom.

Of course, Molly was there, no judgement, just love. That's who she is, her love didn't end at our door, it reached anyone who needed it.

Her love has no boundaries.

She is, and always will be, a beacon of inspiration.

She pours herself into others, never expecting anything in return. She doesn't just make people feel welcome, she makes them feel like they belong.

I've always wanted to be like that because the world needs more people like my mom. She doesn't have a mean bone in her body.

Well...

Except for one moment.

It was a spring morning. I was being a brat, laying on the horn from the passenger seat, impatient for my ride to school. She stormed out of the house, ready to let me have it.

But when she went to flip me the bird, she accidentally gave me a thumbs-up instead. We locked eyes and burst out laughing. The tension dissolved in an instant.

Even in her angriest moments, kindness still wins.

That's my mom.

She worked endlessly to keep us afloat. She would juggle jobs and sacrifice rest, so we didn't have to feel the struggle. But when the house was quiet and the bills were spread like a storm across the kitchen table, I know she cried.

Silently, privately, and always when she thought we were asleep.

Still, we made it through.

"I don't know how," she'd say, "but it's gonna work out. It always does."

And somehow, it always did.

There were no safety nets.

Just faith, resilience, and a mother's love that refused to quit.

Looking back, I think the universe noticed.

She gave so much light, so much goodness, that maybe, in some cosmic way, it gave a little back. Not in riches, but just enough to keep going, and to stay hopeful. Enough to never lose the feeling of home.

But eventually, even that wasn't quite enough.

To survive, we had to open our home to others.

What started as generosity became necessity.

Our little world of three expanded and got more complicated.

Roommates moved in.

Kind, respectful people.

But it changed things.

Our small kitchen became too crowded for spontaneous snack runs or card games at the dinner table.

The bathroom turned into a battleground of schedules.

The heart of our home, the place that once felt so safe, began to feel just a little less like ours.

I missed the quiet, the ease, the freedom to just be.

Even with only one roommate at a time, and always female, I couldn't shake the unease. Especially when their boyfriends visited, nothing ever happened, but something in me bristled. My body knew this wasn't the home it used to be.

I started retreating to my room, tuning in to every creak, every unfamiliar voice.

Maybe I was just being territorial.

Maybe I understood, deep down, that home is sacred.

It's the one place where you're allowed to drop the act, let your socks hit the floor, cry ugly tears, or wear the same ratty pajamas without apology.

With others living there, I couldn't do that.

For someone like me, emotional, loud, deeply sensitive, it felt like a kind of a loss. I've always felt things deeply, maybe too deeply. Even as a kid, I absorbed emotions around me like a sponge, catching every unspoken tension and every shift in energy. I didn't know how to separate their sadness from mine.

So, I carried it all.

At times, it felt like I was suffocating under the weight of it.

In many ways, I'm just like my mom.

My heart doesn't just feel for people, it carries them. That kind of empathy lives deep in me to this day.

Over time, I've learned something important…

We don't have to hold it all.

Life will always throw curveballs, but we get to choose what we carry and what we release. When we let go of the heaviness, we make space.

Space for joy, for peace, for everything that truly matters.

When I was younger, I didn't know how to do that. I caught every emotion and buried it inside until I felt like I was going to explode. The only way I knew how to cope was to let it out loudly, emotionally, and unapologetically.

Whether it was a mean comment at school, a missed goal in street hockey, or a wrong answer on a test, it all hit the same nerve. I needed to feel it and to cry it out.

When strangers lived with us, even kind ones, I couldn't.

I felt like I had to shrink to be quieter, smaller, less me.

I found when emotions stay buried, they build, layer by layer, like lava under the surface.

That's what I became, a volcano.

Not one that erupts in rage, but one that simmers quietly, filling with pressure. And when I couldn't express it, the emotional heat would crawl up my throat, threatening to burn everything in its path.

But that's not who I wanted to be. I wanted to be the kind of volcano that releases gently, lava sliding in quiet waves, letting go without destruction.

I learnt we don't have to erupt or bury it; we just have to learn to release it before it explodes. But I didn't know how to do that yet, not then.

And just when I was adjusting to life with roommates, everything shifted again.

My mom fell in love.

Suddenly, we went from temporary guests to a permanent presence, a stepdad.

He wasn't just sharing our space; he was becoming part of our story.

With him came a quiet shift. The kind that creeps in slowly, until one day, you realize you don't feel quite at home in your own home anymore.

I lost the freedom to exist without tiptoeing.

The couch didn't feel like mine.

The hallway felt smaller.

And my voice felt quieter.

He brought his own issues, unresolved pain and emotions he hadn't unpacked. Instead of facing them, he let them spill into our space.

The tension didn't just visit, it moved in.

The safe place I'd always turned to became somewhere I wanted to escape.

I became collateral damage.

We'll get more into that later. For now, just know this...

His presence changed everything.

Before the darkness took root, before I had to armor up just to get through the day, there was still light.

There was still her, the girl who laughed loudly in a love-filled home, feeling safe. Who grew up with a mom who filled every broken space with warmth.

If we had never lived on that street, I might never have met Megan.

She lived two doors down, and from the moment we connected, we were inseparable. She's more than a best friend. She's my constant, my chosen sister, my mirror.

We've seen each other through every version of ourselves and somehow only grew closer. We fought like sisters too, slamming doors, swearing we were done... only to be laughing an hour later. We shared meltdowns, heartbreaks, secrets, and giggles that still echo in my memory.

She could see when I was spiraling before I said a word. And when I needed to be called out, she didn't hold back.

That's the kind of friendship we had.

After school, Megan and I would race home to what we proudly called the infinite chip cupboard. It was a tiny overflowing corner of our kitchen packed with every flavor imaginable. Salt and vinegar, ketchup, sour cream and onion. You name it, it was in there.

My mom didn't just buy our favorites, she stocked the favorites of every kid on the block. We'd tear into our go-to bags, plop onto the couch, and let the day spill out between bites and giggles. Homework was forgotten, TV humming in the background, life felt light.

No pressure, no stress, just freedom and joy.

Funny how something as simple as a handful of chips can bring that much comfort.

You don't need the whole bag. Just enough to remind you that you're safe, that you're home, that life still holds sweetness.

And Megan?

She was always right there.

We've held each other's hair back at parties, whispered secrets we swore we'd take to the grave, broken rules, nursed heartbreaks, and laughed through more embarrassing moments than I can count.

She's been my rock.

My constant.

My forever.

And I know, no matter where life takes us, she always will be.

But before Megan was allowed to hang out, most of my days were spent running with the boys on the street, most of them friends of my brother, Michael.

Even though Michael is three years older than me, back then it felt like a canyon between us.

They didn't exactly want a little sister around, but they tolerated me. And sometimes they tortured me a little.

Like the day they chopped the hair off all my Barbies.

Barbies were "too girly" to them, and if I wanted to be accepted, I had to ditch the dolls.

So, I did.

Without realizing it, I started changing. Tea parties turned into street hockey. Dresses gave way to grass-stained knees and scraped elbows.

I became a tomboy, tough, fast, always trying to keep up. It wasn't that I didn't want to be girly, but because I wanted to belong.

I'll never forget when they tied me to the hockey net and shot pucks at me. I was fully padded, but it still hurt. I didn't complain though, that would've ruined everything. I had earned my spot; I wasn't about to lose it by being too sensitive.

And then… there was the tree branch incident.

They tied a hockey stick to a rope and slung it on the branch hanging over the deck. The game was to swing off, let go, and see who could land the furthest.

They all took turns, flying through the air, howling with laughter. I begged to try. They kept saying no… until they got bored.

What I didn't know was that they'd weakened the branch just enough that it would snap when it was my turn. I grabbed that stick and jumped, determined to prove I could be like them.

For a second, I felt unstoppable.

Then the branch cracked.

I hit the ground flat on my back, the wind knocked clean out of me.

They laughed like it was the funniest thing they'd ever seen.

To them, it was just a prank.

To me, it was the price of admission.

And I was willing to pay it.

Despite the bruises, the teasing, and the endless attempts to prove I belonged, one of those boys eventually became my very first crush.

He was the first boy who gave me butterflies, the kind that fluttered in your stomach no matter how hard you tried to ignore them.

On the outside, I was tough, blending into their world of hockey sticks and scraped knees.

But inside?

Inside, I was just a girl.

A girl who felt a nervous thrill whenever he was around.

Nathan.

The boy next door.

And oh, did I ever like him.

There was just something about him, outgoing, tall, funny, and easy on the eyes. His smile could light up a room.

And his laugh?

It was contagious, the kind that made you laugh even when you didn't know why. He had this effortless charm; the kind that made my heart skip a beat even when I wished it wouldn't.

I remember daydreaming about him, imagining he'd be my first kiss.

I'd get lost in my own little world, picturing the perfect moment. My heart racing, his lips meeting mine, the air thick with anticipation.

It was magical in my mind.

Thrilling.

Like something straight out of a movie.

But then, Nathan moved away and with him, my little fantasy slowly faded.

As much as I had dreamed about that first kiss being with him, life had other plans. My real first kiss was in grade six, during an innocent game of spin the bottle.

And when I say innocent, I mean the PG version.

We were young.

A quick kiss on the cheek or a brief, awkward press of lips, if you were brave. It wasn't the fireworks moment I had imagined.

No cinematic slow-motion.

No heart-stopping magic.

Yet still, in its own way, it was special.

A moment frozen in time.

One I'll always remember.

Then, something unexpected happened.

My crush, Nathan, came back for a visit.

This time, it was different.

He had visited before, but I was always the little girl tagging along behind the boys.

Not anymore.

A few years had passed, and I had grown up, my body had changed, my flat chest wasn't so flat, and my awkward limbs had softened.

Suddenly, his eyes were on me, and for the first time I wasn't invisible in his world.

My fantasy came to life.

During one of his visits, we found ourselves alone. Caught in a moment that felt different from all the others before.

It happened.

A kiss.

Okay, fine. It was more than just a little kiss.

It escalated into a full-blown make-out session.

Up until that point, I was still new to this kind of intimacy.

Sure, I had imagined it, daydreamed about it in the most romanticized way possible.

But experiencing it firsthand was something entirely different.

He showed me the ropes in a way that felt natural.

Even though my heart was racing, and I was nervous, it was a moment that made me feel both vulnerable and excited.

A strange, electrifying mix of uncertainty and thrill.

But more than the physical…

It was how he made me feel.

For the first time, I felt seen.

Valued.

Appreciated.

And most importantly, I felt beautiful.

It wasn't just about his touch; it was the quiet validation that came with it.

The unspoken message that I was worthy of attention.

I was desirable and someone wanted to be close to me in that way.

It gave me a confidence I had never felt before, one that lingered long after the moment passed.

In its own way, it felt like a powerful gift.

Not the innocent, rushed kind from a childhood game, but an intimate connection.

And just like that, fourteen-year-old me was on cloud nine.

Our house was small, but it was always full.

Neighborhood kids, roommates, laughter, chaos, someone was always coming through the door.

Yet no matter how crowded it got, one thing never changed.

My mom's love.

It wrapped around every corner, filling the cracks, making even the hardest days feel a little softer.

When I look back on my childhood, I don't think about the chipped paint or the second-hand everything.

I think about her, my mom, Molly.

Even with all that love, there was still a space that never quite filled. It wasn't the lack of money, or the cramped kitchen, or the chipped mugs and broken furniture.

It was him.

My dad.

He was there, technically.

Present in the way that checks the boxes, but not in the way a little girl needs her father to be.

Not in the way that fills your heart.

Not in the way that makes you feel chosen.

He missed the everyday magic.

The little things.

The big things.

And... I felt that absence.

Deeply.

As a single mom, she did everything she could to make up for it, and in so many ways, she did.

She was both parents in one.

But no matter how brightly she shined, I still carried the quiet ache of wanting more from him.

And I still do.

CHAPTER 3

Here, Yet Somehow Gone

"You can be surrounded by people and still feel utterly alone."
— *Anonymous*

Do I have daddy issues?
That's a fair question.

If I had to label him, I'd say he was more of a father than a dad.
Yes, he helped give me life, but showing up takes more than that. It's not about biology.
It's about presence.
He left when I was just a year old. Even if I can't remember the moment, I've carried the aftermath ever since.
A quiet ache.
A missing piece.
A man who was around, but never in the way I needed him to be.
He wasn't there at sunrise to greet me with a sleepy hug, or at sunset to tuck me in and sing lullabies as the world faded into night.

He missed the everyday moments. The spilled cereal, the scraped knees, the tears over math homework, and childhood heartbreaks I didn't yet have words for.

Stan was a visitor in my life.

Showing up in the margins, but never really part of the story.

Still, when he did show up, it meant something.

He would take us on long drives with no real destination, just music, stories, and the hum of the road. He loved taking us off-roading. And let me tell you, that was an experience.

The truck would jolt and bounce, flinging mud and dirt as we tore through barely-there trails. Branches scraped the windows, and rocks crunched under the tires. Puddles turned into small lakes that seemed to swallow us whole.

It absolutely terrified me.

Every steep hill felt like we might tip. Every muddy pit was like a trap waiting to pull us under. My knuckles would go white gripping the door handle and my stomach was flipping with every drop.

But deep down… I loved it.

There was something about the way my dad came alive behind the wheel, laughing, wild, completely in his element. It was like seeing a different version of him, carefree, electric, and full of life.

In those moments with the windows down and the wind whipping through the truck, the world blurring in streaks of green and brown, I felt closer to him.

Those wild, muddy rides left a mark.

A messy, unforgettable memory of a dad who, when he was with us, made it feel like it mattered.

It wasn't the steady daily presence I longed for.

But it was something.

Occasionally, we would spend time at the trailer where my dad lived.

It wasn't bad, not exactly home sweet home like ours. It had its own kind of charm. The space was small and modest with just the basics. The couch never quite matched the comfort of our old red one. It was stiff, scratchy fabric that left imprints on your legs if you sat too long.

The tiny kitchen always carried the unmistakable scent of Kraft Dinner, the kind that clung to the air like a childhood memory.

There weren't any frills, no cozy nooks, no special touches, but it was welcoming enough. The trailer felt lived-in, a little rough around the edges with peeling linoleum floors and dented cabinets that creaked when you opened them.

It didn't have the warmth or chaos of our family home, but there was something honest about it.

A quiet kind of comfort.

A space that, while far from perfect, gave us a place to sit, talk, eat, and just be, even if only for a little while.

In a way, that was him.

Simple.

Rugged.

Imperfect.

I remember our visits always started the same way.

Before heading to the trailer, we would stop at the local bar at the top of the street. It was part of his routine, his little ritual.

Just another stop on the way to Dad's place.

He'd savor a cold brew like it was the reward at the end of a long day, while my brother and I made a beeline for the vending machine. We knew the drill.

Was it ideal bringing young kids into a bar?

Of course not.

But at six years old, I didn't know any better.

I was just happy to be with him.

The bar wasn't glamorous, not even close. The place was a strange mix of comfort and chaos, with chipped wooden stools, flickering neon signs, and the faint, ever-present smell of stale beer.

My brother and I would each grab a bag of chips, same choices every time. I always picked Old Dutch Sour Cream and Onion, tearing into the bag with eager little hands as clinking glasses and low murmurs filled the room.

I recall once coming back from the bathroom to find my chips were gone.

And then, I saw an old drunk man a few stools down eating them like they were his.

I stood there, crushed.

Angry, on the verge of tears.

I looked to my dad, hoping for comfort, some kind of reaction.

Instead, he quietly walked to the vending machine and bought me a new bag.

Problem solved... at least on the surface.

What I really needed was reassurance, a hug.

Instead, I got a replacement snack and silence.

That moment stayed with me, not because I lost my chips but because even when my dad was right there, he still felt so far away.

In the summer, he would take my brother and me to the park.

Simple, uncomplicated, and unforgettable.

He'd push us so high on the swings, I swore I might fly right over the top. My stomach would drop, I'd laugh so hard I couldn't breathe.

In those moments, I felt weightless, free, and safe. Soaring through the air, wind rushing past my face, the world spinning into a blur below me. I would grip the rusty chains tighter, eyes wide, heart pounding, flying higher and higher.

There he was.

My dad.

Planted firmly behind me, hands ready for the next push.

Those moments felt like pure freedom. Just a kid, suspended between sky and earth, laughing wildly with my dad steady and strong behind me. Making me feel like I could touch the sky.

We played this game on the big yellow slide called Monster.

My brother and I would climb to the top, daring each other to go first, while my dad crouched at the bottom with a mischievous grin.

Our monster, ready to catch us.

The goal was to slide down fast enough to escape, but more often than not, he'd snatch us at the last second, pulling us into a fit of giggles as we shrieked and wriggled to break free.

It was pure joy.

Nothing else mattered, just laughter, the summer sun, and the thrill of the chase.

No matter how many times we played, it never got old.

When I ran, I was lightning-fast, my little legs pumping furiously as I darted across the playground, racing up the steps of the play structure, heart pounding with adrenaline and pride.

When I made it to the top without getting caught…

I was victorious.

I was untouchable.

The fear of being caught, the rush, the escape, it didn't stay on the playground, it followed me…

Into relationships.

Into life.

I think those moments meant so much to me because they didn't happen as often as I wished they would. Maybe that's why I clung to them so tightly.

As amazing as those memories were, they were rare and far between.

He just wasn't around enough to be a constant presence in my life, the kind of presence that shapes who you are, that turns a father into a dad.

A dad is there for the everyday moments.

The school drop-offs, the bedtime stories, the quiet talks about nothing and everything. It's the little things, stacked over time, that build a bond.

But with him, it was always flashes of love.

Bright, beautiful, but fleeting.

Never enough to create something lasting.

I always felt like my dad abandoned me.

I know people whose fathers disappeared without a trace, and I ache for them. But even though mine was technically around, it didn't feel like enough. He was close enough to touch, but never close enough to lean on.

We talk, even now.

But it's surface-level.

Safe topics about weather, work, family updates. He's never been the one I call when I'm hurting.

Never the one I turn to for advice.

Not then.

Not now.

I was a little girl, grateful for the time I got with him, but always wanting more. I needed more than the surface-level relationship we had, or rather, still have.

Because nothing's really changed.

So why did he leave nearly forty years ago?

Why has he been in my life all this time, yet we've never managed to break through the surface?

What was the lifestyle that pulled him away?

What went wrong in their marriage?

Because if there was love, if there were good times, then why wasn't that enough?

Why did he choose a life that didn't include being there for us in the way we needed?

That's the part I've always struggled to understand.

If I had to sum it up…

He had a lifestyle my mom disagreed with.

And eventually that lifestyle won.

It won against his wife.

It won against his children.

It's not that he didn't love us.

I truly believe he did.

But love alone wasn't enough.

It wasn't enough to keep him present.

It wasn't enough to make him choose us over the pull of a life he wanted for himself.

In the end, he made his choice.

And that choice meant we would never have him in the way we needed.

As I got older, like many kids do, I became curious about my parents' relationship. I wanted to understand the story that shaped my own.

So, I asked my mom.

Her answer was always the same.

"We got married too young."

That was it.

No details.

No context.

No deeper explanation.

Just that quiet, repeated phrase.

Too young.

She never elaborated, and I never pressed. But I always felt like there was more to the story, something left unsaid. I never truly knew what too young meant, not in the way I needed to.

It wasn't until I was seventeen when the cracks in the story finally split open.

One evening, while visiting my dad at his newer, more stable home with his wife, Nancy, I heard a car pull into the driveway.

A sound I recognized, a loud Mustang.

Chad. The biggest drug dealer at my school.

Instantly, my stomach twisted.

By this point, my dad's life looked different, no more trailer, no more bar stops. He seemed settled.

But as I watched Chad grin from the driver's seat like an old friend, the question hit me hard.

What really went wrong?

Stan casually said he was stepping out to lend a tool, his usual excuse.

But I wasn't naïve.

Chad didn't come roaring down our street for a wrench.

I sat frozen on the couch, heart pounding, mind racing.

Everything started clicking, the guys "borrowing tools," the mysterious drop-ins, the way he'd slip out during movie nights.

Those weren't innocent visits.

Suddenly, I wasn't just a kid watching TV. I was a teenager staring down a truth I hadn't asked for. I already knew the answer, but I needed to hear it.

So, on Monday, I approached Chad at school, keeping it casual.

"Hey, pretty sure I saw your car on Arthur Street this weekend."

My heart thundered in my chest, but I kept my voice steady. I couldn't push too hard, not yet.

He looked at me for a second, then laughed.

"Oh, that's just my old man buddy, Stan" he said. "He's one of my top customers."

It hit me like a punch to the gut.

I thought I was ready.

I had pieced it together, the late-night exits, the sketchy visitors, but part of me still hoped I was wrong.

I wasn't.

I had braced myself all weekend, convincing myself it wouldn't hurt if I expected it. But hearing it out loud shattered something inside me.

I wished I hadn't asked.

Wished I'd let the suspicion fade.

It was too late, the truth was raw, and it was mine now.

Humans are wired for truth. It's an instinct buried deep within us. It's a relentless desire to uncover what's hidden, to pull back the curtains and expose what lies beneath.

We despise deception.

It's why we question, why we dig, why we push past uncertainty even when part of us fears what we might find.

We are natural seekers. Always in pursuit, testing theories, analyzing patterns, trying to decode the silver lining that might explain the chaos of life.

We crave meaning.

We're desperate to make sense of everything that happens to us, to connect the dots in a way that brings clarity.

Maybe this relentless drive to know, to understand, goes all the way back to Darwin's theory of evolution. The more we know, the more adaptive we become. Knowledge sharpens our instincts, strengthens, decisions, equips us to navigate our environments, anticipate threats, and ultimately, survive.

In that sense, truth becomes a beacon.

A light cutting through the fog. It offers direction, a framework for understanding not just the world around us, but our place in it.

But the truth?

The real truth?

It's not always kind.

It doesn't always bring the clarity or closure we hoped for.

It can hurt.

It can shake the very foundation we've been standing on.

From that moment on, I needed to know more.

It wasn't just curiosity anymore; it became a mission. I felt like an undercover detective piecing together fragments of a truth that had been hidden in plain sight.

I started collecting clues, lining up facts, revisiting childhood moments that suddenly looked different under this new lens. I traced the fractures in the story I'd always been told, realizing this case needed to be cracked, and I was the only one who could do it.

The more I thought about it, the more it felt like I'd been lied to, not maliciously, but still lied to.

And suddenly, "We got married too young" didn't feel like the whole story.

It felt like a cover.

A soft lie meant to protect me.

But the real story?

It was starting to reveal itself, and I wasn't turning back.

Next on the list was my mom.

I wasn't sure she'd be honest with me. She never had before, not to deceive, but to shield.

But this time, she told me the truth.

No sugarcoating.

No protective spin.

She saw I was ready.

Maybe because I finally looked more like a young woman than the little girl that she'd spent years protecting.

Stan had a lifestyle.

Not just youth or recklessness, a full-blown party life he couldn't walk away from.

Late nights.

Addictions.

A hunger for escape he refused to starve.

The high was his refuge.

The chaos, his comfort.

While he chased the rush, my mom sat in the quiet, hoping he wouldn't wake us as he stumbled through the door.

She clung to reality while he slipped deeper into escape.

And between them?

Two kids, too young to understand that love alone wasn't enough.

My mom was clear from the start.

No drugs, no chaos.

He tried, for a while.

But when she became a mother, her boundaries hardened. Her love had limits, because protecting her children came first.

When he crossed that line, she chose us.

Even if it meant doing it alone.

To her, drugs weren't just dangerous.

They were a betrayal.

Her fear became ours, shaping the way we saw the world. So, when I found out the truth about my dad, it hit harder.

At seventeen, I didn't see addiction as a struggle, I saw it as failure. I saw him as a disappointment.

In time, I realized my reaction was shaped by how I was raised. Her black-and-white view became mine. I judged before I understood. When you grow up believing something is unforgivable, it's hard to imagine a version of the story where it isn't.

But as I got older, I started to see the grey.

Drugs weren't the only reason they split.

My dad was young, nowhere near ready to be a parent, still clinging to a life that wasn't built for responsibility. He wasn't willing to let go of the part of him that thrived on adrenaline and escape.

And being a dad?

That requires change, sacrifice, and showing up when it's hard.

He wasn't ready for that.

I believe things could've been different if he'd been willing to grow.

But the version of him I needed wasn't the one I got.

That version, the one who finally showed up, wasn't meant for me.

My younger half siblings got him. They got the dad who traded chaos for consistency. Late nights for early mornings. The one who packed lunches, helped with homework, stood cheering on the sidelines.

They got the dad I always wanted and deserved.

I'm genuinely happy for them but I'd be lying if I said I wasn't jealous.

Because I am.

I still am.

They got the steady presence. I got the unfinished version. The one who arrived late, left too soon, and was never around in the ways I needed most.

And that kind of absence.

It doesn't just disappear.

It lingers.

Quietly.

Always.

So, do I have daddy issues?

Yeah. I do.

And has it shaped my self-worth?

Absolutely.

At seventeen, I stood at a crossroads, between the version of my dad I thought I knew, and the truth I had just uncovered. Finally understanding why their marriage fell apart was overwhelming.

Yes, my mom had her part. She wanted a picture-perfect life and had non-negotiable boundaries.

I was a teenager, hurt, angry, and desperate for someone to blame.

So, I blamed him.

The drugs.

The chaos.

The choices that pulled him away.

But underneath all that anger was something heavier.

I felt abandoned.

For years I believed, as most kids do, that maybe if I had been enough, he would have stayed.

I carried that guilt like a second skin.

But learning the truth about his addiction was the missing piece.

Suddenly, the broken promises, the emotional distance, it all made sense.

It wasn't me.

It was never me.

It was the lifestyle he couldn't let go.

Still, despite everything, I wanted something more with him.

Maybe it was hope.

Maybe it was love.

Maybe just the stubborn, aching truth that no matter how flawed he was, he was still my dad.

And teenage me?

I wasn't ready to give up that easily.

So, I did the only thing I knew how to do.

I wrote him a letter.

Pen to paper, because sometimes, when your voice shakes and your thoughts are too heavy to say out loud, writing is the only way to speak from the heart.

It wasn't perfect.

It wasn't polished.

But it was real.
Every emotion I had bottled up for years spilled onto the page.
The questions.
The hurt.
The confusion.
The love I didn't always know how to show.
It was my olive branch.
My way of saying, I see you.
I still want something with you.
But I need you to meet me halfway.

That letter was more than just words.
It was a beginning.
Or at least...
The hope for one.

CHAPTER 4

The Letter

"Some letters are best left unsent. Others are written to set you free."
— *Anonymous*

I loved my childhood.

I loved the warmth my mom brought into every corner of our home, the way even ordinary moments felt full.

Laughter echoed through our small, cluttered house, wrapping us in safety and love.

I loved running next door to Megan's, feet pounding, heart racing, not from fear, but pure joy. Her door felt like an extension of home, a place where secrets and giggles lived.

I even loved the boys who toughened me up. The teasing, the bruises.

They built my resilience.

I was learning to be strong in a world that didn't always make space for girls like me.

I was happy.

But no matter how much love surrounded me, there was always a quiet, missing piece. My dad.

He was there, but not close.

Present, but distant, like trying to hold onto a ghost.

I often wonder how life might have looked if my parents had stayed together. Laughter echoing around the dinner table. Bedtime stories told by both, voices overlapping like a beautiful symphony.

I'll never know. The past is set, etched in stone.

But the future?

That's still mine to shape.

I may not be able to rewrite the beginning of my story, but I get to choose how the rest is told.

I hold the pen now.

And that... That gives me hope.

It's hard not to compare the relationship with my dad to the bond my husband shares with our daughter, Maddy.

She's six.

Spirited, strong-willed, full of fire.

And her dad?

He's her world.

She's got him wrapped around her little finger, and he wears that title like a badge of honor. The way he looks at her and how he drops everything just to make her smile. It's the most beautiful thing I've ever seen.

My dad was never my hero.

But Maddy's dad?

He's hers.

And I'd be lying if I said I wasn't jealous.

Not bitter. Just... aching.

Aching for the little girl I once was, the one who longed for that kind of love. The one who watched other girls get lifted into the air, spun around, cherished, and silently wondered what that felt like.

I'm so grateful my daughter will never have to wonder.

But part of me still mourns the version of myself who did.

So, what makes a dad a superhero?

It's not the cape, or the strength, or the power to fix everything with a single word.

It's the moments.

The quiet consistency.

The showing up, again and again, no matter what.

It's kneeling beside her as she fumbles with her laces, guiding her hands, calming her frustration until she gets it. It's seeing her pride bloom because he believed in her until she could believe in herself.

It's saying yes to the extra cookie before bed, brushing through tangled hair without a single tear or scream.

Something I swear I do just as gently.

But when I try?

Cue the dramatic flinching and full-blown bedtime meltdown.

But when Daddy does it, it's chuckles. It's magic.

He reads her the same animal book every night, without fail. Roaring like a lion, squeaking like a mouse, bringing each page to life like it's brand new, even though we both know he could recite it in his sleep.

He could suggest a new book, but he doesn't. Because he knows, for her, it's not just a story, it's comfort. It's home.

That's what superhero dads do.

They show up in the small, selfless ways, the kind no one sees but that shape a child forever.

And one day, when her first crush knocks on the door. He'll stand a little too tall, shake that kid's hand a little too firmly, and drop a not-so-subtle joke that lands more like a warning.

This girl is my world. Her heart is not to be taken lightly.

She'll roll her eyes and mutter, "Dad, seriously?" but she'll get it.

Because beneath the awkward dad jokes and puffed-up chest, there's love.

That's what makes a dad a hero.

Not perfection.

Presence.

She'll grow.

Life will stretch her, pull her in every direction. But she'll always know, deep down, that her dad is still there.

Still watching.

Still holding space.

She'll always be his little girl.

And he'll always be her superhero.

I missed out on so many of those moments with my dad. I never got to see him as a superhero, not in the way a daughter should.

But there's one moment I hold onto.

He taught me how to ride a bike. I remember the sun on my skin, the gravel crunching under my tires, my heart pounding with a mix of fear and determination. I wobbled, I stumbled, but I didn't give up.

I wanted to make him proud.

And when I finally took off, pedaling fast, wind rushing past my cheeks, I looked back.

He was there.

Watching me.

Really watching.

And in his eyes, I saw it.

Pride.

That's the memory I hold onto. Because in a childhood full of absence, that one moment of presence meant everything.

It's important for you to know, I'm not here to paint my dad as a villain, he's not.

He's kind, sensitive, quiet in his ways, and full of heart.

When we stayed at his house as kids, he made bedtime feel like magic. It wasn't just "go brush your teeth."

He'd pull out his guitar, settle in like it was our own private concert, and play. His fingers moved across the strings like he was telling us a story without words. We'd sing along, our small voices blending with his, wrapped in melody and warmth.

In those moments, time stood still.

No past.

No pain.

Just music.

Just love.

There's one song I remember more than any other, "Cats in the Cradle."

A song about a boy longing for his father's attention, learning how to grow up, how to become a man, all on his own. The father, always busy, always preoccupied, never quite making time the way the boy hoped he would.

And yet, despite the missed moments, despite the silence and absence, the boy still idolized his dad. Only to grow up and unknowingly repeat the very same cycle.

It's ironic, isn't it?

That my dad would sing that song.

Because I am that boy. I know what it feels like to sit on the sidelines of someone's life, hoping they'll notice you. Hoping they'll stop and see you. I know what it's like to crave the small, everyday moments that never came as often as you needed.

And yet, when I think back, some of my most cherished memories are the ones where he was there. Falling asleep to the soft strum of his guitar, wrapped in the comfort of a beautiful song.

It sounds like the perfect bedtime, doesn't it?

In many ways, it was.

But the little girl in me didn't want those songs once a month.

She wanted them every night.

That's why it hurt so much that staying at my dad's house was called a sleepover.

That word felt wrong.

Too temporary.

Too much like something you pack for, not something that should define your relationship with a parent.

Sleepovers were for friends.

This should've felt like home.

No packed bags.

No awkwardness.

No whispering thank you for the space.

Just belonging.

Staying at my dad's felt like visiting, like I was a guest.

When I think of a sleepover I picture heading to a friend's house, curling up in a sleeping bag, whispering under the glow of a nightlight, half-eaten snacks scattered around us, and a scary movie flickering in the background. Sleepy laughter, shared secrets, and stories that stretch long past bedtime.

That's a sleepover.

But with Dad?

That should never have been called a sleepover. That should've been home, but it wasn't. Not in the way I wanted.

No matter how beautifully he played, no matter how deeply I loved those bedtime songs, that ache was always there.

The one that whispered, this isn't really your place.

That's what drove me to write the letter.

Not out of spite.

Not to hurt.

But because I couldn't carry it anymore…

The pain.

The disappointment.

The endless wondering why.

I needed to speak.

To say the truths I had buried for too long.

To stop tiptoeing and finally try.

So, I did what I've always done when I don't know what else to do.

I wrote.

I remember sitting on my bedroom floor, knees pulled tight to my chest, pen shaking in my hand.

The letter didn't flow, it poured.

Every word peeled back a layer I'd been too afraid to touch.

Anger buzzed in my chest like a live wire.

Hurt sat heavy in my stomach and that familiar ache of abandonment washed over me like a wave I couldn't outrun.

Resentment.

Sadness.

Frustration.

It all came flooding back, I couldn't keep it buried.

That's never been who I am. I'm not someone who sits in pain and lets it fester. I want to heal, to fix, to move forward, even when the path is steep.

That letter wasn't just emotional release, it was a lifeline.

My way of saying, this is how I feel.

I need you to hear me.

I'm done with surface-level conversations.

Done avoiding the truth.

I want honesty.

Forgiveness.

Something real between us.

So, there I was, seventeen, sitting on my floor, pen trembling, as years of hurt spilled onto the page.

I told him everything…

The loneliness.

The anger.

The ache of wishing he had never left.

And then came the hardest truth.

"It broke my heart when you picked the party over your family."

Because that's how it felt.

Like there was a choice and he didn't choose me.

Sealing that envelope was one of the hardest things I've ever done.

I was scared.

What if it made things worse?

What if it pushed him further away?

But I knew I had to send it.

We'd avoided the truth long enough.

So, I drove to his house, stood at the mailbox with a lump in my throat and let it go.

Then… I waited.

With each silent day, my hope began to fade. I wondered if I'd made a mistake, if I had built a wall instead of a bridge.

But weeks later, a letter arrived.

From the moment I held it, I knew, he read every word, and I knew it had hurt him.

My dad, for all his flaws, has always been sensitive and big-hearted. I never meant to wound him, I just needed him to see, to feel what I had carried for years.

Sometimes healing starts by ripping off the bandage. That letter was me pointing at the pain and asking, "Can we heal together?"

I opened his response with trembling hands and my stomach in knots.

It was nothing like I feared.

There was no anger.

No denial.

Just love.

Vulnerability.

Ownership.

He told me how much he loved me and how much I had always meant to him.

He didn't dodge the truth.

He didn't make excuses.

He took responsibility.

Responsibility for what he had done, what he had missed, and what he wished he could change.

And for the first time… he let me in.

He shared stories of his own childhood pain.

His own sense of abandonment.

The very thing I held against him, he had lived, too.

I had spent years believing he chose the party over us.

But the truth was messier.

The drugs, the late nights, the numbing, it wasn't about thrill, it was about survival.

A way to silence wounds he never learned to face.

While reading his words, something shifted in me, and for the first time I saw not just my pain, but his.

It didn't erase the past, but it gave me something I hadn't expected.

Understanding.

Even the song he used to sing, "Cats in the Cradle," suddenly made sense. It wasn't just a lullaby. It was a quiet confession. A truth he couldn't say out loud. So, he sang it instead.

His letter ended with an apology, honest, heartfelt, and free of excuses. He didn't want to rewrite the past; he wanted to build something new.

A real relationship.

One where he could finally show up as a dad.

And for the first time in a long time, I felt it.

Relief, and the faint, flickering light of hope.

However, tucked inside that same envelope was something I didn't expect, a second letter.

This one was from his wife, Nancy.

The moment I unfolded it; I felt the shift.

Her words weren't warm or understanding, they were defensive, heavy, like a weight pressing down on the hope I had just begun to feel.

She wasn't trying to comfort or connect; she was trying to protect my dad. And in doing so, she dismissed the pain I had poured onto the page.

I understand she was standing by her husband, and I can't fault her for that. But her response made me question myself and the intention behind my letter.

Had I asked for too much?

Was I wrong to send it at all?

I hadn't written to attack.

I wrote to heal.

To open a door, not start a war.

Nancy's response felt like that door slamming shut.

The worst part?

My dad didn't even know she had sent it.

Not until I told my mom, that is. Of course, she went into full protective mama bear mode and made sure everyone knew how upset I was.

Nancy's words chipped away at the progress I thought I'd made. They shook the mindset I had fought so hard to build, the one that believed healing was possible.

The relationship I wanted with my dad, the one I had poured my heart into, suddenly felt out of reach.

Like a foolish dream.

A fairytale I'd written in my head, thinking a heartfelt letter and overdue honesty could actually change things.

I felt stupid.

Naïve.

Like a little girl playing pretend, clutching hope as if it were strong enough to fix what silence and absence had shattered.

It left me stuck, caught between two worlds that had never quite fit together. The fragile bridge I was trying to build now felt unsteady. And for a while, I backed away.

I retreated into old habits, surface-level chats, safe distance.

It was easier.

Once the letters were out and everyone knew, the dynamic shifted. If there had been an elephant in the room before, now there was a mammoth, looming, silent, and heavy.

No one said anything.

So, neither did I.

I buried it.

Pretended none of it had happened.

Nancy's letter didn't help. It scared me off, yes, but I can't blame her entirely.

I wanted a deeper connection with my dad. But I realized I had built walls so high around him that when the door finally cracked open… I froze.

He tried, inviting me for coffee, long drives, little moments to rebuild.

But I hesitated.

Made excuses.

Not because I didn't care.

But because I didn't know how to show it anymore.

I thought one honest moment would fix everything.

But that's not how healing works.

There's no magic wand.

No "poof" that makes years of disconnect disappear.

It takes time.

It takes effort.

And I didn't give enough of either, neither did he.

We had a real chance, and we let it fade.

That's something I have to own now, too.

So, nothing came of the letters.

No big blowout.

No breakthrough.

Just… silence.

And here we are, still orbiting the same surface-level space we've always known.

Decades later and I still don't know how to let him in.

I want to.

I really do.

After years of existing in this emotionally neutral zone, it's become our normal. It's predictable, polite, and just safe enough to keep the deeper stuff out.

I think of that letter as a blueprint, one I poured my whole heart into. I imagined us rebuilding from the ground up, messy but meaningful. But I never laid the first brick; I walked away before anything real took shape.

And now, I sometimes find myself staring at that empty space, wondering if I still have it in me to try again.

I'm not seventeen anymore, I've grown up.

And sharing this now?

It's not about blame.

It's not about pointing fingers.

It's about telling the story the way I lived it, the way I felt it, the way it shaped me.

Healing doesn't come from silence.

It comes from truth.

And sometimes telling your story isn't about hurting someone.

It's about setting yourself free.

So here I am, thirty-eight years old, writing my story and wondering.

Can we still clear the air?

Can we finally acknowledge the mammoth in the room and ask it to leave?

No more small talk.

No more dancing around the pain we've both carried.

I know my dad has his own story.

His own wounds.

His own regrets.

And I've never claimed to be perfect either.

I'm sure there are things he's never said, things he's kept locked away, just like I did for so long.

But here's what I know for sure.

My dad has grown.

Maybe not on my timeline.

Maybe not in all the ways I needed.

But growth is growth, and I see it.

He's poured himself into his role as grandpa with endless time and endless love.

He's shown up in ways I once only dreamed of.

And me?

I've welcomed him in that role with open arms.

But as my dad?

I have never fully opened that door.

Maybe because I believed it was too late, and he missed his chance.

That the version of me who needed him the most had already grown up and moved on.

But the truth is…

I never fully let go of that little girl.

The one who still wonders what it would feel like to be truly seen by her dad.

So maybe it's time.
Time to dust off those old blueprints.
Time to lay the first brick.
Time to stop wondering and start rebuilding.
This time, for real.
Because despite everything.
I'm ready.
Not for surface-level conversation or polite weather updates.
For something honest, something earned, and something real.
And if you're still wondering whether I have daddy issues?
Yeah. I do.
However, I'm done letting them define me.

No matter how old a daughter gets, eight or eighty, there's a part of her that will always ache to be seen through her father's eyes.
We outgrow clothes.
We outgrow homes.
We outgrow so much.
But the longing to feel like daddy's little girl?
That part never really goes away.

CHAPTER 5

First Bell, New Beginning

"The first step toward getting somewhere is to decide you're not going to stay where you are."

— J.P. Morgan

Let's talk about Jody, the teenager, beyond the family dynamics, beyond the letters and unspoken emotions.

Let's talk about the girl with the wind in her hair and dreams in her eyes. She was busy collecting memories like Polaroids and stashing them in a shoebox, while trying to figure out who she was in a world that never paused long enough to ask.

Was I the social butterfly, whose laughter was trailing behind me like perfume?

The loyal type, spending Friday nights on trampolines with my close-knit crew, counting stars and swapping secrets?

Did Megan and I run the halls like a dynamic duo, our inside jokes echoing through the school like our own soundtrack?

Or were there unexpected characters who wandered into my story, changing its course without ever knowing?

And love…

Was there a first kiss under the dim glow of streetlights, a first heartbreak that felt like the world was cracking open, as I cried into my pillow with mascara-streaked cheeks?

Was I the hopeless romantic writing his name in the margins of my notebook, dreaming of forever following one late-night phone call. Or did I keep my walls up, guarding my heart like a fortress with no drawbridge?

Did I sneak out at midnight for teenage freedom?

Was I the girl with a red solo cup in hand, dancing like no one was watching? Or the one wrapped in a hoodie on the porch, deep in a 2 a.m. conversation that meant more than any party?

Maybe I was the athlete pushing through drills under the floodlights. Maybe the artist who was hiding in melodies that said what I couldn't. Or maybe I found my passion in stories, in movement, in the moments that made me feel most alive.

In class, was I the one with my hand raised, eager to be seen? Or the one sinking into my chair, silently begging not to be called on, even when I knew the answer?

Who was that girl?

She was a wild mix of strength and softness, figuring it out as she went.

And every tangled, magical, unforgettable moment was part of her becoming.

High school movies keep getting remade for a reason, those years are juicy. Bursting at the seams with drama, friendship, heartbreak, self-discovery, and transformation.

The teenage brain is a rollercoaster with no brakes, looping through joy, fear, hope, and doubt in the span of a single afternoon. There's a constant tug-of-war between who you are, who you want to be, and who the world expects you to be.

The spark when something clicks. The slump when it all feels like too much. These years are enlightening, no doubt. But they can also be dark, crushing, and lonely.

Everyone walks a different path through those hallways. We're shaped by the people who walk beside us, the moments that catch us off guard, and the choices that define who we become.

Teenage years are complicated.

They're wild.

They're full of lessons we don't even know we're learning. Until we're years down the line, looking back with a mix of gratitude and cringe.

I can still remember exactly what I wore on the very first day of high school, a rainbow tube top. Its vibrant stripes bursting with color, tucked beneath a pair of classic denim overalls.

It wasn't just an outfit; it was a declaration.

A bold, unapologetic entrance into a brand-new chapter.

I thought I looked so cool, strutting through the halls like the world was mine, radiating the confidence only a fifteen-year-old standing at the edge of something new could feel.

That rainbow wasn't just stitched into the fabric, it was stitched into me. I've always loved bright colors, the way they speak without saying a word.

They radiate warmth, energy, and joy.

They don't blend in.

They shine.

And that's what I wanted, to shine.

To walk into a room and bring the sunshine with me.

I was bubbly in the truest sense of the word.

The kind of girl who greeted everyone with a smile.

Who laughed loudly, genuinely, and often.

Who believed that even the tiniest act of kindness could change someone's entire day.

That was one of my favorite things about myself back then.

My ability to be joyful, even when life wasn't easy.

And it wasn't always easy.

But still, I chose optimism. I chose to see the glass half full, to believe in the good, to search for silver linings, even when they felt paper-thin.

I believed in the ripple effect of kindness, in the contagious power of joy.

I still do.

Because the world needs all the sunshine it can get.

Of course, staying positive isn't always easy. Life has a way of knocking us down, of testing our strength in ways we never see coming. I know what it's like to walk through the dark, to wonder if the light is even reachable.

But I've always found my way back, by leaning. Leaning on people who reminded me I didn't have to face the storm alone.

I've climbed out of hard seasons with steady hands holding me, and the warmth of generosity, both given and received. Because I know how powerful it is to have someone in your corner.

Someone who stands tall when you can't.

Who becomes your wings until you're ready to fly again.

Even when you're not ready to speak your truth, just knowing someone's there, quietly and faithfully, can change everything.

It's not always about words.

Sometimes, it's just about presence.

We're wired for connection.

We crave compassion.

We need someone saying, "I've got you," when life feels like too much.

That's why I lead with light.

Why I show up bubbly.

Why I choose love over judgment.

Joy over anger.

Because lifting others up is powerful.

A simple smile, a moment of thoughtfulness, can shift the course of someone's day, maybe even their life.

One of my love languages is giving.

Not for praise or payback, but because making a difference, no matter how small, is enough.

That part of me comes from my mom.

Her warmth.

Her gentleness.

The way she makes people feel seen, heard, and valued lives in me, too.

Helping others has always felt like my purpose.

Some people spend their lives searching for meaning.

But I've always known.

Even as a little girl, I told my mom, "When I grow up, I'm going to change the world."

I didn't know how, I just felt it. Like a spark, a pull, a whisper saying, "go this way."

While other kids dreamed of being astronauts or firefighters, I wasn't dreaming of a job. I was dreaming of impact, of helping people, of healing hearts in some small, beautiful way.

I wasn't inspired by a book, a movie, or a magical mentor. It was just there, planted deep like a seed I was born with. A calling woven into my bones.

I truly think the path chose me.

I still remember a time when I was seven, while other kids played house or dressed up dolls, I set up shop as a therapist. My bedroom became a tiny office with a desk, chairs, and a notepad. I waited for friends to come sit across from me, ready to spill their problems like we were in a second-grade therapy session.

I was ready, ready to listen.

To help, to hand out advice like a tiny life coach in sneakers.

Let's just say… not many kids lined up to play that game. Fair enough, most seven-year-olds can't exactly articulate their problems.

But looking back, it all makes sense.

Even then, I wanted to be a safe place.

Someone people could count on.

Someone who made things better.

No, I never became a therapist. But that girl with the notepad and the oversized heart?

She never left.

She just grew up and found new ways to live out her calling.

We'll get to that soon.

Just know this… the spark never died.

It's still burning.

And my light?

My light is only shining brighter.

So, there I was, teenage me, standing at the threshold of a brand-new chapter.

The first day of high school buzzed with electricity. The air felt charged, full of fresh possibilities like the world was holding its breath for what would come next.

I was excited.

I needed this beginning.

I had convinced myself high school would be the reset button I desperately craved, a chance to step out of the shadows of the past and into something brighter.

Looking back, I was living in denial.

Still, I charged ahead like a treasure hunter, convinced there was gold waiting behind friendships, new experiences, and self-discovery. As an unconquerable pirate sailing uncharted waters, I braced myself for the journey ahead.

I could almost see it, the ship cutting through unpredictable seas, the crew whispering about dangers lurking below. Dark shapes slithered beneath the surface, monsters with unseen claws reaching up from the depths. Deckhands trembled, pleading to retreat, to turn back before it was too late.

Except the gold I sought wasn't something I could hold in my hands. It wouldn't make me rich. It wouldn't buy me status or success.

No, what I was searching for was something far more valuable, I was searching for an escape. The monsters I feared weren't hidden beneath the waves, waiting to attack my ship. They were behind me, lingering in my past, following no matter where I went.

High school was supposed to be my fresh start, a chance to finally outrun those monsters. I was on a mission, and I wasn't letting anything get in my way.

I had a close group of friends, the kind who'd save you a seat in the cafeteria without needing to be asked. I had a quiet boost of confidence too.

That summer, I had met a few older boys, which gave me just enough familiarity to feel like I had a shortcut through the unsettling first-day awkwardness. I wasn't walking in blind, I had backup. Social credibility, even.

Sure, I'd heard the horror stories.

The locker-side hushed tones, the silent social rules, the upperclassmen eye rolls. High school could be a battlefield, a jungle where the villains wore designer jeans and perfect ponytails.

But I wasn't too worried.

I was outgoing, bubbly, and warm.

I thought people would like me.

I hoped they would.

This was my clean slate, and I was ready.

My outfit was perfect, glowing confidence like I was starring in my own coming-of-age film. The sun was shining, the air felt golden. It was the kind of morning that makes you believe everything is going to go your way, and for a little while, it did. I stepped into the building with purpose, heart pounding, sneakers hitting the floor like I owned it.

Lockers slammed.

Laughter echoed.

The scent of cafeteria fries and pencil shavings filled the halls.

I smiled at familiar faces, waved at the boys I had met that summer, and let myself believe the story was beginning just the way I had hoped.

But it didn't take long...

I was in the cafeteria, still glowing with first-day optimism, when an older girl zeroed in on me.

Her steps were sharp, eyes locked on mine like I was a target.

"Are you Jody?" she asked.

There was no curiosity in her voice, only confrontation.

She already knew the answer; this was just the setup.

Behind her stood a cluster of girls with folded arms and tight smirks, like they'd shown up just for the spectacle about to unravel.

I froze.

Confused.

How did she even know my name?

The noise around me faded.

All I could hear was my own heartbeat.

She waited.

I nodded.

And that was all it took.

The energy shifted.

My stomach twisted.

And I knew...
Something had been said.

A rumor had found its way into the air before I'd even had a chance to open my mouth.
It had already run through the halls like wildfire.

Suddenly, I was known.
Not in the way anyone dreams of being known.
No, I was the girl they'd judged by the cover and never bothered to read.

And just like that, my clean slate...
Was vandalized in graffiti I hadn't even written.

CHAPTER 6

The Moment That Broke Me

"You never know how strong you are until being strong is your only choice."

— *Bob Marley*

Before we get to the rumor, let's start at the beginning, with what I used to believe was a relationship.

But that's not the right word.

A relationship implies something mutual.

Shared feelings, shared respect, shared experience.

This was none of that; it was one-sided. From the way it started, to the way it unfolded, to the way it left its mark.

One-sided in pleasure.

One-sided in power.

One-sided in control.

I was just there, along for the ride, swept up in something I didn't understand, didn't choose, and didn't know how to escape.

No say.

No space to breathe.

Just discomfort disguised as attention.

Confusion dressed up as connection.

That's where it all began.
Before the whispers.
Before the judgment.
Before the rumor caught fire.
There was this…
And it would change my life forever.

Like most things back then, it started casually. Just a group of teens bouncing from house to house, laughter echoing through basements, time moving slow and fast all at once.

We were just kids, living for each other, living for the moment.

Most of the group smoked up, it was part of the scene. Nothing wild or rebellious, just expected. I tried it, of course, but it didn't sit right with me. It made me quiet, paranoid, trapped in my own thoughts.

So instead, I stuck to cigarettes. That thin roll between my fingers gave me something to hold onto. A ritual, a way to belong without completely losing myself.

And in that haze of smoke, music, and teenage noise…

He was there.
Watching.
Waiting.

That's where the story really began.
The night I ended up at Devin's house for the first time.
It was small, like mine.

Where my house felt lived-in and loved, his felt cold and still. Like something heavy hung in the air, silent and unspoken. The lights were dim, the energy off, but no one else seemed to notice.

So, I ignored the knot in my stomach and told myself I was being over dramatic.

We were just there to hang out, right?

What's the worst that could happen?

We sat around eating snacks, flipping through MP3s, and pretending the night was ordinary.

Beneath it all was something different, something I couldn't name yet.

I had only met him once before at a local social a few weeks earlier.

If you've never been to a social, picture a dimly lit hall packed with plastic cups, pulsing music, and silent auction prizes lining the back wall. They're usually fundraisers, sometimes for weddings, sometimes birthdays, and sometimes just as an excuse to throw a party.

This one was a sweet sixteen for a girl I didn't even know. I went because that's what we did. We followed the energy, showed up where things were happening.

There he was.

Devin.

With a presence.

Not the loud kind, the heavy kind. The kind that made people tense up the second he entered the room.

He didn't need to say much, his authority did the talking. He was the leader of his group, the one they all orbited. Not out of admiration, but caution.

He had that hardened look, like life had roughed him up early and he'd decided to punch back. His eyes scanned the room like he was always on guard.

He had a bleach-blond buzz cut, sharp features, and an icy stare. His jaw was permanently clenched.

You could sense his temper was simmering just beneath the surface. People walked on eggshells around him, afraid to say anything wrong.

By the end of that night a fight broke out, typical for a social.

This one had Devin's name written all over it. He held the power and everyone else was just spinning in his gravity.

A few days after the social, I heard the gossip.

Devin liked me.

At first, I didn't think much of it, just teenage talk. And besides, my mind was somewhere else. On someone else.

Luke.

He was my teenage daydream. The kind of boy you crush on without even realizing it. He leaned against walls like he had nowhere to be and no one to impress. There was something calm about him, mysterious and magnetic.

Even though I knew he wasn't looking for anything serious, I found myself hoping that I might be the exception. Hoping he saw me the way I saw him.

Even hope without words has a heartbeat.

Luke was the rhythm mine followed.

He was also the boy I lost my virginity to.

It happened quietly, gently, no pressure, no fear. Just a calm certainty that it was the right moment with the right person.

He made me feel safe, seen, like I mattered.

He was exactly what I needed in that moment.

I wished something more came from it, but it didn't. We remained friends, nothing more, nothing less.

Then along came Devin.

The opposite of Luke in every way.

When I heard he liked me, something unexpected crept in.

What if dating him made Luke jealous?

What if seeing me in someone else's arms flipped a switch?

It worked in movies, didn't it?

The girl moves on.

The guy realizes what he's lost.

He comes running back.

Maybe that would happen for me.

Maybe this was my happy ending too.

So, when Devin invited me over one night…

I said yes.

Why not?

And I went.

The night air was cool, but the second I stepped through his door, his attention wrapped around me like warmth. He was dialed in, charming, confident, and effortlessly flirtatious. Every smirk, every glance felt intentional.

I felt seen like I was the center of his universe.

And for a moment, that was enough.

We sat on the futon in his room, cushions soft, sunken and worn like they held secrets of their own. The energy between us hummed with a quiet charge. His hand hovered close to mine, heat radiating and inviting.

Luke never crossed my mind.

I had come in thinking this was about him.

But now?

Now I was here.

Present.

Wanted.

The butterflies were Devin's now.

The hangout started like any other. It was just teenagers packed into a small room, passing snacks, telling stories, half-listening to music buzzing from a speaker in the corner. Smoke clung to the air, the vibe was light and free.

Eventually people started leaving, one by one, until it was just the three of us, Devin, Mitch, and me.

I was fifteen at the time and my curfew was creeping in. Molly was a caring, involved mom with reasonable rules and expectations I respected. I had maybe an hour left, max.

I stayed on the cozy futon, nestled in the same spot where earlier I felt confident.

I felt seen.

But now... something shifted.

A stillness.

A weight.

Like the room itself was holding its breath.

Then he turned toward me.

Slowly.

Deliberately.

His eyes locked onto mine with an intensity that made my skin crawl.

The warmth from earlier, the playful charm and the flirty smiles, were gone. Replaced by something cold.

Hungrier.

I knew instantly, he wanted something.

His gaze didn't waver as he said, flatly, "Mitch, go stand outside the door."

No explanation.

No context.

Just an order.

Mitch didn't hesitate. He didn't blink. He stood up like he'd been trained for this moment, like it was expected.

And just like that, he was gone.

No words.

No goodbyes.

Just gone.

That's when the truth hit me. People didn't question Devin. They didn't push back. They obeyed. He was the kind of guy who thrived on power, and everyone around him played along.

Now I was the only one left in the room.

The energy had changed.

Suddenly, he wasn't the charming, flirtatious guy from earlier.

He was commanding, assertive in a way that sent a shiver through my core.

I felt like I had to obey.

Like saying no wasn't an option.

He leaned in and kissed me.

At first, it was gentle, soft lips brushing mine, almost delicate. For a moment, I felt a flicker of relief, like maybe this wouldn't be so bad.

But I couldn't shake the uneasiness clinging to the edges of my mind. There was a pressure in my chest, something tight and unspoken.

His friend was just outside the door, close enough to hear every movement, every breath. The basement was small, his room tucked at the end of a narrow hallway, a single dim light casting long shadows on the carpet. The walls were thin, too thin to muffle sound. And the air felt thick enough to cut through.

I felt exposed, like I was on display in a space that should've felt safe but didn't. My heart thudded louder with each second, the unease growing harder to ignore.

Then things escalated.

Quickly.

One moment I was sitting upright, nerves buzzing beneath my skin, and the next, he pulled me down with him. The cushions shifted with a muffled thud, and suddenly I was flat on the futon, his body pressing over mine. The weight of him was startling, heavy, and confined like the air had been pushed from my lungs.

His kisses weren't soft anymore.

The tenderness had vanished, replaced by something rougher, more forceful.

His lips moved with urgency, his hands roamed faster and rougher, as if he were chasing something instead of sharing a moment.

My body tensed.

The butterflies in my stomach turned into knots.

"Slow down," I said.

My voice steady, but tight.

Trying to stay calm while everything inside me screamed.

He paused.

Just for a second.

A flicker of stillness, like a match burning out before the flame could catch.

For a breath, I thought he heard me.

That he understood.

But deep down, I knew that moment was already slipping away.

Suddenly it went from a few kisses to… holy shit, how did he get my pants off so fast?

One second, they were on.

The next, tangled around my ankles like an afterthought.

My mind barely had time to catch up.

Everything was moving in fast-forward, a blur of touch and pressure that felt wrong.

All wrong.

"Slow down," I said again.

Sharper this time, my voice cracking under rising fear.

But he didn't listen.

He had a one-track mindset.

Eyes glazed.

Locked in.

Nothing was going to stop him.

I squirmed.

My body twisted beneath his.

Shifting my legs trying to slide out.

Trying to sit up.

Maybe if I could just get to my feet, he would realize and see me. He'd understand this wasn't okay.

But I couldn't sit up.

He pressed down harder.

His weight pinned me like a boulder.

Unmoving.

Unrelenting.

My limbs felt flimsy.

Panic burst through my body like glass shattering from the inside, sharp and sudden.

My throat tightened.

My breath came in short, stuttering gasps.

The room shrank.

The air grew heavy.

I felt stuck.

Helpless.

Like I was slipping underwater with no one to pull me out.

And then, he was inside me.

No protection.

No permission.

Just him.

Using my body like it was his to take.

His to claim.

It happened so fast, too fast for my brain to keep up.

One second, I was twisting away, trying to breathe, and the next, he was already there.

My stomach dropped.

I froze.

My body locked up like a puppet with its strings cut.

Paralyzed.

My heart thundered against my ribcage so loud I could barely hear my own voice.

"I... can we please stop?"

Maybe it was barely above a whisper.

Maybe I said it too soft, hoping he'd see the desperation in my eyes instead.

But he didn't stop.

"I want to stop," I said again, firmer this time.

My voice trembled.

My words felt thin in the thick silence of that small basement room.

But nothing changed.

The warmth and safety I had felt earlier were stripped away, replaced by something cold.

Violating.

I was no longer a girl sharing a moment but an object beneath him.

The ceiling blurred above me.

My vision swam with confusion, fear, and disbelief.

I kept waiting for him to hear me, to realize and pull away.

But he didn't.

He didn't even pause.

It was like he couldn't hear me.

Or worse, didn't care to.

He was locked in his own world, chasing what he wanted, and I was just... there.

A body.

A prop.

A shell to use and discard.

My voice felt like a whisper swallowed by a storm, soft and powerless against the chaos crashing inside me.

I still remember the weight of him, heavy and unrelenting. His body pressing me into the futon like I was nothing more than furniture beneath him. My arms pinned, my legs frozen, my mind racing in every direction, trying to make sense of what was happening.

It didn't last long.

Not by the clock on the wall.

But to me, time split into a thousand slow-motion fragments.

Every second dragged like an hour.

Every breath burned.

It felt like a decade of my life was stolen in just a few excruciating minutes.

Why didn't I fight harder?

Why didn't I scream?

Why didn't I push him off with everything I had?

Fair questions.

He wasn't listening to my voice, but couldn't I have used force?

He was pinning me down, so why couldn't I push him away with the same strength?

In that moment I had zero fight in me.

None.

My body felt paralyzed and disconnected, like it wasn't mine anymore.

Somewhere in the chaos, it had been stolen. He had taken it, claimed it, and I was just there, a passenger inside my own skin.

Maybe it was fear.

Maybe, deep down, I was just like everyone else, afraid of him. Afraid of the rage simmering beneath the surface. Afraid of what he might do if I pushed back too hard.

The what ifs screamed through my mind, frantic and loud.

What if I made it worse?

What if he hurt me more?

But it wasn't only fear.

It was something deeper, heavier.

A kind of emotional suffocation.

I felt powerless.

Like the moment had already swallowed me whole.

Like I was already too far gone to crawl my way back.

I wasn't just trapped physically; I was trapped emotionally.

Mentally.

Completely.

And when your body no longer feels like your own…

When you're stripped of agency, of safety, of voice…

You stop trying to save it.

He finished.

Cleaned up.

Got dressed.

Lit a cigarette.

The flick of the lighter echoed in the silence. Sharp and jarring. Smoke curled into the air, calm and indifferent, like him.

No cuddles.

No eye contact.

No affection.

No words.

Just done.

Like it was nothing.

Like I was nothing.

I sat up slowly. Every movement felt foreign and disconnected. My hands trembled as I reached for my pants, fingers fumbling like they'd forgotten how to work. I pulled them up over what now felt like tainted skin.

A body that had been taken, used, and discarded.

The weight of it all pressed into my chest, heavy and hollow at the same time. I wanted to crawl out of myself. To erase the last ten minutes. To rewind and run.

But I couldn't.

I just sat there.

Numb.

Swallowing a scream with nowhere to go.

The damage was already done.

I felt hollow.

Used.

Like a crumpled page torn from a book and tossed aside.

Devin called Mitch back in, his voice casual, like nothing had happened. Mitch walked in without hesitation. No awkward glance. No shift in energy. Just business as usual.

And me…

I was still on the futon, skin crawling, surrounded by the thick scent of sweat and smoke. The air felt colder now, suffocating. Like even the room recognized something had changed. I sat frozen and stunned, trying to process what had just happened, how fast it had all unraveled. Smoke curled through the room like ghostly fingers.

Mitch lounged against the wall, legs stretched out. He flicked ash into a cracked tray and started rambling about music, school, and some party next weekend. Nothing that mattered. His tone was light and easy, like we were just three teens killing time on a Tuesday night.

But I wasn't killing time.

I was dying in it.

Each drag of his cigarette sent smoke spiraling overhead, thick and suffocating. It clung to me, seeped into my skin like a second layer I couldn't shed. A smell I once found comforting now made me sick.

My body ached.

My chest was tight.

I sat hollow, heart pounding like a ticking clock I couldn't silence.

I wanted to scream but my voice was buried under everything I'd said that night, everything no one had listened to.

And Mitch?

He knew.

He had stood just beyond the door.

Close enough to hear every shift of the mattress.

Every plea.

"Slow down."

"Stop."

"Can we please stop?"

"I want to stop."

Those weren't whispers.

They were clear.

They filled that room, then and now.

But Mitch didn't flinch. Didn't meet my eyes. Didn't say a word. Just lit another cigarette and kept talking.

Sometimes, nearly as painful as the act itself is the bystander who knows it's happening and chooses to do nothing.

I went to the bathroom to put myself back together.

The light above the mirror flickered, casting a pale-yellow hue across the cramped space. The walls were covered in peeling paint, and the air smelled faintly of mildew and smog.

It was the kind of bathroom you didn't want to spend much time in.

But I couldn't leave.

My hands gripped the porcelain sink so tightly my knuckles turned white, like the cold surface might somehow ground me, keep me from unraveling.

My reflection stared back at me through the warped glass.

Same eyes.

Same face.

But everything somehow looked… different.

Like someone had pressed a shadow over my features.

The glow that usually lived behind my smile was gone. My cheeks were flushed, not with warmth, but shame. My lips, still slightly swollen, felt foreign. My hair was tousled, not in the playful, carefree way I liked, but messy in a way that made me want to disappear.

I blinked, hoping the image would reset, that the girl staring back would shift into someone I recognized.

But she didn't.

She looked like someone who'd been taken and left to figure out the pieces on her own.

There was a heaviness in my chest I couldn't shake, an ache wrapped tight around my ribs. My stomach churned with nausea and confusion, but mostly, blame.

Not for him but for me.

Somehow, I had already internalized it.

I felt dirty.

Like I'd crossed a line I never meant to.

Like I had invited something I didn't want.

Even though I said stop.

Even though I pulled away.

Even though I wasn't okay.

The room felt smaller with every second. The mirror began to fog from my breath, a soft mist blurring my reflection. I stayed there, trapped in that tiny space, trying to breathe, trying to think, trying to remember who I was before this night.

But all I could feel was the cold sink beneath my fingers and the silence that followed everything I never wanted to happen.

And then, I heard his voice.

"Jody."

It cut through the silence like a blade, sharp, casual, and inescapable.

He was calling my name, summoning me like nothing had happened.

Like this was normal.

Like I was normal.

I should've left.

I should've run.

His mom was home, just up the stairs. I should have bolted up and told her everything. I could've called my mom, begged her to come get me, sobbed into the phone like a child, because that's exactly how I felt.

Small.

Scared.

Shattered.

But I didn't.

I was frozen.

Paralyzed by fear, confusion, and shame.

And deeper than all of that...

Obedience.

It felt like an invisible string yanked me back into that room. I wasn't making choices anymore; I was just responding.

So, I went.

Step by step, legs dragging like they were made of lead. Each movement felt disconnected like I was watching from above.

I sat down on the futon.

Only now it wasn't soft. It wasn't warm or inviting. It was concrete, cold, and unforgiving. Just like the hollow ache coursing through my body.

Then he reached for me and draped his arm around me like a possessive cloak.

I was his now.

Claimed.

He reached for a water bottle on the coffee table and handed it to me. He uncapped it, passed it to me gently like some kind of peace offering. His movements were calm, practiced, like he'd done this before. Like he knew how to perform care.

He asked me questions, made small talk, leaned in, nodded, listened. His gaze locked on mine. His tone soft and attentive. He pulled me into the conversation with Mitch, who sat there lighting another cigarette like none of it mattered.

Devin made sure I was included now, acknowledged like I'd been initiated into some inner circle I never asked to join.

It was deliberate.

Calculated.

A shift in energy.

A silent message... You're mine now.

I felt it in every breath.

I wasn't a girl anymore.

I was property.

A prize.
A toy covered with fingerprints.
And that was that.

Something in my mind started to shift as I sat there, his arm heavy around me like a chain I wasn't sure I wanted to break.
They call it survival instinct, and that's exactly what kicked in.
My body had endured the moment.
Now it was my brain's turn.
Because if I let myself believe it for what it truly was, I would've crumbled right there on that cold futon.
So, my mind got to work.
Quietly.
Subtly.
Rewiring itself like a security system being reprogrammed to ignore the alarms.
I began feeding myself new thoughts, softer ones.
He really liked me. It wasn't awful; it was passion.
Just his intense way of showing he cared.
I started to believe it.
I told myself I was his girl now.
His girlfriend.
We were official, even if the words were never said.
Because without meaning, it was just trauma.
Just violation.
Just pain.
And I wasn't ready to sit with that.
So, I painted over it.
Used hope as my brush, denial as my color.
I told myself I liked it.
Told myself it wasn't a big deal.
Told myself everything was fine.
Just a boy and a girl.
Just sex.
Something special.

That's what I whispered to myself.
Over and over again.
Until the lie started to sound like the truth.

Everything was fine.
Everything was fine.
Everything was fine.

CHAPTER 7

The Rumor

"Surviving was the first silent decision I ever made."

— Rudy Francisco

Did it work?

Was I able to convince myself that the version I had created, the one where everything was fine... was real?

Yeah.

At least on the surface.

At least for a little while.

When my mom pulled up outside Devin's house, I climbed into the car like nothing had happened. I smiled, chatted, laughed at something she said.

I looked out the window like I was caught in the glow of a new romance, not the aftermath of something I didn't even know how to name.

I brushed my teeth, changed into pajamas, and crawled into bed like it was any other night.

But inside, nothing felt normal.

My body buzzed with static like a TV stuck on the wrong channel. But somehow, I slept.

The next morning, I wore my best "everything is fine" outfit.

Cute.

Confident.

Untouchable.

I walked into junior high like I was floating. Just a few months left in grade nine before high school. A fresh start ahead.

And yet, I was still just a kid.

I should've been giggling through spin the bottle. Sneaking kisses in dark corners during seven minutes in heaven.

I should've been figuring out affection on my own terms, not shoved past the line before I was ready.

I carried that night like a stone in my chest.

But on the outside, I was just another girl counting down to summer.

I told my friends Devin was sweet and thoughtful, how into me he was. And when they asked if we'd slept together, I smiled.

"Yes," I said.

And not just yes.

"Yes… and it was great."

The scariest part was I believed it, or at least, needed to.

That's the thing about trauma.

If you can't face it, your mind finds a way to hide it. You don't rewrite the story to lie, you rewrite it to survive.

You build a version where you were wanted.

Where it was your choice.

Where you had control.

I wore that version like armor.

A week had passed. Devin called every day. We flirted, laughed, talked like we were just two teens in a new relationship.

Everything seemed fine.

I was fine.

That's what I told myself.

Hoping it would be enough.

Then he invited me back.

And why wouldn't he?

I was his girlfriend now, right?

That's the version I'd built.

So going back felt normal.

But something inside me hesitated. Just a flicker at first, a mutter of dread. My body remembered what my mind refused to.

So, I brought Ashley with me. She didn't know why. I didn't even say it out loud, but I needed her there.

Because deep down, I knew I couldn't be alone with him again.

Still, I silenced the warning.

Told myself it was real.

That he liked me.

That he cared.

So, I stayed.

When I walked into his room, his face lit up. Grinning, warm, pulling me into the fantasy I'd repeated so many times it felt like truth.

Soon after, Ashley got a call from her crush, he was nearby.

"I'm gonna go meet him," she said, her voice light and bubbly.

She stood up to leave, smoothing her hair in the mirror.

I asked her not to go, not with panic, not with urgency, but with a tremble in my voice that said more than my words ever could.

From her view, I was fine. I was with my boyfriend. She thought she was giving me a moment of teenage romance… I let her think that after all.

But when she walked out the door, it felt like I had just lost my last lifeline.

There I was.

Alone with Devin again.

Well, technically not alone.

A few of his buddies were still there, laughing and talking. The room felt full, loud, and safe for a moment. There were more people, more eyes, more buffers.

At least, that's what I told myself.

Devin pulled me close, his arm wrapped tight around me like something to show off. Possessive in a way that might have looked romantic to someone else.

Then just as I started to settle into the noise, the illusion of normalcy…

He gave me that look.

The same one as before.

That dark flicker in his eyes.

That silent demand behind a crooked smile.

The air swung.

My body went still.

I knew that look.

I knew what was coming next.

This time, he didn't ask his friends to leave the room. He didn't need to; he had already claimed me.

There were no more formalities, no more pretenses. Just a quiet authority in the way he moved, like he owned the room.

Like he owned me.

He grabbed my hand, firm and deliberate.

Then without a word, led me out.

Past the laughter.

Past the noise.

Past the safety I had talked myself into believing.

Straight to the bathroom.

That same cramped little space just outside his bedroom door. The one with chipped tile floors and a mirror that had watched me fall apart once before.

I knew what was about to happen.

And deep down, I didn't want it to.

Even though I was "his girl" now, even though I had convinced myself this was a real relationship, I wasn't ready.

I wasn't okay.

Just because I'd lost my virginity didn't mean I was suddenly fine with being touched whenever he wanted.

I still had boundaries.

I still had a right to choose.

But to him, I didn't matter.

He never asked.

He just assumed.

Like I was on-call now.

An open door.

A green light that never turned red.

As if once you say yes the first time, you're not allowed to say no ever again.

As if intimacy becomes a debt, a routine, or a package deal.

Like my body wasn't mine anymore… it was his.

But that's not how it works.

Just because you've been intimate before doesn't mean you owe anyone access.

Consent isn't a one-time pass.

It isn't permanent.

It isn't automatic.

To him, it wasn't even a question.

It was already decided.

And despite my gut screaming to run, I followed him.

Every step felt like dragging through wet cement, heavy and resistant. The hallway stretched ahead like a tunnel, dark and narrowing, swallowing me whole.

My body moved, but it wasn't mine.

It felt borrowed, like I was floating outside myself, helpless to change course.

The bathroom door loomed, a chipped white frame with rusted hinges. When he opened it, harsh light spilled into the hall, casting our shadows across the floor. My legs were numb. The air was sharp and cold. It smelled like mold and stale body spray.

I caught a glimpse of myself in the mirror, just a blur of fear disguised as calm.

Then, I heard it.

The voices inside my head.

Clear.

Loud.

Urgent.

"Stop."

"Don't follow him."

"Don't follow him."

It echoed like sirens, but I tried to bury it beneath the lies I'd been feeding myself.

That it was too late.

That saying no wouldn't matter.

That this was love.

That this was just what girlfriends do.

So, I stepped inside, the door shut behind me like the closing of a trap.

He kissed me.

Everything moved fast.

Too fast.

There was no tenderness.

No affection.

Just urgency, reckless and consuming.

His hands gripped my waistband hard.

He yanked my pants down so quickly I flinched, startled and scared.

Before I could process, he spun me around.

My hands braced against the cold counter.

It was happening.

Again.

No warning.

No pause.

Just him, taking what he wanted.

The pain was immediate, sharp, breath-stealing.

My body tensed.

I gasped.

"Please... slow down."

I whispered, barely audible.

"Can you be gentle?"

I held onto hope.

He cared about me, right?

We were together so he had to care.

People who care don't hurt you.

Right?
Wrong.
The fear I had buried erupted like a flood.
This was not okay.
This is not okay.
I am being raped.
"I want to stop."
This time, I didn't whisper. I yelled it.
"STOP."
And for a moment, just a flicker, he stopped.
His grip loosened.
The pressure lifted.
Relief bloomed in my chest, fragile but real.
But before I could even exhale, he was back.
Rougher.
More relentless.
And this time...
It wasn't just more of the same.
This time, it was different.
He forced himself somewhere else.
Somewhere untouched.
Unimagined.
Somewhere sacred.
No warning.
No hesitation.
Just violation.
The pain was blinding.
A scream rose in my throat but never made it out.
I went still.
Completely still.
My body no longer felt like mine.
He had taken more than my voice.
More than my safety.
He had taken something sacred.

Something that had always been mine.
Until now.

And in that moment, something in me broke.
A part of me was stolen.
Something that can never be returned.
It only lasted a few seconds but that's all it took.
A few brutal, unforgiving seconds to destroy something sacred.
A part of my spirit, gone.
My soul, splintered.
My self-worth, shredded.
My dignity, ripped from me like a page torn violently from a book.
I wasn't whole anymore.
I was hollowed out, a shell of the girl I'd been just moments before.
And that missing piece?
It wasn't replaced with healing.
It was filled with emptiness.
With disgust.
With hate, not just for him, but for myself.
With guilt that didn't belong to me, and shame that clung to my skin like smoke, like something I couldn't scrub off no matter how hard I tried.
This time, I couldn't repress it.
Couldn't shove it into the corners of my mind or pretend it hadn't happened.
This was real.
Too vivid.
Too raw.
I couldn't dress it up in a prettier narrative or lace it in denial or delusion.
There was no "maybe."
No gray area.
No excuse that could make sense of it.

No love story could save me from the truth.

He had raped me.

Not once.

But again.

It was without care, without hesitation, and without a single shred of remorse.

No matter how tightly I'd wrapped myself in the idea that we were together, that I was his girl, that this was love, none of it was real.

Safety had been an illusion.

Consent had never been part of the conversation.

And love?

Love wasn't even in the room.

It was never love.

It was power.

It was control.

It was rape.

And that truth hit harder than anything I had ever felt in my life.

Growing up in my generation, society painted rape as something vulgar and violent.

End of story.

A dark alley.

A stranger in a mask.

A weapon.

Screams echoing into the night.

Torn clothing.

Bruises.

Flashing lights.

Dramatic music swelling in the background.

I started to really think about what defines rape.

What makes it real?

What makes it count?

Because my experience?

It wasn't like in the movies.

So… was it still rape?

I had gone to his house willingly.

I'd convinced myself it was a relationship.

I didn't scream, I didn't claw my way out of the bathroom, I didn't run, I didn't call for help.

But I told him to stop, I said no, I asked him to slow down.

And still, I told myself, it wasn't enough.

I sat with that shame.

I swallowed it.

Let it grow.

Maybe I led him on.

Maybe I didn't fight hard enough.

Maybe I was just a stupid, naive girl who put herself in that situation.

Maybe I deserved what I got.

And for a long time, I believed those maybes.

No one teaches us that rape doesn't always look like it does in the movies.

No one tells us it can happen in familiar rooms, behind closed doors, with people who say they care.

No one tells us it doesn't always leave bruises you can see, but it always leaves a mark.

On your body.

On your mind.

On your soul.

It took a long time.

A lot of unlearning.

A lot of talking myself down from guilt and out of shame.

Twenty-four years later, I finally said it.

I said the words out loud.

I was a victim.

And I was raped.

If someone says "stop," "no," "slow down," "don't," anything along those lines... It's rape.

If their body language or facial expressions say no, say stop, say I don't want this... It's rape.

If someone doesn't fully, clearly, willingly consent... It's rape.

If they're blacked out drunk at a party, barely able to speak or stand, and someone takes advantage of them... It's rape.

If someone says yes at first but changes their mind and it continues anyway...It's rape.

Let's be clear...

If you're flirty, really flirty, if you're teasing, touching, sending signals all night long, but then you say no, and they don't stop?

It's rape.

Wearing a short skirt or a low-cut top isn't an invitation.

It's not automatic consent.

Women are allowed to flirt.

They're allowed to feel sexy.

They're allowed to move their bodies, flaunt their confidence, own their sexuality.

But none of that, not once, means they deserve to be taken advantage of.

No means no.

Silence means no.

Uncertainty means no.

Only clear, willing, uncoerced, fully present yes means yes.

There are no blurred lines.

No gray areas.

No such thing as "not fighting hard enough."

No such thing as "deserving it."

No such thing as "it wasn't that bad."

There's one undeniable truth... I was raped.

And I'm not alone.

I did not deserve it.

And if you're a victim, neither did you.

Society needs to stop pushing the narrative that rape only "counts" when it's violent, when it leaves bruises, when it's committed by a stranger in a back lane.

Because when that's the only version we validate…

We silence the rest of us.

What about survivors like me?

The ones who didn't scream loud enough.

Who didn't fight hard enough.

Who walked in willingly, but never truly consented?

What about the girls who convince themselves it wasn't really rape, because it didn't match the script the world gave them?

Rapists don't stop.

They don't question themselves.

They keep going because it's subtle.

Because girls like me carry the blame for them.

Because we stay quiet.

We bury it deep.

We suffer.

Every. Single. Day.

Fuck that.

Enough.

We already suffered when it happened.

Why are we still the ones suffering long after?

Why do we carry the shame?

Why do we carry the guilt?

While they get to move on like nothing happened.

It's time for society to wake up.

Rape is rape.

Victims deserve more than silence.

We deserve truth.

We deserve healing.

We deserve justice.

We deserve our voices back.

If you've been sexually assaulted, please don't be another silent statistic.

I know how hard it is to say it out loud.

I know the fear.

The shame.

The crushing weight of wondering…

Will they believe me?

Will they judge me?

Will they twist my truth into something else?

But your story?

It matters.

Your voice has power.

You are not alone.

I never want anyone to go through this.

I never want anyone to carry this void.

Because this changes you.

It lingers.

It shapes you in ways the world may never see, but you feel it, and you battle it daily.

The more we speak up…

The more we take back control…

The more we reclaim our power.

Before writing this book, I couldn't even say the word. I could barely whisper it.

But now I'm saying it.

Loud.

Clear.

Unapologetic.

Rape.

I am a victim of rape.

And I hope my voice, this voice, can save someone else.

The next victim.

Who walks into a room and doesn't see it coming.

Even if one survivor reads this and feels less alone, I've already started to change the world.

And that little girl inside me, the one who always wanted to help people, can finally breathe again.

Now back to that night.
What happened after?
Did I see him again?
Did I tell anyone?
Things didn't go back to normal.
He saw it in my face, I was broken, and he couldn't flirt his way out of it.
There was no smirk, no cocky joke, no charm strong enough to erase the emptiness in my eyes.
I don't even remember getting dressed or leaving. It was all a blur. My limbs felt foreign like they didn't belong to me. I think I just grabbed my stuff and left.
He didn't walk me to the door.
I just remember being cold.
Not the kind that makes you shiver, it was deeper.
In my bones.
In my soul.
My body was in shock.
I climbed into my mom's car in silence. She chatted gently, her voice soft and familiar. She asked how my night was, casually, warmly, like moms do.
I didn't respond.
Just stared out the window, watching streetlights blur.
I wanted to disappear.
I pressed my forehead to the glass and prayed the night would swallow me whole.
Inside, I felt disgusting.
Used, like trash.
I didn't tell her.
Not my mom.
Not my best friend.
No one.

Not because I thought they wouldn't believe me, but because I was terrified they'd look at me differently.

Because I already did. I didn't recognize the girl sitting beside my mom.

The girl in the mirror.

I felt like a ghost, haunting my own life.

So, I stayed silent.

And let the shame settle in.

Weeks passed and I started to notice it, the shift…

The quiet mumbles. The glances that flicked away too fast. Friends who paused when I entered a room. Eyes that wouldn't meet mine. My name muttered, hidden behind hands.

I already saw myself as broken.

Now they did too.

Then came his version of the story.

It didn't explode, it leaked.

A comment here, a laugh there.

Breadcrumbs of cruelty building a lie.

I wasn't just the girl who "hooked up" with Devin.

I was that girl.

The one who "loved it."

Who "begged for it."

Who "liked it rough."

The one who "took it in the ass."

His lie got to them first.

In that bathroom, he knew exactly what he'd done.

Maybe the first time he told himself I didn't mean it when I said stop.

But the second time?

He couldn't deny it when he saw my fear, confusion, and tears.

I was folding into myself, and he knew it.

Still, he made a choice not to face it, not to own it.

Instead, he rewrote the story.

Cast himself as the guy I couldn't get enough of.

He cast me as the slut.

He stripped away my truth and replaced it with a lie loud enough to drown me out.

And the worst part?

I wasn't going to tell anyone.

That night was my secret, my shame.

I buried it so deep; I could barely admit it to myself.

But his lie?

It was a warning.

A dare wrapped in a rumor.

Stay silent… or it gets worse.

The horror wasn't just the rumor.

It was knowing that he knew I wouldn't speak up.

That he'd already taken so much, I had nothing left to fight with.

My voice.

My safety.

My light.

His words were just smoke after the fire.

Embers trying to spark where the flames had already burned me down.

He thought he had silenced me.

But one day, I knew I would scream.

And when I did, I would never be silenced again.

Months passed.

I got good at pretending and burying it all beneath fake confidence and perfect smiles.

I told myself I had to keep climbing, keep building a life that looked okay.

But inside, that void was growing.

The basement trauma had taken root, stretching deeper and darker. I knew if I didn't start climbing out, I might never come back.

Then came high school.

My fresh start with new friends and new hallways.

A new version of me.

I held on to hope.

Devin's rumor followed me like a shadow.

And you know how rumors work…

They grow legs, they twist, and they stretch until they're unrecognizable.

So, there I was, sitting in the cafeteria wearing my rainbow tube top and denim overalls.

Trying to design my own clean slate.

Then, she appeared.

An older girl.

No warning.

No notice.

"Is it true?" she asked, loud enough for the room to hear.

"You're that massive slut who loves getting double-teamed in the ass?"

It hit me like a brick.

My stomach dropped.

My heart pounded.

I could barely breathe.

But I had to say something.

So, I sat up tall, smiled, and said…

"No."

One word.

All I had.

She laughed right in my face.

"Okay, whatever."

Her job was done, she walked away.

Silence fell.

Only stares, laughter, and gossip as the cafeteria collapsed around me in slow motion.

And just like that, I wasn't the bubbly girl in the colorful top anymore.

I was that girl.
The target.
The rumor.
The slut.

CHAPTER 8

Dysfunctional Relationships

"Until you heal the wounds of your past, you will bleed on people who didn't cut you."

— *Anonymous*

As I looked around the cafeteria, it felt like every pair of eyes had locked onto me, piercing through my skin, digging into my soul.

The whispers buzzed like static, but to me, they were deafening.

It was like the world had cranked up the volume, not to drown me out, but to spotlight my shame.

My body sank into the chair. I wished the floor would crack open and swallow me whole. But instead, I sat there, center stage, stripped bare under a cafeteria spotlight.

Her words had hit like a slap, but it was the stares that cut deeper.

I didn't know how the rumor traveled.

I had left that friend group behind and stopped speaking to most of them. Somehow, the lie made it across the city, across schools, slipping through cracks like smoke. It wasn't even the same school. It wasn't even the same part of town.

Yet before I could introduce myself, I had already been defined.

I was supposed to be starting over, instead I walked into a public execution.

Leading up to that moment, I had been climbing. I was clawing my way out of the crater Devin left in me. I pictured the summit, bathed in light, untouched by shadow, free from the ache I carried.

And for a moment, I thought I was close.

The first day had started strong.

My feet were steady.

My lungs full.

I was rising.

But I hadn't reached the top.

And that cafeteria moment?

That was the avalanche. The harness snapped. The safety rope vanished. And just like that, I was falling. Not all the way. Just dangling. Clinging to the face of the mountain, knuckles white, chest pressed hard to stone.

Below me, the pit stirred. The same one that opened in that basement. The same one I'd been trying to escape ever since.

Then the rumor itself hit me in full.

It wasn't even the same fucking rumor.

Somewhere along the way, it had mutated, twisted into something even worse.

"Double-teamed?"

"In the ass?"

It was grotesque, cruel, and completely false.

But it didn't matter. The rumor had spread, and it had stuck.

Now I wasn't just the girl from before, I was a spectacle, a punchline, the walking embodiment of someone else's fiction.

And the worst part?

It worked.

When I found out who brought it here, who made sure it reached my new school.

It wasn't Devin.

It was Ashley.

My best friend.

Or at least, the friend I thought she was.

She didn't just let the rumor travel.

She delivered it.

And that betrayal cut deeper than all the stares combined.

She knew I was hurting. She saw me retreat. And still… she did it anyway. It felt calculated, intentional, and razor sharp.

Sometimes, betrayal doesn't come only from enemies. It can come from the people standing right beside you. And that kind of betrayal cuts the deepest.

So, what happened after that?

Did I transfer schools?

Hide out in bathrooms?

Disappear?

Somehow, I got lucky, I started dating Cory.

He was a popular senior with a good reputation. And like magic, the shaming stopped. Not because people grew a conscience. It was because he made it known, subtly and firmly, that I was off-limits.

In high school, that's all it takes, social currency is real, and it carries power.

So yeah… the whispers didn't vanish.

But the boldness did.

For the first time in months, I could finally breathe.

I made it to the summit.

But I didn't climb there on my own. I was carried by someone else's status, someone else's protection.

When I got there, it wasn't what I imagined.

It wasn't freedom. It was quieter, sure. But the ache was still there. The shame still lingering. The trauma still tucked away beneath the surface, behind a prettier view.

I never faced it.

I just kept climbing, smiling, laughing, and surviving. I wasn't running anymore, I was outrunning. And for a while, that was enough.

But let me say this... I despise rumors.

They are poison. They start small, slip through cracks, and infect everything. They rewrite truth. Distort reality and ruin lives. Especially in adolescence, when self-love is already so fragile.

What might feel like harmless gossip to you or to someone else...

It's their world collapsing.

So, if you've ever repeated something just for the thrill of it...

If you've ever laughed when someone else's name came up...

Think again.

Words are not harmless.

They have power.

They can heal, or they can destroy.

So, lead with kindness.

Please.

Always choose the kind of power that builds someone up.

Not the kind that tears them down.

Let's talk about relationships, or more specifically, the patterns I kept falling into.

I call them dysfunctional for a reason.

It wasn't some perfect love ballad.

It was chaotic.

Off-key.

I was drawn to bad boys, but not the Devins of the world. Not the truly dangerous ones. My body remembered; my gut knew better.

The ones I fell for were charming, a little reckless, but never cruel. Life-of-the-party types with swagger on the outside and sadness in their eyes.

They didn't seem shattered, just cracked. Cracked enough to need fixing and I was the fixer, the healer.

That was my pattern.

My poison.

The nice guys never stood a chance. I dated a few, but it never lasted. If you had your life together, came from a good home, knew how to be compassionate, I didn't even see you.

Not because you weren't enough, but because I believed I wasn't.

I thought I was damaged.

That if you got too close, you'd see it too.

So, I chased what felt familiar... chaos.

Brokenness didn't scare me; it felt like home.

Yeah, my dad had something to do with it.

That old cliché about girls choosing men like their fathers, I lived it.

Charismatic, untamed, and emotionally unavailable.

And without even realizing it, I kept choosing that same man.

Without fail.

The boys I dated weren't cruel, they were emotionally distant. Deeply sensitive beneath the surface but unsure how to show it.

They didn't ask for help, but needed it. They appeared whole to the world but were crumbling in private.

And that was my guilty pleasure.

If I couldn't fix my dad, maybe I could fix them.

To me, love wasn't supposed to be easy; it had to be earned.

What better way to earn it than by becoming everything someone just a little broken needed?

Some of them were addicts, party boys chasing the next high.

I had one rule, no drugs.

They promised they'd quit for me, and I believed them. But the truth always came out, lies and denial on repeat.

And then I saw it, I was doing exactly what my mom had done.

Setting boundaries.

Clinging to promises.

Hoping love would be enough.

Turns out, the apple doesn't fall far from the tree after all.

Realistically I couldn't save them.

No matter how much they cared for me, the addiction always won.

They cared in their own way, but their needs always came first. I was the one on standby, waiting behind while they took center stage.

There were unanswered texts, missed birthdays, promises shattered on impact.

I kept fighting for people who wouldn't fight for me.

And even when I knew that, I stayed.

Hope is heavy, and I carried it like a damn champion.

I didn't want to be someone's everything.

I just wanted to matter.

I was always second place.

They would show up drunk. Forgot important days. Blackouts became routine. I cleaned up the mess. I became the babysitter, the driver, and the lifeguard.

I held them up, broke up fights, tucked them into bed. I wasn't a girlfriend; I was a buffer between them and their destruction.

And yes, I got cheated on… More than once.

I wasn't asking for perfection, just consistency, respect, and effort.

This wasn't about one guy.

It was a pattern that followed me through high school, into my twenties.

A shadow I couldn't shake.

Looking back, most of them weren't bad people. Just young and immature.

Emotionally unequipped.

They made stupid choices.

They hurt me because they didn't know how not to. But in their own messy, fractured way… they loved me.

In private, I was everything. The late-night drives, the way their fingers traced lazy patterns on my back, the whispered "I love you's."

I felt like the center of their world.

Until the second we stepped into public, the switch flipped. Suddenly, I was invisible, like love had a curfew. I hadn't changed, so why did they? I never asked for grand gestures. Just something real, something steady, and something safe.

Some of them grew up. They got there eventually. They started thinking before acting. They stopped being one version for me and another for everyone else. They stopped loving with conditions.

They started loving me the way they loved their mothers, with gentleness and care.

When I finally got the love I wanted, I should've been relieved.

Right?

But then, out of nowhere, I was caught.

Not physically.

Emotionally.

Mentally.

And the second that realization hit, I ran.

Just like I did on the big yellow slide, playing monster with my dad. His laughter behind me, my heart pounding as I sprinted away. Even back then, I hated being caught.

It made me feel trapped.

Powerless.

That same little girl still lived inside me. She still ran when love got too close. The closer someone came, the faster I sprinted. Even when it felt good. Even when it felt safe.

Because love, to me, had always come with conditions.

With risk and pain.

I wasn't running from them.

I was running from the part of me that didn't believe I deserved love.

You may be wondering… what is wrong with me?

I'd spent years craving commitment. I stuck it out through mayhem, through immaturity, through late-night apologies that always came too late. I patched up broken pieces.

So now, when I had everything I said I wanted, kindness, consistency, and commitment, what did I do?

I ran.

It sounds backwards, I know.

But trauma doesn't follow logic, it rewires you. And somewhere along the way, I learned that steady love wasn't mine to keep, it felt foreign. And when something feels unfamiliar, even if it's good, it's terrifying.

So yeah, I bolted.

Not because I didn't want love, but because I didn't know how to trust it. It felt like standing on the edge of a cliff with no handrails, no parachute, just trust.

And trust has never come easy to me.

I've been hurt.

Deeply.

I've cried into pillows, screamed into the dark, felt heartbreak in my bones.

But I was never fully destroyed, because I never fully gave myself away.

My heart had backup armor.

But what if I didn't?

What if I let my walls fall and handed someone the rawest, most delicate parts of me?

The thought alone made my chest tighten. I already felt like I was barely held together, stitched with invisible thread and stubborn hope.

You can chip at glass for years, scratch it, scuff it, wear it down, but it still holds. It still reflects the light and remains whole, even if imperfect.

But the second you shatter it?

That's it.

You're left with fragments.

Jagged, dangerous pieces that won't fit back together, no matter how hard you try. Even if you manage to glue them in place, the cracks will always show.

That's exactly how I felt.

I was that piece of glass, flawed, chipped, maybe a little cloudy in places, but still intact.

Still standing.

Until I wasn't.

What if he changed his mind?

What if he saw the wreckage beneath the smile and decided I wasn't enough?

My dad left.

So, he could too.

That's the story I knew.

The one my heart rehearsed on loop.

But here's the twist, the one that hurt most... I was the one leaving.

I became what I feared.

I left before I could be left.

I broke hearts so mine wouldn't be broken.

I became the villain, not because I wanted to be cruel, but because I was terrified. I stayed through havoc. I stayed through damage. I helped them grow, evolve, become the version I always believed in. Then, when I finally got what I wanted, I'd leave.

The worst part, as scared as I was of commitment, I was more afraid of being alone.

If things got too good, that creeping panic would set in.

And with it, a backup plan.

Someone on the sidelines. Someone I could text, flirt with, vent to when things with my boyfriend felt heavy. I didn't cheat, not physically, but emotionally there were blurred lines. Safety nets. Plan B's.

Because being alone was unbearable.

From fifteen through my twenties, I was single for maybe three weeks. Always moving from one relationship to the next. Never stopping long enough to reflect, to breathe, or to heal.

Why couldn't I just be alone?

You'd think someone afraid of commitment would crave solitude.

I didn't.

Being alone wasn't freeing, it was terrifying.

I was always on edge. Checking locks and peering out windows. The fear I carried wasn't just emotional, it was physical.

What happened in that basement rewired me.

I didn't just fear loneliness, I feared danger.

My first thought when I heard a sound at night wasn't theft, it was rape. Even with every door locked, the alarm on, cameras running, I didn't feel safe. I hated passing windows after dark. Even with the blinds shut, I felt exposed.

People talk about fight or flight. No one talks about freeze.

And freeze is what I know best.

If it ever happened again, would I move?

Would I fight?

Would I survive?

That's what no one sees. That's why true solitude, being really alone, is still my greatest fear. Not because I don't love my own company, but because I still don't fully believe I can protect myself if something goes wrong.

And here's the hardest truth of all…

That trauma doesn't excuse how I've treated some of the people I've cared for. It doesn't justify the way I left, the way I pulled away, the way I broke hearts without giving closure.

But maybe now, you understand why.

Relationships made me feel safe and protected. Like I wouldn't end up back in that basement.

Even if it wasn't the right relationship.

Even if it wasn't love.

It was enough to feel okay, for a little while.

I've made mistakes.

Big ones.

I've hurt people who didn't deserve it.

And I'm not proud of that.

I've always believed my purpose is kindness, lifting others, and spreading joy.

So where was that version of me in those moments?

I didn't ghost them. I ended things face-to-face with words, not silence.

But I still left.

And no matter how gently you break a heart, it still breaks.

You know that cliché, "It's not you, it's me?"

This time it really was me.

If you're wondering if I finally stopped running…
Yes.
I've been married for twelve years and I'm still in it.
So yeah, I broke the pattern, but it wasn't easy.
It still isn't.
Loving fully and staying steady takes work.
Trusting love, even safe love, is still something I'm learning.
But here's what I know for sure…
I deserve to be fully loved.
And I'm done running.

CHAPTER 9

Beautiful Chaos: Transition Into Adulthood

"Everyone is a genius. But if you judge a fish by its ability to climb a tree, it will live its whole life believing it is stupid."

— *Albert Einstein*

Three years later, high school ended, and I stood at the edge of something new.

Graduation felt like the final scene in a book I had written one hard-earned page at a time. Highlighted textbooks, scribbled margins, late-night cram sessions, and waves of self-doubt I'd fought through.

As I stepped onto the stage, lights hot on my face, applause swelling around me, I clutched my diploma like proof, not just of grades, but of survival.

I was proud of the girl who kept showing up, weathering the storm.

The honor roll?

Let me tell you, that didn't come easy, especially math.

Math was my Everest, where formulas blurred and numbers danced just out of reach. I spent hours hunched over notebooks, erasers worn thin, pencils shaved to stubs. I wanted it to click, I needed it to. But no matter how hard I worked, math and I were never friends. We were distant acquaintances in a strained relationship.

Sadly, it wasn't just math.

I've always felt like my brain worked differently.

While others soaked up knowledge like sponges, I tried to catch raindrops with open hands. Some stuck, most slipped through.

I wasn't lazy, I wanted to learn.

I was present, but I had to work harder and dig deeper, finding the backdoor route to understanding. That's just how my brain works. It takes the scenic route, but it gets there.

And now, I've actually learned to love that about myself.

Yes, I was chatty.

Okay, very chatty.

I needed constant reminders to pipe down.

Talking was how I connected, how I thrived. Socializing wasn't about attention. It was about energy, belonging, and learning through people, not just pages.

My mom still tells the story...

Little Jody at the park, wandering off and coming back minutes later with a new best friend like we'd known each other forever. That's who I've always been, a social butterfly with a heart wired for connection.

I never craved the spotlight. I could share it, step back when it wasn't my moment, or cheer others on from the sidelines. I knew how to read a room, how to show up when it mattered most.

But beneath all that, I struggled.

Especially with reading.

In grade four, my teachers noticed what I already knew, something wasn't clicking. My mom enrolled me in a resource class. Literacy wasn't as confusing as math, but it was still hard.

Reading and spelling felt like decoding a language that didn't belong to me. Phonics didn't land. Words bounced on the page, and my eyes would dart around, skipping lines. I'd lose my place, then lose the meaning.

Spelling?

A disaster.

Letters jumbled, patterns vanished, nothing stuck.

Reading out loud?

A nightmare.

I'd stumble, mispronounce, then feel the heat rise in my cheeks while shame twisted in my stomach. If I earned a dollar every time someone teased me for saying a word wrong, I'd be a trillionaire today.

My biggest fear in school wasn't failing a test, it was hearing my name called to read out loud. The panic started before I even opened the book. Hands clenched, face flushed, breath shallow, voice cracking. I imagined everyone watching and judging. I wanted to vanish.

So, I buried it.

I carried that fear like a secret through every grade.

Eventually, though, I faced it head-on.

I stopped letting it define me. That secret fear is what led me to become a teacher. I majored in English. I chose the very thing that once terrified me, not to chase perfection, but to prove that fear didn't get the final word. I know what it feels like to choke on words, to be seen for all the wrong reasons.

I know that dread, that desperate wish for a fire alarm, any interruption, to save you from speaking. I remember gripping the desk, my heart pounding, voice trembling.

Now, I teach with the same compassion I once needed. I'll never put a student through that kind of humiliation.

Before I found my voice, before I stood at the front of a classroom, I still felt kind of stupid.

High school didn't make it easier. I needed tutors, extra help, and no matter how hard I tried, reading and spelling remained uphill battles.

I was haunted by that same troubling question...

Why is this so hard for me?

What I didn't know then was, I simply learned differently.

My brain wasn't broken, it just danced to its own rhythm.

The struggling didn't mean I wasn't smart; it meant I was resilient.

Now, I get to help students discover that same rewarding truth for themselves.

But back then, I was desperate to hide it.

So, I faked needing glasses. I even convinced my mom. We went to the optometrist, and I faked my way through the exam. Not because I needed glasses, but because I needed an excuse.

"Oops, forgot my glasses."

Boom.

No reading today.

I mastered the craft of strategic forgetfulness. Those glasses never showed up in English class. They worked just fine in art, where I could squint at still-life sketches with perfect clarity.

I knew it wasn't subtle, but it was survival. And every time I pulled it off, I felt like a genius. Because when you're drowning in fear, even the smallest hacks feel like lifelines.

Then, in university, during an education class on learning disabilities, I saw myself.

The lesson was on dyslexia, and suddenly, everything clicked.

The dancing letters, the skipping lines, the struggle to sound out words, the frustration, and the exhaustion. It was all there on the slides and in the textbook, staring back at me.

Just like that, I realized this wasn't just something I had. This was something I'd been living.

No one had caught it.

Not even me.

It was a moment of heartbreak and clarity all at once.

Back to my final year of high school, the year everything finally came full circle.

The late nights hunched over my notebook.

The tears.

The quiet "Can I even keep up?"

Every ounce of effort led me here.

And somehow, through all the confusion and insecurity, the combination of my hard-earned grades and outgoing personality earned me the ultimate honor…

Valedictorian.

Me.

The same girl who faked needing glasses to dodge reading out loud.

The one who sat in resource class feeling like she was always one step behind.

The girl who worked twice as hard just to feel average.

And yet… there I was, standing in front of my graduating class, about to deliver my speech.

Even now, it still doesn't feel real.

It wasn't just a title.

It was proof.

Proof that I wasn't defined by fear, shame, or struggle.

I was defined by the fight, the relentless, quiet push to keep going when everything felt stacked against me.

Holding that title wasn't just about grades. It was about perseverance. Like the girl who once whispered her fears had found her voice and was now standing tall, microphone in hand, ready to speak. And without a doubt, it remains one of the greatest honors of my life.

What made it even more meaningful was my mom had been valedictorian too. From the moment I found out, I dreamed of following in her footsteps, not out of pressure, but admiration. She believed in me, even when I didn't believe in myself.

Of course, the road to that stage wasn't smooth.

Just minutes before my speech, a teacher pulled me aside.

She asked about scholarships, university plans, what I'd be doing next.

I told her the truth.

I was taking a year off to work.

Her smile tightened.

"Oh. So, you're just an average Joe."

The words hit harder than I expected, and in that moment, I felt small.

None of it…

My effort, my growth, my grit, mattered unless I stepped into the "right" future on someone else's timeline.

It wasn't that I lacked ambition. I wanted to go to university, I planned to. But dreams cost money, and money wasn't something we had in abundance. My grandma saved what she could, but it wasn't enough.

If I wanted that education, I had to earn it.

Despite her comment, I still walked on stage.

When I delivered my speech, I didn't only speak for the straight-A students or the scholarship winners.

I spoke for every student who fought like hell to be there.

At first, "average Joe" echoed in my head like a stubborn tick.

But I didn't let it shake me.

That teacher didn't know what I knew. I had a damn good speech.

And I was ready.

Reading out loud used to terrify me when the words weren't mine.

But public speaking?

That's different.

Give me time to prepare, and I thrive.

The fear was never the crowd, it was the unknown. The risk of tripping over a simple word while everyone else breezed through it. That's what paralyzed me.

When I speak my own words, I come alive.

In high school and university, I leaned into that. I started asking to present instead of writing essays. The first time I asked, teachers looked stunned, what kind of student wants to speak in front of the class?

This kind.

And every time, they said yes.

Every time, I got an A+.

That's the thing, you don't have to be good at everything.

But if you know what you're good at, lean in and own it.

Success doesn't always come with a pen in hand.

Sometimes, it shows up with a mic.

When I got to university, I tackled my learning challenges head-on. I rewrote notes, recorded lectures, studied until sunrise, and found what worked for me. I even scored 100% on two exams. Graduated just shy of a 4.0 GPA.

Yes, I struggled.

But I overcame.

And I'm damn proud of that.

I stopped chasing someone else's strengths and started embracing my own.

Comparison is a thief.

It steals your joy, your energy, your fire.

So, stop wishing for someone else's gift.

Use what you've got.

That's where your power lives.

My valedictorian speech went better than I could have imagined. As I stood on that stage, pouring my heart into the words, I felt something deeper than pride.

I felt unstoppable.

Afterward, that same teacher approached me.

She looked me in the eye, clearly stunned, and said, "Wow… that was really amazing."

It wasn't just what she said. It was in her face, the surprise, the shift, the realization.

I smiled, because in that moment, I proved something, not just to her, but to myself.

That even the so-called "average Joe" could be valedictorian.

That labels don't define us.

That potential isn't always obvious.

And sometimes, the ones who fight the hardest…

Shine the brightest.

I survived high school.

Despite a brutal first day that nearly unraveled me, I made it through. I outran the rumor that could've destroyed me. I buried it in the rearview and somehow in the process I found joy, friendships, and laughter again.

I loved high school.

I really did.

But I would be lying if I said there wasn't a part of me still feeling damaged. No matter how much I accomplished, no matter how many milestones I hit, I never quite felt good enough.

I was always moving, dodging bullets no one else could see.

I was staying just busy enough to keep the weight from catching up.

If I slowed down, if I let myself breathe, the pain might catch up too.

You can only outrun the darkness for so long.

Eventually, no matter how fast you run or how brightly you smile, the cracks start to show.

Quietly yet relentlessly, it finds you…

In the pauses between laughter.

In the silence between accomplishments.

And when it does, you have to stop.

To sit in the stillness.

And face what you tried so hard to leave behind.

Healing doesn't come from running, it comes from standing still long enough to finally feel it.

CHAPTER 10

The Trigger

"His words didn't echo. They rooted."

— *Anonymous*

It was a crisp fall day, the kind where the air carries just enough bite to remind you winter is coming. Leaves spun in amber and crimson swirls, sunlight spilling through the window in that fleeting, golden way only autumn allows.

I was at my kitchen table, lost in the rhythm of my thoughts, coffee cooling beside me, fingers typing out a chapter that felt raw and real.

The kind of writing that only happens when the world is quiet, and your heart is wide open.

But time has never been on my side.

Before I knew it, the clock nudged me back to reality. I had to close the laptop and slip into another role.

Teacher, coworker, functioning adult.

The words would have to wait.

By noon, I was driving down the highway on my way to work. The sky was heavy, muted gray. The sun tried to break through but couldn't. The air felt thick, like it was holding its breath.

Then I saw them, flashing lights, red and blue, pulsing like distress signals through the haze.

Something serious.

My grip on the wheel tightened.

Police cars scattered like chess pieces across the highway while officers directed traffic into a slow, reverent crawl.

And then... I saw it.

A car, or what was left of one, crushed inward like a soda can. The front end was mangled and metal twisted grotesquely. Glass sparkled across the pavement like shattered ice. Debris everywhere, open wires, a single tire yards from the wreck.

I scanned the scene for signs of life.

No movement.

No bodies.

The ambulance was already gone.

And then I saw him.

A boy.

Just standing there, talking to a police officer.

Or trying to.

He wasn't speaking, not with his mouth, and not with his eyes. His face was pale, eyes glassy, arms limp. He looked like he had watched his entire world collapse in front of him.

He wasn't just standing.

He was stuck.

Frozen in time, caught in the moment his innocence shattered.

Teenagers walk through life with this beautiful, fragile belief that they're invincible. It's not arrogance, it's biology. They race forward, taking risks, laughing at danger.

Grief, loss, consequence... those belong to other people.

Until they don't.

Until the moment the illusion breaks.

Maybe it happens in a hospital waiting room. Or in a quiet phone call. Or on the side of a highway, where lights flash and metal still smokes.

But it happens.

And once it does, everything changes.

That boy had just been thrown into the deep end of a truth no one asks for. His world would never look the same again. He would move differently, see differently, and live differently.

While watching him, I remembered my own moment.

I was fifteen.

In a basement bathroom.

When your invincibility disappears, it's like a light switch flips, a sharp, jarring, and fluorescent truth.

You realize you are not safe.

That the world can break you in an instant.

And once you know that unsettling reality, you carry it.

Forever.

After that night, I became cautious, controlled, a rule-follower.

Not for image, but survival.

I wasn't trying to be perfect; I was trying to stay safe. I didn't chase mayhem. I didn't flirt with rebellion. I had been to the edge, and I barely made it back.

Yes, it probably saved me from some foolish, risk-taking behaviors.

If I could take it back, if I could live even one more year in that blissful bubble of innocence…

I would.

I like to believe everything happens for a reason.

It's what I tell myself on the days the "why" still lingers.

I am proud of who I've become, of my strength, compassion, and fire. But the pain didn't vanish. It just buried deeper.

And sometimes, I still wonder…

Who would I be if I hadn't been sexually assaulted?

Would I love differently?

Trust more easily?

Feel safer in my skin?

I'll never know.

And that, not the trauma, not even the pain…

That is the hardest part.

The not knowing.

The life that might have been.

Just like the moment you lose your invincibility; triggers don't come with warning labels. They strike like lightning, fast, ruthless, and disorienting.

One minute you're grounded, believing you've got a handle on things. The next, something, a glance, a word, a memory knocks you off course.

That's the power of a trigger.

It doesn't ask.

It interrupts.

At that point in my life, teetering on the edge of adulthood, I was already quietly battling my self-worth. But no one would've known. I wore confidence like armor. My smile, my energy, and my ease with people were all part of the disguise.

Underneath, my foundation was fragile.

My worth felt conditional, like something that could be revoked if I slipped up.

Still, I told myself I was doing okay.

I'd made it through high school. I had a job, friends, a full social calendar.

Most days, I liked who I was.

I looked in the mirror and thought, I'm holding it together.

And then he came along.

The first real trigger.

The man who shattered the mirror I had only just begun to see clearly in.

He cracked open the way I saw my body, my beauty, my worth.

He planted a seed of doubt so deep it took years to unearth.

His name was Grant.

My stepfather.

Before I go further, I need to say this…

He wasn't a bad man.

He was a man at war with himself, and I was caught in the crossfire.

I was collateral damage.

When he entered our lives, it felt like a fresh start. He was funny, lighthearted, quick with a joke. He made my mom laugh in a way I hadn't seen in years.

For a moment, I wondered, could this be my second chance?

A real father figure?

At first, maybe it was.

He teased me, paid attention, made me feel seen. But fairytales fade fast. His depression crept in like a slow fog. The warmth disappeared. The air in the house changed. One minute calm, the next suffocating.

He wasn't cruel, not intentionally. He was sick. I understand now that depression isn't something you simply "get over." It's a weight, a shadow. It requires work, therapy, accountability, and the willingness to face your pain.

Grant wasn't willing.

He wasn't ready to do the work, to face his own darkness.

And when pain isn't dealt with, it spills.

It stains.

It touches everyone nearby.

I don't think he realized how sharp his words could cut. How his silence could feel like punishment. How his presence could darken an entire room.

But it did.

Because unhealed wounds don't stay quiet.

They fester. They spread. And eventually, they can hurt people who had nothing to do with causing them. I became one of those people.

Living with him became unbearable. Our home lost its warmth. I started tiptoeing through my own life, afraid to make a sound. The TV was too loud. I left a glass out. The door wasn't closed all the way. I was parked wrong in the driveway.

Any small thing could ignite him. Instead of talking, he lashed out. He would let frustration stew until it exploded, and usually in my direction.

Sometimes I buried it.

I blamed myself.

Convinced myself I was the problem.

Other times, I walked away.

But there were moments I snapped.

I'm emotional, and that was still my home.

Everyone has a breaking point.

Still, he never owned it. Never sat down to talk it through. No accountability, no growth. Just complaints, taken straight to my mom.

"This family isn't working. Maybe I should leave."

And my mom?

She just wanted peace.

She just wanted him to stay.

So, guess who always had to apologize?

Me.

No matter what.

And once I did, he'd act like nothing happened.

"Hey Jody, wanna go for a drive?" and I'd go.

We'd smoke a cigarette together, something my mom never knew about, and for a few moments, it felt like we were rebuilding. He knew how much I craved that bond. A father-daughter connection. I clung to it, even after all the pain.

My mom was stuck in the middle. Torn between the love of the man she married and the love for the daughter she raised. He and I clashed like we were both fighting for her loyalty.

At first, it was manageable. Just growing pains and power struggles. But eventually, the tone shifted. The digs became personal. Not about dishes or the driveway anymore.

They were about me, how I looked, how I moved, who I was.

He started chipping away at my confidence, not with yelling, but with subtle jabs that built up like tiny cracks.

And over time, I began to believe him.

I'd come home excited about school, goals, dreams, and he'd crush it with four belittling words.

"Good luck with that."

Dismissive and condescending.

Enough to make me question my worth.

And the worst part was I cared. I cared because I wanted him to be the dad I never had. So, his words cut deeper. I took them as truth and my self-esteem slowly deflated.

Then one day he took it one step further.

He called me fat.

That's when everything changed.

Before that, I was happy in my body.

Sure, I was a teenage girl, I had insecurities, awkward phases, off days, but I didn't obsess. I didn't fear the mirror or count calories.

My confidence wasn't tied to the scale or the flatness of my stomach. It came from who I was, my energy, my friendships, the way I made people laugh, the light I brought into a room.

I noticed other girls not for their size, but how they moved through the world. My body wasn't the lens I used to measure my worth.

I liked what I saw.

I felt beautiful.

And that feeling?

It was mine.

Until he took it from me.

It started small. Offhand jokes tossed out with a smirk, just sharp enough to cut, easy enough to brush off.

If I grabbed a donut, he'd grin,

"Watch out, I can see the pounds adding up."

I laughed it off.

At first.

But the words stayed.

They echoed louder each time I looked at my plate.

And then came the moment I'll never forget.

We were standing in the kitchen. I don't remember the conversation.

But what he did?

What he said?

That's burned into memory.

He leaned over, pinched the side of my stomach, looked me dead in the eyes, and laughed.

"You're getting chubby," he said.

"Better be careful, or you're going to blow up soon."

Something inside me snapped.

My self-esteem, once strong and steady, suddenly shook.

For the first time, I questioned my reflection.

Not because I felt uncomfortable in my skin.

But because of what he saw.

And it didn't take long before I started seeing myself through his eyes.

I began analyzing every bite.

I learned about "good" vs. "bad" foods.

I read nutrition labels like they held the secrets to my worth.

I counted calories.

Skipped dessert.

Halved portions.

Punished myself for feeling hungry.

And just like that, the way I viewed my body, and its value, changed.

The irony was my body was doing exactly what it was supposed to. I was eighteen, transitioning from girlhood into womanhood. My hips were widening. My face was softening. My body was maturing naturally and beautifully.

Yes, I gained a few pounds.

But that didn't break me.

His words did.

Paired with the secret I was already carrying, his comments were poison. My fragile sense of self didn't just crack, it shattered. The mask I wore so well was torn away, leaving me raw and exposed.

And in that moment, something flipped.

Not gently, not gradually.

Sudden and sharp like a rusted switch yanked down in the dark.

The light inside me dimmed.

That was the beginning.

The moment my eating disorder took root.

Grant was the first trigger.

And everything unraveled from there.

The disorder that would drag me to rock bottom, started here.

With one moment, one comment, one humiliation that completely distorted how I saw myself.

That was the moment I began to doubt my worth.

To fear weight gain.
To become self-conscious in a way I never had before.
And the worst part?
It wasn't just anyone saying those things.
It was him.
The man I thought might be my fresh start. The father figure I longed for. The one I pinned my hopes on. His words weren't careless, they carried weight. It was enough to make me question everything I once believed about myself.
Enough to override my reflection.
Enough to reshape my self-worth.
If there's one thing I've learned over the years, it's this…
The only opinion that truly matters is your own.
Not everyone's going to like us, we're not meant to be everyone's cup of tea.
And that's okay.
We're meant to be different.
Not every relationship is supposed to fit.
But I didn't know that back then.
I was desperate for his approval and his love.
A dad.
So, everything he said?
I absorbed.
Completely.
His words didn't just sting.
They stuck.
And slowly, they started to define me.

Funny enough, that wasn't the first time someone called me fat.
As a teen, I did some modeling.
My grandma had modeled locally and got me into it. Up until then, I was a total tomboy, no makeup, no fuss, just casual clothes and zero interest in anything "girly." Modeling changed that. I learned how to do my makeup, pose for the camera, and for a moment, I liked stepping into that version of myself. It felt kind of nice to feel pretty.

Most of my gigs were small and local, but I still remember the thrill of getting pulled out of school for shoots. The fashion world, though, wasn't always so glamorous.

I'll never forget this one shoot.

Gray pants, green bikini top, camera on me.

"Lean forward and laugh," the photographer said.

I did.

His face dropped in disgust.

"Too many rolls. Stand back up."

That was my first experience with fat-shaming.

I was embarrassed, sure, but it didn't stick.

Not then, not yet.

Because when you like yourself, words can sting, but they don't leave scars.

It's different when it comes from someone you love.

I went on a modeling trip to Vancouver with my mom and brother. Our first time on a plane. My mom had sacrificed a lot to get us there. I wish we had explored more of the city and made memories as a family. But the trip revolved around me and my runway shows.

And for what?

I walked every runway, did every showcase... and didn't get a single callback.

I was told I looked "too plump."

"Too healthy."

Too healthy?

Since when was health a flaw?

One night, a group of us went out for dinner. I ordered a sandwich with fries, no second thoughts. But some girls barely touched their food. Plain salads, dressing on the side. Hollow eyes staring at full plates they wouldn't eat. And the way they looked at my meal, there was judgment, yes, but also envy. They wanted to eat like me. But they just couldn't.

At the time, I pitied them. I didn't yet understand how hunger could become a badge of honor, how eating fries could feel like rebellion.

But little did I know, I was already on that path.

Step by step, quietly and unknowingly, I was heading in the same direction.

The truth about eating disorders is they don't discriminate.

They don't care about your age, gender, grades, background, or dreams.

They slip in quietly, just a whisper, a suggestion, a nudge.

And once they take hold, they don't let go.

They wrap around your thoughts like barbed wire, twisting your reality until you can't remember what "normal" ever felt like.

This was the start of my descent.

I was already fragile.

Already chipped.

My stepdad's words had been cutting me down for months, quick and sharp like shards of glass.

And just like splinters, they buried themselves deep.

Unnoticeable at first.

But over time, they festered.

The pain spread slowly and quietly, until it reached places I didn't even know could hurt.

His words rewired the way I saw myself.

Your weight is the problem.

That's the belief I clung to.

Lose it, and maybe you'll be good enough.

So, I started the cycle.

Got a gym membership.

Worked out religiously.

No… Obsessively.

What started as "being healthy" quickly became a form of control. At first, it looked like self-care. "Better choices, clean eating."

But that's the lie eating disorders sell.

The truth?

I had already crossed the line.

Food and exercise didn't support my life anymore, they started to control it.

And I let them because control felt safe.

I used to move my body for joy. For energy and for fun. Yet somewhere along the way, movement became punishment. And the deeper I fell, the harder it became to climb back out.

Growing up, horseback riding was my greatest joy.

Yes, that was me.

A full-on horse girl.

My aunt owned a farm just outside the city and took us under her wing. While my siblings dabbled, I fell in love. It wasn't just a hobby; it captured a piece of my soul.

My aunt, a quiet horse whisperer, saw something in me.

A spark.

A natural ability.

And coming from her meant everything.

I started on a sassy little buckskin pony named Cinnamon.

She was fast, stubborn, and perfectly matched to me.

As I improved, she moved me up.

Bigger horses.

Higher goals.

Competitions.

And with every ride, I felt it.

Pride.

Power.

Peace.

Riding wasn't about burning calories or chasing perfection. It was about connection. About freedom. Put me on a horse in an open field and I felt grounded, yet soaring. It was therapy. It was empowerment. It was mine.

And then, it was gone.

My aunt's divorce ended my riding days too soon. I didn't just lose a hobby; I lost a sanctuary. And the timing couldn't have been worse.

That's around the time when Grant came into our lives.

My stepdad.

My first trigger.

The joy I once found in movement slowly slipped away, replaced by something darker.

Sometimes I wonder, if horseback riding had still been part of my life, would things have been different?

Would I have moved my body for joy instead of punishment?

Maybe.

But the truth is, my eating disorder found a crack and sank its teeth in deep.

And once it took hold, it didn't let go.

Even the purest joy, like the kind I felt on horseback, probably wouldn't have stood a chance.

Because an eating disorder doesn't care about joy, it devours it.

The slippery slope began.

By this point, my eating disorder had wrapped itself around me like a snake, tightening its grip with every passing day. The venom wasn't in my bloodstream, but it might as well have been. It was in my thoughts, my habits, my choices. It poisoned my joy, hijacked my confidence, and destroyed parts of me I didn't even know were vulnerable.

My stepdad's words were the first strike.

But they weren't the last.

There were more.

More comments.

More glances.

More echoes of the same cruel message…

You are not enough.

Each moment dragged me further down, until the darkness wasn't just following me anymore.

It was living inside me.

No longer a shadow, but a presence, heavy and constant.

It shaped how I saw myself, how I moved through the world, how I breathed.

I had a one-way ticket on a runaway train, firing down the tracks with no brakes, no map, and no way to turn back.

Up ahead, waiting at the final stop. With cold tile and a dimly lit light, and the girl I'd become, curled up on that bathroom floor.

My rock bottom.

CHAPTER 11

Slippery Slope

"It is the false hope of control that keeps us clinging to the very thing destroying us."

— Cheryl Strayed

What else triggered my eating disorder?

It wasn't a dramatic collapse or a loud cry for help.

It was slow and quiet, a gradual unraveling that snuck up on me while I was busy trying to hold it all together.

I didn't even see it happening at first.

It started subtly, small changes I overlooked. A growing unease in my body. Anxiety that showed up without warning. Moments of overwhelm that came on fast and fierce, leaving me breathless and on edge.

I tried to manage it.

I told myself I was fine, that I had a grip on it.

But stability is slippery when you're already cracked.

I was cracked, worn down, and tired from absolutely everything.

It was like trying to keep a wild animal caged inside me.

At first, I was the zookeeper who called the shots. I had the key. Each day, the animal grew stronger, fed by self-doubt, insecurity, and unprocessed pain. It would pace behind the bars, restless and waiting. I could feel the tension and pressure like the whole thing could snap at any second.

And then one day… it did.
The cage didn't just open.
It shattered.
And with it, I lost my control.
The eating disorder wasn't something I managed anymore.
It managed me.
It consumed me.
And I was powerless to stop it.

When it comes to eating disorders, it's not just about looking in the mirror and thinking you're fat.
That's the surface-level assumption; the oversimplified story people tell.
It runs deeper.
So much deeper.
Yes, body image plays a role, but at its core, an eating disorder is a storm of contradictions. A complex web of pain, control, fear, and worth.
It's not just about the body you see.
It's about the battles no one else can see.
Yes, social media plays a huge part. It floods us with impossible beauty standards, selling the lie that thin equals worth. That if your waist is tiny, your skin flawless, your features symmetrical, then you'll be loved. Then you will matter.
Social media trains us to define our worth by appearance, specifically perfect appearance. Effortless beauty, flat stomachs, long legs, and radiant skin. If we're not glowing and camera-ready 24/7, we feel like we're failing.
But here's the sick part.
Even the celebrities we idolize don't look like the versions of themselves we see. Their skin is smoothened, their bodies sculpted, their flaws erased. What we're consuming isn't real, it's manufactured, filtered, and fabricated. Still, we hold ourselves to those impossible standards.
And don't even get me started on diet culture. It disguises itself as wellness, while feeding us constant messages.
Carbs are the enemy.

Dessert is weakness.

Skipping meals is discipline.

Being smaller means being better.

It's manipulative.

It's dangerous.

And it's everywhere.

When you grow up in a world that ties your value to how you look, it's only a matter of time before that belief burrows in. And once it does, it's a long, hard road to unlearn.

Sure, things are shifting. Brands are pushing body positivity. Beauty at every size, and I love seeing women embrace themselves unapologetically.

It's powerful and it's necessary.

But let's be real, this change came after decades of damage.

The pressure to shrink ourselves was already deeply embedded long before this movement gained traction. We're still unlearning generations of toxic messaging, and not everyone escapes it unscathed.

So yes, I believe social media can be toxic. It can make people question their worth, hate their reflection, even develop eating disorders.

But that wasn't my story.

My eating disorder didn't come from comparing myself to influencers or chasing a curated ideal.

My trigger wasn't something I scrolled past on a screen. It lived inside my home. It wore the voice of someone I trusted, someone whose words cut far deeper than any filtered image ever could.

It was never about wanting to look like someone else. My disorder didn't bloom from a simple desire to be skinny.

It took root in something far more complex, a crumbling sense of self-worth.

A slow unraveling of who I thought I was.

With that unraveling came a hunger for control, something I felt slipping through my fingers more and more each day. Despite my best efforts, nothing seemed to go my way.

University was overwhelming. Assignments piled up, deadlines loomed like walls closing in, and the high grades I was maintaining were slipping further out of reach. There were too many demands and too many expectations. For someone who learns differently, it felt like climbing an endless hill, always behind, and always breathless.

I couldn't control the pace.

I couldn't control the pressure.

But I could control what I ate.

I could control how much I exercised.

In a world spinning out from under me, that became my anchor, my illusion of power, my false sense of safety. It wasn't about being thin; it was about feeling like I had a handle on something.

I was juggling three jobs just to afford tuition. The exhaustive lectures, assignments, and work shifts were crushing me. I was burning out, fast. My relationship at the time was crumbling too. There wasn't enough time.

Not for school.

Not for work.

Not for love.

Not even for myself.

I gave everything I had, and it still wasn't enough. Life was happening around me, and I was stuck in the passenger seat, powerless to grab the wheel.

Drowning in insecurity.

Suffocating under pressure.

Watching even the simplest things unravel in my hands.

The worst part wasn't just one thing, it was everything. Collapsing like a house of cards, leaving me exposed and fragile, stuck in the belief that I was never good enough.

The girl I used to be, the high school version of me, she was confident. She accepted her body. She didn't let a number on the scale define her.

When everything started slipping, when life no longer felt steady, my disorder saw its chance. It was never just about body image; it was about control. It was about trying to reclaim stability in a world that suddenly felt unrecognizable.

And when you combine that kind of desperation with unhealed trauma…

It's a dangerous mix.

A perfect storm.

My disorder found me vulnerable, fractured, and aching for something to hold onto.

And once it buried its claws, it didn't let go.

From what I've come to understand, eating disorders exist on a continuum. On one end, there's anorexia, where food is restricted to life-threatening levels. On the other, there's obesity, where the body consumes far more than it needs to function. Most people fall somewhere in the middle, in that space of balanced eating.

I won't call it healthy eating, because to me, health isn't about rules or numbers.

It's about tuning in.

It's fueling your body when it's hungry, honoring cravings without shame, and recognizing fullness without guilt.

It's knowing that food isn't good or bad, it's just food.

Balance is everything.

Eat only apples and you miss essential nutrients.

Eat only cookies and the same happens.

It's not about punishment or restriction.

It's about understanding that all food has a place.

Each bite eaten with intention helps us feel nourished, satisfied, and connected.

That said, some foods are more nutrient-dense than others.

I know that. I have an eating disorder brain.

At my worst, I wasn't just counting calories, I was tracking every vitamin, gram of sugar, fat, fiber, and protein like my life depended on it. It gave me a sense of power, but it also fed the obsession.

Now, I focus on balance, something I never could do back then. Letting go of extremes and embracing flexibility. That's what's helped me rebuild a healthier relationship with food.

I know not everyone sees it this way, and that's okay.

But removing the "good" and "bad" labels is how I stay in recovery.

It's how I stop myself from slipping.

It's my strategy.

And honoring what works for me matters more than trying to fit anyone else's definition of health.

This mindset brings me peace.

And peace is something I fought hard to earn.

The girl in this chapter had a long road ahead before she could ever see food this way.

The second you start shifting toward either extreme on that continuum, restriction or overconsumption, you step into disordered eating. A lot of people hover near the middle, dipping one way or the other, and still manage to function. But the closer you get to the edges, the more your body suffers.

When I became anorexic, my body went into survival mode. It was starving, searching for fuel, clinging to whatever it could find. Between the restriction and obsessive over-exercising, there was nothing to hold onto. I was demanding more and more from a body I refused to nourish. Running on empty and expecting it to perform like usual.

But here's the truth…

Push too far toward the edge, and your body doesn't just rebel, it begins to shut down.

Your organs weaken.

Your heart slows.

Your body starts to give up.

And if you don't stop it, if you keep going, it ends the only way it can.

You die.

I was like the showgirl in the magician's box, an illusion, a spectacle, something to be marveled at. He'd twirl me around, shift the box pieces, rearrange my body from head to toe. The drumroll-built suspense, the audience held their breath, eyes locked on the stage. One by one, the magician opened the box, and parts of me disappeared. Gasps filled the air. The crowd was entranced.

But what they were really waiting for was the finale, the dramatic return. The moment I'd reappear, whole, radiant, as if nothing had ever been taken. The crowd would cheer, the magician would bow, and the act would end.

My finale was not that pretty.

There was no applause, no gasp of relief. If anything, the audience would've demanded a refund, because the girl never came back together.

Her body remained fragmented.

The missing piece.

Gone.

Vanished.

She was slowly dying, fading before their very eyes. The magician had no choice but to resign.

I haven't talked much about the other eating disorders yet...

Bulimia nervosa, binge eating disorder (BED), avoidant/restrictive food intake disorder (ARFID), OSFED, pica, and rumination disorder.

Each is unique, with its own symptoms, struggles, and misconceptions. And while I brushed up against some behaviors from a few, binging, purging and abusing laxatives, I was never diagnosed with bulimia.

My eating disorder took a different form.

I was diagnosed with anorexia nervosa, more specifically, athletic anorexia.

Fasting, extreme restriction, obsessive calorie counting, excessive exercise, and a rigid, punishing routine I followed with military precision.

I'm not an expert on the other disorders, they weren't my lived experience, but I believe that despite the differences in behavior, there's a shared emotional thread running through all of them.

Because at the core, the eating disorder brain speaks the same language.

It whispers the same lies.

It feeds the same fears.

It thrives in cycles of obsession, guilt, punishment, and self-destruction.

The details may vary, but the emotional roots are eerily similar.

Once ED takes hold, no matter the form, it is unforgiving.

Some people live in the in-between, disordered eating that doesn't cross into full diagnosis. They teeter on the edge, functioning but fragile.

Mine started there, but ED didn't want part-time control. It went all in. It dragged me to the far end of the spectrum where my body stopped functioning properly and where I stopped feeling like myself.

From here on out, I'll refer to my eating disorder as ED. It's a common term in the community, almost like naming the intruder.

The liar.

The voice in your head.

Because that's exactly what ED is.

It wasn't just a disorder.

It was a constant companion.

It followed me everywhere, in the mirror, at the dinner table, at the gym. It whispered that it was keeping me safe, that if I just obeyed, I'd be enough.

ED told me what to eat, when to eat, and how much.

It called me lazy and weak.

It punished me when I slipped, praised me when I restricted, clapped when I pushed through exhaustion.

And at my lowest, ED wasn't a whisper.

It was the only voice I could hear.

It convinced me I was in command.

But… I never was.

ED was.

And yes, I do talk about ED like it's separate from me, because that's exactly what it feels like.

Like I'm possessed.

Like an imposter has taken up residence inside of me, making my decisions, dictating my thoughts, ruling my body.

It's a daily war for control.

Every day, it's me versus ED.

I'm not a doctor. I'm not a therapist. I'm not an expert. I'm just a girl who lives with one. And I can only speak from that place with honesty, vulnerability, and without sugarcoating.

Because I know I'm not alone.

Others have fought this war too.

Others still are.

And if that's you, I want you to know… you're not alone.

So how did I get pulled in so deep?

We know the spark, my stepdad's words.

That was the match.

From there, it started small.

Counting calories, eating a little less, building a strict food routine.

It felt manageable at first.

Contained and in charge.

Then came the exercise.

Daily movement wasn't enough anymore, it had to be structured, intentional, and merciless. I created a gym plan and followed it religiously.

At this point, I was still in what some might call a functional disorder.

My eating was disordered, yes, but I could still function.

I still went out with friends. I still showed up to work, to class.

My body hadn't slipped into survival mode yet.

I was silently and subtly losing weight.

And then…

Somewhere along the way, I hitched a ride on the runaway train.

The one headed straight to my worst.

And once I was on it, there was no slowing down.

Numbers on a Scale — A Disclaimer.

I've always hated talking about numbers when it comes to my eating disorder. I've tried to avoid defining my experience by weight because a number on a scale isn't a universal measurement of health.

My natural, healthy weight is different from yours, different from anyone else's. We all have unique bodies, genetics, and metabolisms. No single number can capture that complexity.

A number cannot tell the whole story.

It can't define what's "healthy" or "unhealthy" across the board.

What's safe for one person might be dangerous for another.

So, if I mention numbers, it's only to describe what became unhealthy for me. I avoid specifics because we should never define ourselves by them.

Your self-worth cannot be measured on a scale.

You are so much more than a number.

We all are.

Before my eating disorder, I barely stepped on a scale. The only time I weighed myself was at the doctor's office, quick, routine, and forgettable.

Growing up, we had one scale in the house, tucked under my mom's dresser. I think it was once white, but over time it faded into a worn-out beige, its surface scuffed and dull from years of use. It wasn't digital. It had that old-school ticking dial, the kind that wobbled before landing on a number.

And when the scale became my new best friend, those few agonizing seconds watching the dial teeter, my heart would pound.

My breath would catch.

Anxiety swallowed me whole.

That number, that meaningless, arbitrary number suddenly had the power to decide everything.

That dresser became a destination, a ritual. I visited it multiple times a day.

The scale wasn't just an object.

It was a judge.

A dictator.

The keeper of my self-worth.

Imagine waking up each day with a singular mission…

To master every behavior.

The day was a test, and I was desperate to pass.

Every pound lost, half a pound even, felt like a monumental win.

"I did it."

"I'm successful."

My excessive exercise.

My restrictive eating.

It was all working.

Every drop in weight brought a surge of twisted gratification.

A false sense of control.

A warped kind of pride.

An intoxicating wave of self-fulfillment that felt like victory.

Looking back, it breaks my heart that my greatest sense of achievement came from starving myself.

From shrinking.

As if getting smaller made me more worthy.

But it was never enough.

No matter how much weight I lost, I was never enough.

That scale ruled everything.

When the number stayed the same or worse, increased, I unraveled and suddenly, I was a failure. If I ate too much, if I slipped even once, the weight of self-hatred crashed into me.

The disappointment was unbearable.

Suffocating.

That one moment of failure felt like proof I was weak and undeserving. My body was in survival mode, begging for nourishment, but my mind wouldn't let go. I was trapped in a relentless cycle where success was never enough, and failure felt like the end of the world.

My self-worth?

Shattered.

I told myself I was the one guiding the reins.

But ED was running the show.

Before the obsession began, before the restricting, the rules, and the control, my natural weight floated between 125 and 130 pounds. That was my body's happy place, the weight it maintained when I ate normally and moved in ways that brought me joy.

When I turned eighteen, I gained a few pounds, as most people do. I was probably around 135 to 140, nothing drastic, nothing unhealthy. Just a normal part of growing into a woman.

But I didn't see it that way.

I started cutting back and exercising more.

Eventually, I dropped back to 130, technically still within a healthy range for my body.

But my mindset was no longer healthy.

I wasn't eating to nourish.

I wasn't moving to feel good.

I was becoming obsessed with food, weight, and control.

I use the term "healthy range" loosely because, to be honest, I've never fully agreed with the BMI scale. BMI only considers height and weight, assigning a number to place you on a health spectrum.

But it leaves out so much.

Genetics, ethnicity, cultural influence, muscle mass, fat distribution, bone density. All of these shape our bodies in ways BMI simply doesn't account for.

I'm not saying BMI is completely useless, it has scientific merit and can serve as a starting point for identifying risk factors. But it's far from the full picture. It's a broad brush trying to paint a deeply nuanced portrait.

And when it comes to bodies, especially bodies in recovery, there is no one-size-fits-all formula.

As my slippery slope got deeper, the number on the scale kept dropping, pound by pound, little by little.

So, what happened next?

How low did that number go?

How far did I fall?

This disorder was slowly killing me.

But how did it get that far?

What pushed me past the point of no return?

What was the turning point?

Let me tell you about my second major trigger.

I call it…

The trip from hell.

The trip that took the lack of control I was already battling and amplified it to a level I didn't know existed.

The trip that turned a spiraling disorder into a full-blown freefall.

CHAPTER 12

Downhill Spiral

"You can't selectively numb emotion. When you numb the dark you numb the light."

— Brené Brown

I couldn't have described it better; it really was the trip from hell.

From the moment it began, I felt like I'd been thrown into the eye of a tornado.

Chaotic, disoriented, and powerless.

Just when I found my footing, another gust knocked me off course. Plans unraveled, tempers flared, and disasters piled up like wreckage in a storm.

But nothing could've prepared me for what was waiting back home.

That's when the real destruction began.

The tornado didn't just toss me around, it tore through the very foundation of my life.

Everything that once felt steady, safe, and whole was ripped apart piece by piece. I could almost hear the wind howling through the cracks as my world collapsed. I was spinning, spiraling, reaching for anything to hold onto, but there was nothing.

Everything started unraveling.

The faster I spun, the tighter ED gripped me.

And the tighter it held on, the deeper I sank until I was fully consumed.

Trapped in a place so dark it felt like there was no way out.

The force was too strong.

Suddenly, all that was left were the ruins.

Long story short, I started dating Tyler and things were going well, too well.

Not that he was perfect, he wasn't. He still had that bad-boy edge I'm forever drawn to, flaws and all. But he treated me well, really well.

And that scared the hell out of me.

Which, of course, meant only one thing…

I ran.

It's basically my signature move. The second something feels real, steady, or good, I get that familiar pang in my chest, and I'm out.

So, true to form, I let fear take the wheel and drove straight into my favorite detour…

The exit.

The only problem?

We had already booked a trip to Panama.

And now… we were broken up.

My first instinct was to cancel and cut my losses. No way we could travel together now, it felt impossible, but he insisted.

"It'll be fine," he said.

"We'll go as friends. You've already paid, why waste it?"

He even reassured my family, promised to look out for me, said we'd still have a great time. And I let myself believe him.

So, there I was. Twenty years old, stepping onto foreign soil for my first time. My passport practically brand new, pages crisp and unmarked. Up until then, the furthest I'd traveled was to the lake and a short modeling stint in Vancouver.

This felt different.

A real adventure, a leap into the unknown. A whole new experience waiting to unfold.

Bags packed, dropped at the airport, and before I knew it, we were off.

Then somewhere between the first layover and the next, the real problem surfaced.

Tyler hadn't truly accepted the breakup. He wasn't treating this like a friendly getaway. In his mind, this was our trip, our chance to fix things, to fall back into what we'd had. He'd convinced himself this was what we needed to rekindle it all.

There we were, not even in Panama yet, already arguing in some in-between airport about our relationship. I had to break up with him, again, this time spelling it out in painfully clear terms.

We were just friends.

We were moving on.

Separately.

I thought we had settled this.

I was stunned he had imagined anything different.

He wasn't happy, obviously. And to be fair, I had hurt him. Even though I'd made my position clear before we left, he'd clung to a different version of the story.

One where we were still… us.

And now here we were with the entire trip still ahead.

From that point on, things only went downhill.

First, let's talk about who I am.

I'm a Type A planner. I plan everything, always have. I thrive on structure, I need organization, I have to know what's coming next. It's how I function.

So why, of all things, did I think backpacking through a foreign country with zero concrete plans was a good idea?

The moment we landed, it hit me.

I was completely out of my element.

The first half of the trip was a disaster.

We bounced from hostel to hostel, scrambling for places to stay, missing buses, getting stranded in random towns that weren't even on the itinerary, assuming we ever had a real itinerary to begin with. And to top it off, I was stuck traveling with someone who clearly didn't want to be around me.

All the excitement had drained from the trip. What was supposed to be an adventure felt more like a slow-motion disaster I couldn't escape no matter how badly I wanted to.

I was done.

I wanted to go home.

I was wandering through a foreign country with no real plan, no safety net, and with someone I no longer trusted to look out for me.

Panama itself was stunning. Everywhere I looked was like a postcard. Lush jungles, golden beaches, waterfalls that looked like they'd been pulled from a dream.

But even paradise has its shadows.

The stories we heard in hostels didn't help. Fellow travelers shared warnings. Tourists stabbed and robbed in broad daylight. We were told where not to go, what streets to avoid. Suddenly, the beauty I'd come to see started to feel... dangerous.

I couldn't shake the unease in my gut. I found myself constantly looking over my shoulder, hyper-aware of every stranger who walked too close. That quiet fear lodged itself deep inside me, heavy and sharp, growing stronger by the day.

Eventually, we traveled west across the country and caught a ferry to a coastal town on the Pacific side.

That's where I met Sarah, Jennifer, and their parents.

To my surprise, things finally started to brighten.

Their family welcomed me like one of their own, and I think I stayed longer on that trip because of them.

They had actually planned their vacation thoroughly. Every detail was mapped out, and because of that, they were getting a completely different version of the country than I was.

Their days were full of laughter, sunshine, and ease.

Surrounded by their energy felt like a bubble of peace I didn't want to leave.

When we arrived at our next destination, a quiet little town tucked into the hills, Sarah and Jennifer's family had rented beautiful cabins at the top of a gated hill. It was serene, secure, and stunning.

I was so jealous.

I would've done anything to stay with them. To feel peace and safety, to finally rest.

But Tyler and me?

We had to find yet another hostel.

And of course, it was just days before Christmas and the town was nearly full.

There was only one place left with vacancies.

How do I even describe this hostel?

A Nightmare.

That's the first word that comes to mind.

Why a nightmare?

Where do I even begin…

As we approached the hostel, an eerie tension settled over me.

Police were everywhere. Flashing lights bouncing off uneven pavement, officers huddled in hushed, serious conversation. The building looked like something out of a horror film. It was rundown with peeling paint and barred windows that made it feel more like a prison than a place travelers would willingly choose to stay.

The air felt thick like the place was clinging to something dark.

And that was before I learned what had happened.

Just days earlier, a girl staying at the hostel had been kidnapped by a group of men. She'd been horrifyingly beaten, raped, and then… returned.

They threw her out of a car right in front of the hostel doors like she was nothing.

Like she was disposable.

By the time we arrived, she'd already been rushed to the hospital, but the police were still there trying to piece together the trauma she'd endured.

Out of all the damn towns we could've stumbled upon, out of all the places to stay, we landed here.

Of course, just my luck.

It felt like the universe was playing a cruel joke.

Testing how much more I could take.

It's wild how fast a trigger can hijack your body. A scent, a sound, a flicker of emotion, a random moment. Then suddenly, you're not in the present anymore.

You're back there.

Back in the fear.

Back in the version of yourself you've worked so hard to outgrow.

The one who barely survived.

You lived through something you were never meant to endure, and sometimes your body remembers before your mind does.

To call this a trigger doesn't cut it.

It wasn't a memory.

It was a relapse.

It pulled me under, fast and hard.

It wasn't just the horror of what had happened to her.

It was what had been unburied in me.

Fifteen-year-old Jody.

That basement.

The memories I'd buried so deep.

I almost convinced myself they weren't real.

I had become an expert at pretending it never happened, layering distraction over denial over survival.

Trauma doesn't care about your coping mechanisms.

It finds cracks and it slips through.

This time, I had nowhere to run, and it dragged me down with it.

There wasn't another ferry until morning. It was getting late and sleeping on the streets wasn't an option.

So, there I was, stuck.

I was forced to spend the night in that nightmarish hostel, with an ex-boyfriend who was barely speaking to me. The weight of what had happened there pressed down on my chest like a boulder. The air felt uneasy and the walls too close.

No matter how badly I wanted to escape, I couldn't.

I had never felt so trapped, physically, emotionally, and mentally.

And yet, even in the midst of my own panic, I couldn't stop thinking about her.

The girl who had survived the unthinkable.

My heart ached for her, for what she'd endured, for the way her world had been shattered so violently, so inhumanely.

How terrified she must have been.

How broken she must have felt.

How do you come back from something like that?

If she couldn't... what did that say about me?

I thought I was broken.

I thought I was damaged beyond repair.

But what she had lived through, I couldn't even comprehend.

The thought alone made me nauseous.

And even now, all these years later, that night still twists my stomach into knots.

The image of her ingrained in my mind.

She became part of the weight I carry.

For the rest of my time in that town, I avoided the hostel as much as humanly possible. I clung to the few pockets of safety I had found, mainly the family who had, unknowingly, become my refuge. I spent my days with Sarah and Jennifer, lounging at their serene hillside cabins where everything felt calm, predictable, and secure. Or I was stretched out on the beach, letting the sun warm my skin and silence my thoughts.

Despite the fear, the distress, the disarray, I found myself laughing again. Smiling effortlessly. Feeling flickers of genuine happiness, I hadn't expected and almost didn't believe I deserved.

On Christmas Eve, they invited us out to dinner. One of those cozy restaurants where the air smelled like herbs and garlic, where candlelight danced against rustic wood walls, and every dish looked like it had been crafted meticulously with love.

Everyone ordered hearty pasta.

Creamy sauces, fresh seafood, twirled noodles that looked like they'd melt in your mouth.

I still remember the smell.

Buttery, warm, and comforting.

The kind that stirs your hunger with a single breath.

I ordered a salad.

Just shrimp and greens.

I was deep in my restrictive phase, and pasta had become the enemy.

No matter how hungry I was, how much I wanted, how much I needed just one bite, I couldn't do it. There was a wall inside me, invisible and unbreakable. One I didn't know how to demolish.

By the end of the night, my stomach was hollow with hunger, but the fear of losing control screamed louder than the physical ache.

So, I smiled, laughed, and played along while the war inside me raged on.

After dinner, we went dancing at a local bar. It was a familiar spot to the family. They knew the locals and the safe tucked-away places. And they were right. The people were warm, welcoming, and full of life.

It should've been the perfect night.

The kind that lets you forget the heaviness.

The kind that feels like freedom.

But I couldn't shake the unease creeping through the back of my mind.

Where were those men?

The ones who had taken that girl.

Were they here now?

Watching?

Blending in?

Laughing at the bar?

Standing at the next table to me?

Brushing past me on the dance floor?

The thoughts buzzed like static, sharp, persistent, and impossible to tune out.

As the night wore on, the music slowed, the crowd thinned, and the party faded. Everyone was heading back to their rooms, ready to call it a night.

My heart sank.

It was time to return to the hostel.

Back to the place that made my skin crawl.

But at least I wasn't going alone.

By this point, Tyler and I had started to find common ground. The tension had softened, the edges dulled. And though I hated to admit it, that gave me a small, fragile sense of comfort.

Maybe, just maybe, things were starting to turn around.

I don't know how long I had been asleep. Maybe a few hours, maybe less, but something jolted me awake. A bright light was shining into the room, too sharp, too intrusive, slicing through the darkness like a blade.

My eyes adjusted.

And then I saw it.

The door was open.

Wide open.

Not cracked.

Not ajar.

Wide open.

Not locked.

Not secured the way it had been when I closed my eyes.

Panic surged through me so fast my hands began to tremble. My breath caught as I whipped my focus toward the other bed, instinctively reaching out, ready to shake Tyler awake, to tell him to shut the door, lock it, to do something.

But he wasn't there.

He was gone.

He had left the room.

Left me alone.

Left the door wide open in this frightening hostel where the unthinkable had already happened to another girl just days before.

And now I was exposed, unprotected, and terrified.

Something inside me snapped.

I started shaking, uncontrollable tremors rattling through every inch of my body. My mind was racing too fast, the fear gripping too tight, pressing against my chest like a vice.

I felt it in my gut, in every nerve screaming inside me.

This is it.

They're coming for me.

Just like they got that other girl.

I was next.

And there was no way out.

I launched myself out of bed, legs moving on pure adrenaline.

I bolted for the door so fast my feet barely touched the floor. I slammed it shut and locked it tight, hands fumbling, heart pounding, breath ragged.

I used to think I was fast as a kid, running from the monster during playground games.

But that speed was nothing compared to now.

This wasn't a game.

This was survival.

The door was now locked, but it didn't matter.

A lock wouldn't stop them.

Nothing would.

That certainty crawled beneath my skin, cold, sharp, and paralyzing. I could feel it.

They were coming.

It was only a matter of time before the handle turned.

Before they forced their way in.

The lock felt fragile and useless.

A false sense of safety waiting to snap.

I curled into a ball on the bed, arms tight around my knees, spine pressed to the wall. I stared at that door like my life depended on it, because in my mind, it did.

I stayed that way.

All night.

Eyes wide open.

Muscles tense.

Listening for every little creak, every footstep, every whisper of movement outside.

Waiting...

But no one came.

No one burst through the door.

No one dragged me into the dark.

And yet, the fear didn't fade with the sunrise.

It stayed, etched into my bones.

As night gave way to morning, birds chirped outside. The sunlight spilled softly into the room, warm and golden, deceptively peaceful.

And I was still here.

I hadn't been taken.

I was safe.

But I was alone.

Tyler was still gone, and I had no idea what I'd just woken up to on Christmas morning.

Logically, I knew the chances of those men returning, especially with police involvement, were slim.

But logic didn't matter.

Fear was louder.

So much louder.

It echoed through every inch of me, drowning out reason, suffocating any sense of calm. And it wasn't just about the hostel anymore. It wasn't even just about what had happened to that poor girl.

It was everything.

All of it.

Everything I had buried.

Everything I hadn't healed.

My past.

The trauma I'd locked so deep I thought it might stay there forever. But it was awake now.

The demon I'd spent years silencing had been stirred. And no matter how hard I tried, I couldn't shove it back into the dark.

It was out.

It was alive.

And it wasn't going anywhere.

I couldn't pretend anymore.

I couldn't smile through it.

I couldn't distract myself.

I couldn't downplay the weight of it all.

Everything was not fine.

And for the first time in a long time…

I stopped trying to convince myself otherwise.

At some point, I found myself on the beach. I don't even remember deciding to go. I just ended up there, sitting in the sand, staring at the waves as they rolled in and out, steady and indifferent.

My body was shaking, my chest was tight, and my hands trembled in my lap. Then came the tears, silent at first. Then harder, until I was sobbing, feeling everything and nothing all at once.

Then out of nowhere, I started saying my goodbyes.

It wasn't planned.

It wasn't even conscious.

The words just spilled out, uttered softly into the wind like a prayer, or a plea. Some part of me truly believed I wasn't going to make it home from this trip.

My ex was gone, I was alone, and I felt helpless.

And the worst part?

I couldn't even fight it.

I'd always seen myself as strong, smart, and resourceful. The kind of girl who figured things out.

But in that moment, I had nothing.

No strength.

No plan.

Just fear and the quiet goodbye of a girl who didn't think she'd make it back.

I was broken.

Numb and frozen, despite the sun on my skin and the heat of the sand.

It felt like I wasn't even there, like I was floating above myself, watching from far away.

I didn't move for hours.

I just sat there.

Heavy.

Hollow.

And then… something shifted.

I can't explain it.

I swear someone was with me.

Not physically but spiritually.

I've always been more spiritual than religious. I truly believe the ones we've lost never fully leave us. And in that moment, I sensed them.

A presence.

A gentle whisper:

"You're not alone. You're not going to die here. You can get up. You will go home."

And somehow, I did.

I stood up, wiped my face, and forced my body to move.

Every part of me felt like it could collapse. The exhaustion wasn't just from lack of sleep, it was from carrying it all.

The memories I couldn't outrun.

The dread that sat heavy in my body.

The war I was waging inside my own mind.

But I kept going.

One step.

Then another.

And I knew exactly what I had to do.

I needed to call my mom.

My poor mother. It was Christmas Day, when she saw that long-distance number flash on her screen, she probably thought I was calling to say Merry Christmas, not to ask for help.

The second she answered, I broke down, completely. I could barely get the words out between sobs. I told her everything. How Tyler had left me, how I was stranded, how I didn't even know how to get back to the main city, let alone the airport.

I begged her to get me out. I had no strength left to pretend I had things under control. I was scared, broken, and all I wanted was my mom.

My mom, being the rock she is, didn't panic. She didn't spiral. She just went into action. We made a plan. She'd handle the flights and logistics, and all I had to do was get to the main city.

For the first time all morning, I felt a flicker of purpose, a sliver of control. The fog began to lift, just enough to breathe. I was going to ask that kind family for help. Surely, they'd point me toward the right bus or ferry.

But before I could, Tyler showed up.

He looked like hell, like he'd crawled out of a 24-hour blackout.

While I'd spent the night paralyzed by fear, reliving trauma I'd buried deep, he'd been out partying.

A full-blown bender.

Not concerned.

Not sorry.

Just drunk, high, and too selfish to care.

Another addict boyfriend.

Check.

I lost it.

I screamed at him, rage spilling out like a dam cracked wide open. He rolled his eyes and told me I was overreacting. And maybe to him, I was. But it didn't last. Because beneath the fury was something louder, my desperation to get out.

When you've lived through trauma and your brain tells you it's happening again, you don't argue with it. You don't reason your way out of survival mode. All I knew was I couldn't take the risk. Because if something like that ever happened again, I wouldn't survive it.

At first, I didn't think he'd help. He looked annoyed like I was ruining his fun. Then he called his mom, Claire, to say Merry Christmas. Instead of the pleasant festive greeting he was expecting, she laid into him.

Claire and Molly had grown close while we were dating, and my mom had already filled her in. He didn't care what I had to say.

But his mom?

He listened to her.

"Don't you dare leave Jody again. You take her back to the airport. Right now."

So, he did.

We boarded the ferry, then a bus, then another. Each mile brought me closer, closer to the main city, closer to the airport, closer to home.

With every turn of the wheels, the weight on my chest lifted, just a little. I wasn't there yet, but I was moving. And for now, that was enough.

I wish I could say relief came with distance, but it didn't. My body was still in fight-or-flight. My nerves were raw. My mind looping every awful moment like a film I couldn't shut off.

Yet, I couldn't bring myself to paint Tyler as a monster.

I don't believe most people are truly evil.

He wasn't.

Just like Grant wasn't.

Just like my dad wasn't.

They were all carrying their own pain, their own wreckage, none of which had anything to do with me. But somehow, it still found its way into my life.

They never cleaned up their messes and I just kept getting caught in the crossfire.

And as if I hadn't been through enough, getting out of Panama was anything but smooth. From the second I stepped into that airport to the moment I landed back home; it was madness.

Flight info got scrambled.

My ticket had errors.

And at one point, I lost my damn passport.

It felt like the universe was testing me, seeing how close it could get to breaking me completely.

Meanwhile, my mom, my rock and savior, was back home moving heaven and earth to get me out. It was the holidays.

Flights were packed. Options were slim but she didn't stop. She worked around the clock with a travel agent, called every number she could find.

She pulled every string.

She was unstoppable.

She was love in motion.

And if it weren't for her, I don't know how much longer I would've been stranded, scared and unraveling, in a place that no longer felt like an adventure, but a trap.

I still remember that final flight home.

For the first time since Christmas Day, my body stopped shaking. It was like my nervous system had been stuck on high alert for days, and now, as the plane cut through the night sky, I could finally breathe.

My heart slowed and my hands steadied; the fear began to loosen its grip.

For the first time in days, I had a sliver of stability.

I kept telling myself:

"You made it. You made it. You're almost home."

Even as relief washed over me, the weight of everything I'd been through still pressed down.

The fear, the isolation, the unhealed past.

It was all still there.

That trip had cracked something open.

I wasn't okay, but at least I was almost home.

The moment we touched down in my city, I broke.

Tears streamed down my face as I rushed through the airport, and the only thought in my head was this…

I needed my mom.

Not as the grown woman I was trying to be, but as the little girl I still carried inside me. I needed her arms around me. Her voice telling me it was going to be okay.

After everything, I just needed to feel safe again.

But what happened next blindsided me.

When I finally hugged her, she broke. Full-body sobs shook through her. At first, I thought it was relief that she was overwhelmed to see me home, alive.

But it was more than that.

She wasn't just crying because I was safe.

She was crying because she had been fighting to get me home.

Fighting for me while fighting with him.

The tension between Grant and my mom at the airport could have snapped like a wire pulled too tight. And in that moment, something hit me even harder.

They had no room left for my pain.

They were drowning in their own.

Grant had threatened to leave her.

He told her I should lie in the bed I made. That I needed to figure it out alone. That she should stop rescuing me.

But my mom knew.

She heard the fear in my voice, felt the urgency in my words, and she did what mothers do when it matters most.

She chose me.

It wasn't the first time Grant and I had battled for her love. We had spent years in a tug-of-war, always pulling her in opposite directions.

But this time, she didn't stand in the middle.

She stood with me.

And Grant?

He threatened to walk away.

He let his pride win.

I have tried to understand it. He came from hard beginnings. He believed in tough love, but there is a difference between tough love and abandonment, between letting someone learn and leaving them to drown.

There was no lesson here.

Just a girl in crisis, desperate for help.

And he didn't care one bit.

So, there I was, finally safe in my mother's arms, and I couldn't even tell her what I had been through.

Not the fear.

Not the trauma.

Not the memories clawing their way back from the dark.

Her world was already cracking open.

There was no space left for my pain, too.

So, I buried it.

Stuffed it down.

Tucked it into the shadows with every other part of myself I didn't know how to face.

Then came the guilt.

Grant had blamed me.

And if there is one thing I have always done well, it is believing the worst things he says about me. And it didn't take long before I started to believe it too.

I had ruined their marriage.

He had a bag packed and one foot out the door.

So, I did what I always did.

I tried to fix it.

I apologized.

Told Grant it was all my fault, and I begged him not to leave. I don't even remember exactly what I said. Just that I made sure it was enough.

Enough to make him feel right.

Enough to make him stay.

Enough to get things back to normal, even if that version of normal came at the cost of my own truth.

And it worked.

On New Year's Eve, symbolic and cruel, they were smiling again. Back together, celebrating and toasting to a fresh start.

And me?

I had never felt more shattered in my life.

That night marked the true beginning of my downward spiral.

The freefall into my rock bottom.

I had no control.

No one to turn to.

And piece by piece, everything around me began to collapse.

I clung to the only thing I thought I could control, my body.

My eating disorder quickly became an obsession.

No longer a slippery slope, I slid all the way down, and the darkness was there to catch me.

It consumed me.

It was all I thought about.

All I cared about.

The number on the scale.

The portion sizes.

The calories burned.

And still, the pressure kept building.

So, I dove deeper.

Deeper into exercise.

Deeper into restriction.

Deeper into perfectionism.

Every pound lost still wasn't low enough.

Every bite of food felt like too much.

Every hour spent burning calories never felt like enough.

Thirty days after I got home, I was forty pounds lighter.

And that was just the beginning.

I was possessed.

Trapped in my own body, no longer the one calling the shots.

ED was fully in charge now.

It dictated my choices.

My thoughts.

My worth.

And no matter how much I obeyed, how much I gave…

It still wasn't enough.

I still wasn't enough.

And ED had a mission.

It wouldn't kill me quickly.

It wanted to break me slowly.

To starve me of everything: food, joy, light, and life.

Until all that remained was a hollow shell and the echo of who I used to be.

And the worst part?

I let it.

I welcomed it like a friend.

Like the only thing that truly understood me.

What I didn't know then, what I couldn't see, was that the darkest part of the storm hadn't even hit.

Not yet.

Because the real battle?

The real unraveling?

Was still to come.

CHAPTER 13

Living in Denial

"I'm fine. A lie I told myself so often, I started to believe it."
— Beau Taplin

My obsession wasn't just a habit.

It was now my entire existence.

Every action, every thought, every decision was ruled by one unstoppable desire...

To be thinner.

Smaller.

Less.

I lived by numbers.

I'd set a goal weight, reach it, and instead of feeling proud, I'd lower the target again.

And again.

I should've celebrated those milestones.

But the number was never low enough.

If I could just lose a little more. Be a little smaller, even just a few pounds less...

Then I would be happy.

Then I would love myself again.

The happiness never came.

I wasn't the only thing disappearing, my focus slipped and my energy vanished. Functioning, especially in school, something I already struggled with, became nearly impossible. Learning had always been hard. Try concentrating when your body is starving, when your brain is fogged by hunger and all you can think about is food.

When can I eat?

How little should I eat?

How long can I hold off before I finally let myself have something?

And then the moment would come.

The moment I allowed myself to eat.

The sensation was powerful.

The second food hit my lips, it was like euphoria, like I was in a trance.

Careless and free.

For a split second, my body felt relief, like I had finally given it what it needed. A wild surge of serotonin rushed through me. And just for a moment, it felt like life was returning.

Light.

Energy.

Hope.

My body clung to every bite, screaming thank you, begging for more. It tried to conserve, process, and distribute. Desperate to do what it was designed to do.

Function.

Live.

Survive.

I never gave it enough.

That's it.

That's all you're getting.

And then it would retreat.

Back into survival mode.

Back into darkness.

Back into the war.

Just as quickly as the relief came, the starvation phase swallowed me again. My body hoarded what it could, terrified it wouldn't get more.

And worse than the crash?

The guilt.

It came roaring in like a tidal wave.

Suddenly, I felt disgusting.

Like I had failed.

Like I was undoing everything I had worked so hard for.

I couldn't win.

And my poor, overworked, starving body…

It was falling apart.

You know that hollow ache when your stomach growls?

Now imagine it magnified by a thousand. My stomach didn't growl, it screamed. My muscles ached. My joints throbbed. This wasn't hunger anymore, it was full-body pain. But instead of listening, instead of stopping, I pushed harder.

I ate less.

Exercised more.

Ignored the pain.

Told myself I was stronger than my body's cries for help. That I was still in control.

I skipped meals.

Pretended I forgot to eat.

Lied about my food intake.

"Oh yeah, I already ate."

"Actually, I'm not that hungry."

But it wasn't just about eating less.

I started cutting out entire food groups. Carbs, fats, sugar.

They became the enemy.

Only safe foods were allowed.

Low-calorie.

Low-fat.

Clean.

I created rigid rules that dictated everything.

What I could eat.

When I could eat.

How much I could have.

No food after 6PM. No exceptions.

I remember nights buried under university essays, pouring myself a glass of white wine, hoping it would take the edge off and help me focus. Yeah... alcohol on an empty stomach? Not a good idea. The buzz hit fast, and the hunger made it worse. I'd reread my work the next day and think, what the hell was I even trying to say?

Then came another rule: I have to burn X calories before I can eat. Non-negotiable.

My immune system wasn't just weak, it was barely functioning. Every common cold struck me with full force. But it didn't matter how sick I felt. That was never an excuse; I still had to exercise. And not just once a day. You heard me right.

Throughout the day.

Morning.

Afternoon.

Night.

Fever?

Didn't matter. Coughing, sniffling, aching all over? Still didn't matter.

Rest days weren't allowed.

Rest was weakness.

And on the days when I did exercise, but didn't hit that invisible, ever-shifting target?

No food.

Just guilt.

And hunger.

But the punishment didn't end there.

After every meal, I had a ritual. A strange, obsessive routine I couldn't skip. The second I was done eating, I'd head straight to the bathroom. I wasn't purging yet, not physically, anyway. I was

163

still deep in the throes of obsessive anorexic behavior at this stage.

I'd stand tall, arms stretched high until I felt the burning pull through my core. In my mind, someone was tugging my arms upward, another pulling at my legs. Not to break me, just to stretch me out. To flatten my stomach and undo the damage. Take back what I'd just put in.

Then I'd twist my torso side to side, convincing myself I was helping digestion. Speeding it up, fixing the fullness and erasing the shame.

But worse than those moments in the bathroom were the ones outside. When I had space to move, to walk, to roam.

That's when ED thrived, because in my mind, I was walking it off. Trying to erase the guilt. Trying to un-feel the food sitting in my stomach like a weight I didn't believe I deserved to carry.

I remember one moment so vividly. I was visiting my brother at his new condo. Mom and I had just gone out to eat. Even though I'd ordered the safest thing on the menu, it still felt like too much. Too many ingredients. Too many unknowns. So instead of celebrating with him, instead of admiring his new place, I was outside power walking laps around the condo complex. Arms flailing, breathing heavy, pacing circles, over and over again. Michael kept calling, begging me to come inside. I wasn't listening, I was on a mission, and nothing was going to stop me.

Looking back, I'm sure his neighbors were peeking through their windows, wondering what the hell was this girl doing.

But that's the thing about an eating disorder...

It consumes you. It becomes your whole world. It turns your focus inward. Selfish and self-centered. And suddenly, there's no room for anyone else.

Just you.

And ED.

The rules went on and on...

I must eat the exact same meals every day.

If I eat one "bad" food, I've failed the entire day.

I can't have more than X calories.

If I ate too much yesterday, I have to eat less today.

If I break a rule, I must punish myself.

Certain foods mean instant weight gain.

Each day brought new rules, stricter limits, and harsher expectations. My routine got tighter, yet still, it wasn't enough.

Anyone could see these rules were irrational. But ED had me convinced they were truth, so I followed them. All of them, without hesitation.

Because that's what ED does.

It commands.

And I obeyed.

Then came the rituals. The disordered habits that kept the rules in place. They weren't quirks, they were coping mechanisms. Methods of discipline.

An internal drill sergeant dictating my every move…

Ripping food into tiny pieces.

Eating with a specific utensil, never switching.

Pushing food around the plate instead of eating it.

Taking painfully small bites.

Eating in a set order: veggies first, protein last.

Chewing excessively, counting every bite.

Using the tiniest plates and bowls to make portions look bigger.

And the gum.

Always the gum.

Sugar-free, one piece after another. I was starving but not allowed to eat. So, gum became the in-between. The fake fix. Sure, Hubba Bubba tasted better, but it felt too sweet. Too indulgent. Too risky.

From the outside, these rituals might've seemed harmless, but they weren't. They were quiet reinforcements of the disorder's grip. The longer I followed them, the tighter that grip became.

Eventually, eating in front of others became nearly impossible. Too vulnerable, too exposed. So, I withdrew. Being alone felt safer. There were no questions, no stares, and no confusion. Just me, staring at a plate of food.

Feeling joy.

Feeling hate.

All at once.

With time, I started pushing my friends away. Socializing almost always meant food. Grabbing a bite, gathering around snacks, laughing, talking, and just being together. But I couldn't enjoy any of it. All I could think about was the food. How much I wanted it, even just a bite, and how I wasn't allowed.

The internal war was constant.

Desire vs. denial.

The longer I sat there pretending to be present, the more consumed I became.

Even something as simple as grabbing a drink at the bar felt like rebellion. Alcohol? Empty calories. I had to be mindful of everything.

So, to avoid the triggers…

I avoided everything that made me feel joy.

My friends.

My laughter.

My happiness.

ED didn't leave room for any of it.

And just like that, I started shutting down every relationship I had.

Everyone who cared.

Everyone who loved me.

Everyone who just wanted me back.

But ED was a jealous bitch.

The only relationship I was allowed to have was with it.

My friends tried. They stuck around, even when I shoved them far away. They didn't know how to help, but they wanted to. Some asked if I was okay. Some made jokes about my weight, trying to lighten the mood.

None of it worked, because I didn't think anything was wrong.

I wasn't sick.

I was just a little skinnier.

That's all.

I canceled plans one too many times, and eventually they stopped checking in. I couldn't blame them; my walls were up. No matter how hard they tried, there was nothing they could do.

There's no manual for what to say to a friend who's slowly dying from an eating disorder.

Then there were the ignorant ones.

The ones who thought they had all the answers.

"Just eat something. It's not that hard."

"Someone give this girl a burger already."

Oh, trust me, if it were that easy, I would have eaten the damn burger.

My body was starving.

But I was trapped.

Stuck in a trance I couldn't escape.

A hostage.

At ED's mercy.

And my reality?

It was shattered.

My eyes were open, but I couldn't see straight.

I was blind to the truth.

ED had pulled me into another world. And in that world, ED ran everything. The mayor. The sheriff. The doctor. The principal. The store owner. ED was the town. A town built on fear and lies.

And the worst part?

I believed it was safe.

I believed I belonged there.

ED convinced me it was protecting me. It became my safety blanket. The thing I clung to when I felt unworthy, unlovable, and not good enough.

Letting it go?

Terrifying.

The idea of stopping.

Of recovering.

Of gaining weight.

Felt scarier than the disorder itself.

Because if I stop…

Who am I without it?

What if I recover, and I'm still not happy?
What if I realize I was never enough to begin with?

Readiness is everything.
The first, most crucial step in recovery is realizing that no one can be forced into it.
Like any mental illness, the desire to heal has to come from within. You can offer love, support, and encouragement. You can show up, check in, and hold space. But unless the person wants to change, and chooses to, progress will always hit a wall.
And that's one of the hardest things to witness.
Standing by, watching someone you love spiral, knowing that no matter how deeply you care…
You can't carry them to healing.
They have to want it.
They have to choose it.
For themselves.
And at that point in my life?
I wasn't even close.
I had no intention of stopping.
Not even when my body started to shut down.

At the time, I was working part-time as a server at a bar. But that didn't last long. You can only faint so many times while carrying a tray full of drinks before you realize, maybe your body is trying to tell you something.
Something loud.
Something urgent.
But I wasn't listening.
The fainting spells became more frequent. Hunger pains turned into something worse, a stabbing, persistent agony deep in my gut. At first, I brushed it off. Another reason to push harder, restrict more, stay diligent.
Pain had become normal.
Expected.
Part of the process.

But then I found out something more.

My eating disorder wasn't just destroying my mind.

It was destroying my body.

I had developed gallstones from rapid weight loss.

That unbearable pain in my stomach was my gallbladder failing.

I needed surgery.

I had no choice.

Up until then, I'd been avoiding my family doctor. Even in denial, I was aware of what I was doing and what she would say if she saw me. But the pain forced me back. The moment I walked in, she didn't waste time. She brought up eating disorders. Mentioned treatment programs. Asked questions I refused to answer.

I denied everything.

Said I was fine.

Said it was just the gallstones and that became my perfect excuse.

The gallstones gave me an explanation for the weight loss that didn't involve the truth. In some twisted way, I saw that as an opportunity. Now I had a reason to eat plain, bland food.

Which to me meant...

Cut out fat.

Cut out flavor.

Keep cutting.

The pain never stopped.

It followed me morning, noon, and night. And eventually, I wasn't even sure anymore. Was it the gallstones? Or just my body, starving itself into oblivion?

Either way, I used it.

"It's just my gallstones."

"This isn't my fault."

But the truth?

I had changed my eating long before they ever showed up. Maybe I thought I was clever. But looking back, I don't think anyone really bought it.

Time passed, and I eventually had the surgery.

But even that wasn't simple.

My surgeon, someone who'd done this procedure countless times, was hesitant.

I was too malnourished, too underweight, and too weak. The risks were high. Much higher than they should've been. He told my mom that operating on me was like doing a heart transplant on an eighty-year-old woman. My body wasn't built to withstand it. But the surgery had to happen.

He expressed concern about my ability to handle anesthesia. He warned her my healing would likely be slower than normal, and I was at serious risk for complications.

I remember standing right there in the room, present, yet completely invisible. I was twenty years old. Legally able to consent to my own procedure. But he didn't speak to me. He spoke about me, to my mother, as if I were a child.

Maybe he was right. Because I wasn't really there, not fully. I was sleepwalking through life. Drifting through every moment in a fog. Too hollowed out to speak up. Too far gone to even absorb what he was saying.

My mom stood tall, calm, and strong. She listened without flinching, without tears. No fear in her eyes. Just a mother, standing firm, protecting her daughter the only way she could. The surgery needed to happen. He was one of the best and she wasn't going to settle for less. She buried her fear, her anxiety, her heartache, and showed up for me in every way I couldn't show up for myself.

At one point, he finally turned to me. Looked me dead in the eyes, steady, kind, but unwavering, and told me he wouldn't do the surgery unless I promised him one thing…

That I would start eating.

Once the gallbladder was out, I had to fuel my body.

That was the deal.

He wasn't mean but he wasn't soft either. There was conviction in his voice. He was drawing a line. For the first time in a long time, someone wasn't asking. He was telling me.

And what did I do?

I smiled, I nodded, I played the part.

Gave him the answer he needed to hear.

"Of course," I said. "Once the pain's gone, I'll eat."

But behind my back, my fingers were crossed.

There was no way I was going to start eating.

Why wasn't that moment, the surgeon's concern, the risk, the plea, a red flag?

Why didn't it shake me awake?

It should have, but it didn't.

I was too deep.

Still strapped in.

Still clinging to the lie that I was in control.

The surgery itself went fine.

My body handled the anesthesia.

But the recovery… that was another story.

It was anything but smooth.

I ended up back in the hospital multiple times with internal infections. They put me on strong antibiotics, which only made my stomach issues worse.

What should have been a few weeks of healing turned into months of complications.

My body was failing me.

It couldn't heal.

It was exhausted, weak, and constantly in pain.

It didn't have the strength to recover.

The lack of proper nutrients had slowed everything.

My ability to fight off infection, to rebuild, to bounce back.

I had given my body nothing.

No fuel.

No care.

Just a surgery it wasn't prepared for, and no tools to recover from being cut open and stitched back together.

So yes, I broke my promise to the surgeon. I never meant it anyway. I said what I had to say to get the surgery, to make it happen, to get him off my back.

There was never a plan to start eating, no matter how badly my body needed it. Because as much as I needed healing, needed strength, nourishment, and rest, there was something louder.

ED's voice.

Sharper.

Stronger.

More convincing than ever.

In my ear…

"We're not done yet."

"We've only just begun."

With every hospital visit, every time my mom rushed me in after another fainting episode, it got harder to ignore what was happening.

I never remembered going down. One second, I was standing. The next, I was on the floor. Curled in on myself, clutching my stomach, pain slicing through me like a thousand knives. My gallstones were gone. So it wasn't that. This was something else, this was starvation.

I let my mom pick me up. She helped me stand and guided my disoriented body to the car for another trip to the ER. Another day in the cycle and no matter how terrified she was, she stayed strong. My rock. But deep down I knew, with every collapse, she feared I wouldn't get back up.

I remember the sting of the needles, how they jabbed me over and over, searching for veins that had grown thin and withered from malnutrition. I remember the IVs, sliding into my arm, pumping fluids into my hollow body. My body must've loved those IVs. That was the most nourishment it had received in what felt like forever.

And those warm hospital blankets were glorious. My skin was paper-thin, and my bones always chilled to the core. Wrapped in those blankets, cocooned in artificial warmth, I finally felt something that resembled comfort. Something that reminded me, just for a moment, what it felt like to feel safe in my body.

I think it was my fifth trip back to the hospital when I finally broke.

I couldn't take the pain anymore.

Couldn't take the looks.

The pity.

The concern.

The quiet helplessness in their eyes.

Couldn't take the whispers from nurses who thought I was asleep.

Back on my first visit, I heard two of them talking.

"She's so sick."

"It won't be long before her organs shut down and her heart stops."

"That poor girl... she's dying."

I heard every word.

And still, when I got discharged, I went home and restricted harder. Their words didn't scare me straight. They lit the match. They didn't put out the fire, they fed it.

By the third visit, a doctor stopped sugarcoating my condition.

He looked me dead in the eye and said what the nurses had only whispered.

"Your organs are close to shutting down."

"Your digestive system is failing. Your stomach lining may be permanently damaged."

He explained how my nutrient-starved body couldn't absorb food properly. How the only way to stop the fainting, the pain, the hospital trips, was to eat.

That was the answer.

It was simple and straightforward.

Just eat.

All I heard was...

Do the one thing that feels impossible.

The thing that could save me... was also the thing I feared most.

To eat.

During my next visit, yet another doctor looked me in the eyes and said...

"If you keep going this way, you might not live past another birthday."

This time, he didn't just warn me about short-term risks.

He talked about long-term damage.

Things that might never heal.

Even if I got help.

Even if I survived.

"There's only so much the body can do to repair itself after this much damage," he said.

At first, I was annoyed. Here we go again, another speech. Well-rehearsed and well-delivered. But not winning any Oscars with me.

And then he said the one thing that stopped me cold...

"You might not ever be able to have kids."

That hit differently. It wasn't about pain, weight, or health anymore. It was about something sacred. Something I'd always wanted.

To be a mom.

A mom like mine.

Warm, fierce, and safe.

After hearing him say it might never happen felt like a knife to the chest. For the first time, I didn't zone out. I didn't roll my eyes. I listened.

He explained how years of starvation pushes the body into survival mode, and when the body stays there too long, it stops doing what isn't essential.

Like reproduction.

"A body that's been through what yours has is at much higher risk for infertility."

I had spent so long shrinking myself, chasing less.

That I never stopped to think about what else I was shrinking.

My future.

My ability to carry life.

My chances at motherhood.

And suddenly, I wasn't so sure I was the one running the show.

What if it was already too late?

Oddly, it wasn't the warning that I might die that got to me.

It was the idea I might never become a mother.

Even through all the delusions, I still pictured a future.

One where I'd hold a baby.

One where I'd be okay.

ED never wanted me dead.

It wanted to own me.

It didn't want to share.

Despite how hard that realization hit, I still wasn't ready. Wrapped in that warm hospital blanket, clutching the truth like a lifeline, I let ED pull me back in. Its voice roared louder, sharper, and stronger. And just like that, the doctor's words were pushed aside. Silenced and tossed in the pile with all the others.

So, I returned.

One week later.

My fifth visit.

Same hospital.

Same story.

Despite every plea, every warning, I still hadn't changed.

Another bed.

Another IV.

More tired eyes peering down at me, wondering if this would finally be the turning point.

I don't even know what else they could've said, I wasn't hearing any of it.

Until something shifted.

I can't explain it exactly.

Maybe it was the real Jody, still buried deep, fighting her way to the surface.

Screaming to be heard.

I looked around that tiny room. The IVs in my arm and my mom's voice behind the curtain, begging the doctor not to discharge me. Not yet. She knew, just as I did, that once I looked stable, I'd be sent home. Back to the storm.

I saw the doctor's shadow stretch across the curtain. I knew he was about to say the same things. The same warnings. The same facts.

And I broke.

Not because of what he was about to say.

But because I couldn't hear it again.

"Yes, I'm dying. I get it."

"My body's shutting down. I might not have kids. I know, I know."

I was tired of people telling me about my body. I lived in it. I knew what it felt like. And yeah, things were bad, but not as bad as they thought.

I still believed I had control.

The only thing I couldn't control was the pain.

So maybe, I thought, they could help with that.

Not recovery.

Not weight gain.

Just pain relief.

Let me go back to ED, but without the agony.

It sounds ridiculous now, like a fantasy or a fairytale. How could I keep all my ED behaviors and still have them make me feel a little healthier? I knew there wasn't a medication for that. Logically, I knew it wasn't possible. But for some reason, I believed anyway.

So, I gave them a small win. I decided to work with them, just a little. Enough to get me back to functioning. I knew the only way to do that was to admit I was sick.

By then, I wasn't in denial anymore.

Not completely.

Every complication after surgery, every hospital visit over the past few months had slowly chipped away at the illusion.

It was during that last hospital stay when the bubble finally burst.

Despite brushing off everything the doctor said, I remember coming home that night. My behaviors hadn't changed. My rituals and my rules were still there.

But my mindset?

It had shifted slightly.

Just enough to let in a flicker of something new.

Hope.

I wasn't just thinking about food anymore; I was thinking about the future. Wondering what life with ED would really look like. Maybe just the two of us, forever. The doctors still hadn't fully convinced me. But their words didn't make me roll my eyes anymore. I heard them. Not loud and clear, not fully. But louder than a soft hush. And, for the first time, I didn't ignore them.

I started wondering.

Could they be right?

Could I actually die from this?

Will I ever be a mom?

There was a tug-of-war in my head, but one thing had become undeniable.

It was time.

Time to step outside of denial.

Time to admit what everyone around me already knew.

I was sick.

And more than that…

I was tired.

Tired of hiding.

Tired of the lies.

Tired of carrying this disease like it was some twisted badge of honor.

I wasn't ready to let it go, not even close.

But I knew I needed a new way to carry it.

Something had to give.

So, there I was, sitting in that hospital bed, watching the doctor slowly approach. Then just as he took a breath, preparing to speak, I cut him off.

If I was going to admit it, it had to be right then.

Before ED's voice got too loud.

Before it pulled me back under.

Before denial buried me all over again.

There was still a spark inside me, a flicker of stubbornness that hadn't gone out.

And in that moment, it lit up.

ED was still screaming in my head, but the urge to speak was louder.

I was done with the pity.

Done with the looks.

Done with people tiptoeing around me like I was made of glass.

I needed to say it.

Out loud.

For real.

So, I did.

I took a deep breath.

Clenched my fists.

And let the words go.

Raw, undeniable:

"I have an eating disorder."

CHAPTER 14

Rock Bottom

"Rock bottom is not the end. It's the place where the ground stops falling."
— Kat Lehmann

My mom walked into the room just as the words slipped out of my mouth.

I finally said it.

Not just to the people around me, but to myself.

Hearing it out loud made it real.

In that moment, I knew there was no turning back.

I couldn't pretend I had said something else.

I couldn't shove it back down.

It was out there.

Spoken.

Admitted.

Exposed.

As terrified as I was, as much as I wanted to run, I also felt something else.

Relief.

Not overwhelming.

Not life changing.

But just enough.

Enough to take a breath.

A real one.

Deep, honest, and unshaken by denial. I was still trapped, still tangled in ED's grip. But for a moment, the pain eased, and I could finally breathe.

My mom walked over and sat on the edge of the hospital bed. She took my cold, brittle hand in hers. Firm, but gentle.

She didn't speak.

Not right away.

And then the tears came.

Quiet, steady tears.

Not a breakdown. Not a collapse. Just the release of everything she'd been holding. The fear, the heartbreak. The weight of watching her daughter fade before her eyes.

And I cried too.

For the first time in a long time, we weren't just mother and daughter.

We were two hearts.

Both hurting, both holding on.

Together.

When my eating disorder first began, my mom had been in denial with me. She didn't want to admit her baby girl was struggling. Not like that. Of course, deep down, she knew. A mother always knows. It took time for her to fully grasp the depth of it. The severity, the darkness I'd been living in.

She had tried to talk to me, gently and carefully, but I shut her out before she had the chance. So instead, she waited. She stayed close. Present, watching, and hoping I'd be the one to finally say it. And when that moment came, she didn't say "I told you so." She didn't scold, she just held me. She had always been ready, even when I wasn't.

Saying it out loud made it real for both of us.

A reality we weren't fully prepared to face, but one we could finally stop hiding from.

"I have an eating disorder."

The words hung heavy in the air.

And just like that, the room shifted.

The energy changed.

Everything changed.

The doctors and nurses, who had once been firm, warning me, pushing me, trying to get me to see what I refused to.

Suddenly, they looked different.

They weren't angry.

They weren't frustrated.

They were calm, hopeful, even.

Like a collective breath had been released.

Like everyone in the room had been holding on, waiting for me to say it.

Now the ball could start rolling.

Before I even left the hospital, they handed us pamphlets for clinics, treatment programs, and recovery plans. A referral was already lined up. Everyone around me exhaled, convinced I was finally on the road to recovery.

But what no one realized was this…

Just because I admitted I had an eating disorder didn't mean I was ready to recover.

The thought of gaining weight?

That was still the scariest thing in the world to me.

Scarier than dying.

Scarier than never having kids.

The idea of even putting on one pound felt like being trapped in a shrinking room, gasping for air.

So, no.

I wasn't ready.

Not even close.

I went home at my lowest weight ever.

Eighty-two pounds.

And I had a tail.

Yes, you read that right.

A tail.

My tailbone had become so sharp, so unforgivingly exposed, that it actually stuck out above my butt. A small, grotesque ridge of bone. Pushing through where flesh used to be. It was like my body had grown a reminder, a permanent, physical badge of how far I had fallen.

My entire frame was sunken in. Hips protruding like blades, ribs like staircases. My collarbones casting shadows beneath my skin. I looked like a sketch someone had started, then gave up halfway through.

A hollowed-out version of what I once was.

There was basically nothing left of me.

Just skin, bone, and a disorder that had taken over everything in between.

Clothing draped off my body like I was a child playing dress-up in someone else's wardrobe. Even the smallest sizes in the store swallowed me whole.

I started wearing children's clothing, because at least then, I could feel the fabric against my skin. Tiny kid-sized pants fit like awkwardly long shorts. The proportions were all wrong.

Waists tight, legs too short, but they had the one thing I needed most. A waistband that stayed up on its own. No more threading shoelaces through belt loops, no more double knots cinched tight. Only to keep my once-favorite jeans from falling down.

Those jeans… Oh, I had loved those jeans. I wore them daily. They had once molded to me, faded just right, soft in all the perfect places. They had been mine, a part of me.

But now, the thought of ever fitting into them again felt like pure torture. Despite how much I had adored them, I could not, would not allow myself to grow.

Not one inch.

Not one pound.

The idea of gaining weight was a suffocating concept.

A panic attack wrapped in denim.

So instead, I wandered around in bright, bold children's clothes. My body drowning in neon cotton, while my tailbone played peek-a-boo every time I moved.

I wasn't in denial anymore. I knew exactly what was happening. But I was still fully committed. Still married to this thing inside me.

Me and ED.

Still together.

And I wasn't leaving.

Before I move on, I need to say this. This is the last time I'm going to talk about weight in numbers. Because weight is just a number. We all have different bodies, different shapes, different sizes. What's healthy for me might look completely different on someone else.

None of those numbers ever really mattered anyway.

They didn't define my worth.

They didn't define my health.

They didn't define me.

So, from here on out, we leave the numbers behind.

I was eventually named a candidate for an eating disorder program.

My body was failing, frail and exhausted, crying out for help, yet I was still placed on a waitlist. The demand was overwhelming. So many others, just like me, silently suffering and desperately waiting.

I remember feeling shocked by how many people were fighting the same internal war. In a strange way, it was comforting I wasn't alone. But it was also devastating. So many of us, minds turning against our bodies. Bodies bearing the weight of our pain.

There I was, no longer in denial, but not quite ready to let go. I knew I'd eventually walk through those treatment center doors. I was over eighteen so no one could force me.

It had to be my decision.

And it was… sort of.

I agreed to go.

But my intentions weren't exactly pure.

Part of me hoped the center would ease the pain, lift the weight of my self-loathing, maybe even help me look healthier without touching the one thing I couldn't let go of, my eating disorder.

I wanted to keep it.

I wasn't ready to surrender the control.

The twisted comfort it gave me.

I was open to treatment, but only on my terms.

The rest, I wasn't ready for that part yet.

The waitlist felt endless.

It was three months long, but in my condition that wasn't just a waiting period, it was borrowed time.

Still, there was no space for me. The program was full, weak bodies and weary hearts lined up, hoping for their turn to be saved.

And so, I waited.

I waited knowing that every day on that list was another day my body slipped further away.

During this time, my mom stepped in, fully and fiercely, without hesitation. She took personal days from work, more than I could count, just to stay home with me. The secret was out, and she wasn't about to let me slip through the cracks.

She watched me like a hawk.

Every bite.

She was there.

She became my shadow.

My protector.

My babysitter.

It was suffocating, but it was love.

A mother's love in its rawest, most desperate form.

At first, I hated it.

Her hovering, her eyes on me.

I felt like I couldn't breathe beneath the weight of her constant presence. But eventually, I adjusted and got used to it. And somewhere in that moment, something changed.

I was still restricting, but now, I began binging and purging regularly.

That was new.

Until then, my disorder had revolved around mastery…

Rigid restriction.

Obsessive calorie counting.

Relentless exercise.

But now, my body was too weak.

I could barely stand, let alone work out.

So, ED adapted.

It evolved.

And, like always…

I listened.

With my mom home, I was forced to eat more.

Not a dramatic increase but the quality altered.

Hard.

Looking back, I can't believe what I put into my body.

It was vile, random, and coarse.

ED gave me permission to dabble in cravings as long as I promised to get rid of it after.

I craved everything: sweet, salty, creamy, and crunchy.

So, I threw it all together in the most disgusting combinations you can imagine. Then I'd make it disappear.

Try not to gag when I tell you about my daily breakfast.

I'd start off scrambling egg whites, normal enough.

Then I'd add:

Crab meat

Tuna

Ham

Cheese

Blueberries

Cinnamon

Strawberry yogurt

But wait, it gets worse.

Once it was on my plate, I would spread a thick layer of peanut butter on top.

And as a final touch, chocolate chips and rainbow sprinkles.

Yeah. Let that sink in.

It sounds revolting.

And looking back, I agree, it was.

But in that moment, it was perfect.

Not because it tasted good, but because it tasted like freedom. An outrageous collision of flavor and control. It satisfied something in me, not my hunger, but my desperation.

That breakfast would've been a "scary food."

And to my ED brain, it wasn't just breakfast, it was bingeing.

Logically, I knew the portion was small, nowhere near a real, balanced meal. But to ED, it was massive, excessive, and mortifying.

I "allowed" myself one meal a day.

That was it.

The rest of the day, I survived on "safe" snacks.

A plain can of tuna.

A dry chicken breast.

No seasoning, no sauce.

Just protein swallowed with shame.

Yes, it sounds like barely any food, because it was.

But to ED it felt huge, disgusting, and weak.

By day's end, I wasn't relieved I had eaten, I was repulsed.

Bloated.

Guilty.

Dirty.

Because in ED's world, eating wasn't nourishment.

It was failure.

It was weakness.

And I couldn't shake the feeling that I'd lost my power.

For the first time in what felt like forever, I'd given in to a craving. Those wild, random omelets reintroduced something I hadn't tasted in years… flavor.

Real flavor.

And for one fleeting moment, I let myself enjoy food again.

But the guilt was unbearable.

That's when I started purging.

It didn't take long for my mom to catch on. She hovered outside the bathroom, listening and waiting. I couldn't escape her vigilance, so I needed a quieter plan. Something that seemed more natural.

Enter: Milk of Magnesia.

A laxative.

Recommended dose, one tablespoon.

What did I do?

I drank an entire jumbo-sized bottle.

Every day.

Let's just say, my colon was very clean.

It became my new ritual, my secret weapon.

And in the moment, it felt like I mastered a new technique.

But in reality, it was just another form of self-destruction masked in silence and swallowed whole.

Eventually, my mom caught on again. She stopped buying it. Refused to let another bottle into the house. By then, I'd been drinking it daily for nearly a month. I thought I was outsmarting my body. Manipulating digestion. Mastering control. But all I was doing was damage to my gut, my health, and my future.

Now, nearly twenty years later, I'm still feeling the effects.

I developed irritable bowel syndrome (IBS), something I now manage daily. Was it the Milk of Magnesia? The years of restriction, bingeing, and purging? Maybe all of the above. I'll never know for sure.

But one thing's certain.

The damage doesn't disappear just because the behavior stops.

ED took a serious toll on my body, one that didn't vanish when treatment began.

For the next decade, I needed daily medication just to help my stomach function. To manage digestion, acid reflux, and the consequences of a damaged stomach lining.

My body had to relearn how to process food, something that should've come naturally. But nothing about recovery felt natural.

My organs had been through hell.

They didn't bounce back.

I had spent years breaking them down.

I couldn't expect them to heal overnight.

I may have survived my eating disorder.

But my body bore the brunt of it.

And even now, it's not fully healed.

But I'm alive.

I'm here.

I made it through.

And that's what matters most.

Before reaching this stage of recovery, I was still deep in destruction, headed straight for the moment I crashed on the bathroom floor.

Still on the waitlist.

Still trapped in the in-between.

My mom had discovered all my tricks.

Every single one.

I was being watched, monitored, and managed. I was forced to eat but I couldn't purge, sneak laxatives, or exercise. Every outlet ED once used to give me control was suddenly gone.

And I had never felt more helpless.

I was stuck in a body I hated, stuffed with food I didn't want, stripped of every coping mechanism I had. I was drowning in my own skin, suffocating in silence, with nowhere left to turn.

The worst part of the day was bedtime. That's when everything hit the hardest. My body ached a deep, relentless pain. And at night, it was unbearable.

My mom would rub Tiger Balm on my back and neck, trying to soothe the pain. Trying to numb the hurt. But it was never enough. I'd crawl into bed trembling and shaking uncontrollably. I was freezing because there was no fat left on me to keep warm. The cool sting of the balm only made it worse. Blankets weren't enough. Nothing was. So, I layered up.

Two pairs of thick wool socks. Fleece pajamas. A big fleece housecoat. A toque pulled tight over my head. Mittens, because even my fingers felt like ice.

My body couldn't fall asleep on its own, it was too busy fighting to stay alive. Sleep wasn't something I eased into; it was something I forced. Every night, I took a sleeping pill, praying it would knock me out before the ache swallowed me whole.

And as I lay there in the dark, wrapped in layers and desperation, I wished for an escape. I felt stuck in an endless loop, trapped between survival and surrender. I wasn't getting into treatment fast enough. It felt like I never would.

And even if I did, I wasn't sure I was ready.

It all felt hopeless.

I spent so many nights lying there thinking...

If I close my eyes tight enough, maybe I won't wake up tomorrow.

Maybe I'd finally be free from the pain, the heaviness, the grip of this disorder.

I just wanted to disappear.

I had no fight left in me.

I was done.

At that point, even death seemed better than this.

On nights I couldn't sleep, I'd creep out of bed and turn on our old dial-up internet. I'd sit at the family computer, in the stillness of night, and play Sarah McLachlan's "I Will Remember You."

On repeat.

Over.

And over.

And over.

Some nights, I cried.

Other nights, I just stared at the screen, numb and hollow, letting the lyrics wash over me. Wondering if I'd ever find a way out. Wondering if anyone would remember me if I didn't.

That song held two meanings.

In one version, it was a farewell.

A song for the girl who didn't survive, who lost her battle.

Her eulogy wrapped in melody.

Soft.

Sorrowful.

Final.

But in the other version, it was future me speaking to present me.

"I will remember you."

I imagined a stronger version of myself, one who made it out.

Who looked back at that cold, broken girl in the chair and whispered,

"I'm not her anymore. I survived."

Most days, that version felt impossible.

The rare moments I believed in recovery were drowned by fear.

Because a life without ED was unimaginable.

I didn't know who I was without it.

I was terrified.

Terrified of gaining weight.

Of my body changing.

Of losing the one thing I thought gave me control.

It didn't feel like there was a way out.

And even now, all these years later, that song can still bring me back.

Back to that quiet room.

That humming computer.

That fragile girl, bundled in layers, hovering between life and death.

But now, I can look back at her…

And remember.

As much as my mom stayed home to care for me, there were days she couldn't miss work. She always tried to keep those shifts short, just half days when possible. But one day, she was gone from morning to late afternoon.

I remember slowly waking, peeling off the layers I'd slept in. Layers meant to fight off the cold my body couldn't. Even getting dressed was a workout. A kids' size extra small hung off me like a sheet. I was drowning in fabric.

Everything took twice as long. I moved like a zombie, weak, hollow, and exhausted. Then came the first battle, the staircase. Only a dozen steps, but it felt like a mountain I was descending from. My legs trembled; my heart pounded from the effort.

But none of that mattered.

Because the scale was waiting.

Before brushing my teeth, before using the washroom, I went straight to it. Tucked beneath my mom's dresser.

That number dictated everything.

I'd take a deep breath, step on, and brace myself.

If the number stayed the same or dropped, I felt a flicker of success. But if it went up, even slightly, panic took over. The day unraveled before it even began.

One weigh-in was never enough.

I'd step on that scale at least ten times, resetting with every tiny fluctuation. I wasn't "allowed" to continue until the number matched perfectly, again and again.

Luckily, that morning, it stayed the same.

I dodged the bullet.

No spiral... yet.

Next on the agenda, I would normally head to the kitchen to make my infamous omelet. My twisted version of indulgence, packed with bizarre combinations meant to satisfy cravings without breaking my rules.

If the scale stayed the same, I earned my extras. Sprinkles, chocolate chips, a dollop of peanut butter. My illusion of indulgence. If the number went up. No chance. Everything got stripped down, bland and joyless, a meal swallowed in shame.

But that morning, even with the green light, I wasn't feeling it. There were no cravings, there was no appetite. And with no one hovering, no one there to force me, I didn't see the point.

So instead, I decided to shower.

Not a bath, not one of those supervised ones where my mom would wash my hair, or my brother would wait outside the door.

No, I wanted to stand. I wanted to feel something.

I stepped into the shower, pulled the curtain closed, and cranked the heat.

Scorching hot.

So hot it should've burned my skin.

But I didn't flinch.

For a moment, the heat masked everything. The ache in my bones, the cold that never left, the emptiness inside me. Even if it hurt, it was a pain I could handle. I was numb inside. The heat didn't scald, it felt nice and comforting. Not unbearable at all.

I ran my fingers through my hair, and clumps came loose in my hands. Thick strands, slipping away without resistance. Every day there was less. My brush already full, blonde locks tangled like they'd simply given up.

My hair, like my body, was losing the fight.

Just like me.

I don't know how long I stood there, letting the steam wrap around me, breathing in the thick, damp air. But I know it was a while. My legs weakened. Standing became harder. My body was giving out. But the heat felt like peace.

No pain.

No chill.

No hunger clawing at me.

Just stillness.

Just warmth.

So, I stayed. As long as I could.

Eventually, I knew I had to get out. The hot water would run out anyway.

I shut off the water, opened the curtain, and reached for a towel.

That's when it hit me.

The dizziness.

The spin of the room.

I gripped the counter, trying to steady myself.

But my body wouldn't cooperate.

My vision blurred.

My knees buckled.

The world tilted.

And then I collapsed.

I hit the bathroom floor.

Landing at rock bottom.

There I was, naked, shivering, and all alone.

Nothing but skin and bones, sprawled out on the bathroom floor.

Thoughts of suicide flooded my mind as my eyes drifted toward the blade resting on the edge of the tub.

But I couldn't move.

I had no control over my body.

No power to choose whether to live or to die.

I was ED's hostage more than ever.

I wasn't living.

I wasn't dying.

I was just… trapped.

Ready to disappear, yet unable to go.

As much as I wanted it to end, death wasn't an option.

Not because I didn't want it, but because I couldn't do it myself.

That wasn't my path.

I was meant to struggle.

To suffer.

To feel every agonizing second.

There was no way out.

My body was numb.

My brain was numb.

My heart was numb.

I felt like an empty shell, like all the life had been sucked out of me.

And yet, somehow, my heart was still beating.

So, I just lay there, breathing, barely.

My mind was racing, but time stood still.

I felt like I was trapped on a Ferris wheel. Spinning round and round, never stopping. It never malfunctioned. Never broke down enough to force me to act. If it had, maybe I would've signaled for help. Maybe I would've jumped. Maybe I would've been ready. But I wasn't. I wasn't at the top, or the middle, or the bottom. I was just endlessly spinning.

Each slow, predictable loop pulled me deeper into an invisible void. A silent darkness that wrapped around me like fog. A ride

I didn't remember getting on, one I couldn't escape. And eventually, even the Ferris wheel began to rust. Its paint chipped; its parts wore down. Disintegrating into scraps of metal.

Just like me.

My body was fading, nothing more than a hollow silhouette, bones and limbs barely holding me together. And it made me wonder…

What happens when a Ferris wheel breaks down? Does the carnival tear it down? Toss it like garbage? Or does someone come along, give it a fresh coat of paint? A second chance at life? Or does it just sit there abandoned?

A landmark of what once was. Something people glance at in passing. A relic. A memory. Something that used to be full of life, full of joy, full of purpose. Now, just a rusting reminder.

As I lay there, too weak to move, I imagined it.

My tombstone.

Towering above my grave.

A final destination.

A quiet end.

Would I become a historical landmark?

A monument of what once was.

Finally at rest.

Finally, still.

No longer spinning round and round. Trapped in an existence of pain with no escape. Just stillness, silence, and peace. A grave that didn't ache. A body that didn't scream. A mind that didn't spiral.

For a moment, the thought didn't scare me.

It comforted me.

So… how did I get up?

How did I get off the Ferris wheel?

How did I find the strength to stand again?

To climb my way out of rock bottom?

Because clearly, I did.

I'm here.

I'm alive.

I'm writing this memoir.

But what was strong enough to pull me back?

What force was powerful enough to breathe life into my hollow frame?

To crack through the numbness and whisper, "Keep going."

To make me believe, even just a little, that I was worth saving?

What gave me the strength to fight ED?

To choose life when every part of me wanted to disappear?

What gave me hope?

What made me believe in myself?

Let's just say…

I saw an angel.

And by that, I mean.

My mom came home.

My strong, brave mom.

Through it all, I'd been so consumed by my disorder, by my own suffering, I never stopped to think about her.

I never asked:

"How is she feeling?"

"How is this affecting her?"

"Is she okay?"

My mom was my rock, my anchor, my constant. No matter how deep I sank, she stayed strong. Not just for herself, but for me. She never showed weakness. Never backed down.

She was on a mission to protect her daughter, and she refused to let me go.

She was my guardian angel.

My wings when I couldn't fly.

She gave up her entire life to take care of me. She would've done anything to save me.

And in that moment, when she found me on the bathroom floor…

I broke her.

I heard the back door open. The jingle of her keys. Her bag hitting the counter.

Then, her voice.

"Jody?"

She started calling my name, her voice echoing through the house.

I didn't answer.

I heard her.

I wanted to respond.

But I couldn't.

I didn't even have the strength to whisper.

Then came her footsteps.

Closer, faster, more urgent.

And then… she turned the corner.

She saw me.

Naked.

Shivering.

Crumpled on the floor.

She ran to me, panic in her voice, tears already forming.

She dropped to her knees, hands trembling as she tried to lift me. I could feel the fear. Sharp, frantic, and breaking.

She thought she'd have to call an ambulance. Thought this was it. Another emergency. Another moment she didn't know if I'd survive.

She reached for her phone.

And that's when I screamed.

"Mom, just let me go!"

"Just let go!"

"I'm done, just let me die!"

I didn't move.

I just lay there crying, pleading, begging her to say goodbye.

Then in that moment, my strong, unbreakable mother collapsed.

It was like her legs gave out beneath her.

Like the weight she'd been carrying finally became too much.

I had never seen her like that.

Not ever.

She shattered before my eyes.

Tears poured down her face like a storm that had been building too long.

She screamed.

"I'm not saying goodbye to you!"

"I'm not burying my daughter!"

"I refuse to bury you!"

She yelled it, again and again.

A mantra.

A battle cry.

The only strength she had left.

It hit me.

I had drained her.

The fight she'd carried for both of us had finally broken her.

And I did that.

I was so consumed by my pain; I hadn't seen hers. Hadn't noticed the cracks forming. The quiet unraveling. The way she was breaking beside me, while holding me together.

And now there she was.

On the floor.

Sobbing.

Screaming.

Broken.

Because of me.

Something then gave way.

That was my turning point.

Watching the strength drain from her stirred something inside me. Because in taking her strength, my guilt, and more importantly, my love, gave me back a flicker of my own.

I couldn't do it anymore.

I couldn't watch my mom cry.

Couldn't hear her scream.

I couldn't be the reason she was breaking.

So, I did the only thing I could.

I GOT UP.

Not because I was strong.
Not because I was ready.
But because she had carried me for far too long.
It was now time for me to carry something.
Even if it was just the weight of standing.

I don't remember the rest of that evening in detail. I know it followed the usual routine, eating with her watching, Tiger Balm massaged into my aching body, layers of clothing bundled tight to keep me warm. And then, her putting me to bed.

But that night… something was different.

She always tried to be optimistic at bedtime, wrapping herself in this bright, hopeful energy. A forced kindness cloaked in a big, warm smile.

Most nights it annoyed me.

"How can she be so positive with everything that's going on?" I used to think.

But now, looking back, I see it for what it was. Her strength and her armor were the persona she wore, night after night, just for me. I was angry. I was broken. But still, she tried to bring a little light into our dark world. Just a spark. Just enough to keep me going.

Except tonight, there was no spark.

She couldn't fake it anymore.

She wasn't hopeful.

She wasn't strong.

She looked… defeated.

She told me she loved me. Told me how much I meant to her, that she never wanted to lose me. She kissed my forehead. And said, "Good night."

Up until that night, I hadn't really felt anything. For months, my emotions had been numb. Dulled by exhaustion, hunger, and pain.

But tonight, I felt something.

I felt for her.

And my heart broke.

That's the thing about eating disorders.

They don't just destroy the person who's trapped.

They destroy everyone who loves them.

Everyone who fights for them.

Everyone who refuses to let go.

It takes a toll on everyone.

And on this night, my mom hit her breaking point.

She wasn't just watching me suffer anymore.

She was suffering with me.

Dragged into the darkness, right beside me.

She was there, at rock bottom, too.

The next morning, I woke up. Something had clicked. It was like a light bulb switched on. Not bright enough to light the room, but just enough to spark something inside me.

A flicker of hope.

Of fight.

I can't explain it, but for the first time in a long time, I felt the faintest trace of strength.

Not for me.

For my mom.

Her voice from the night before echoed in my mind.

"I won't bury my daughter."

And in that moment, I made a promise.

She never would.

I still didn't care about myself. Not yet. But no parent should have to bury their child. Not the woman who gave up everything to save me. There was still a chance. I had a choice. I had to believe I was still in there somewhere. That the girl I used to be, full of life, full of light, could come back.

For months, I had felt powerless. But suddenly, there was a spark. A tiny flame. And maybe, just maybe, I had enough fuel to ignite it.

I remember that moment clearly, lying in bed and, for the first time in ages, not being disappointed I had woken up.

Not mad that death hadn't taken me.

I just lay there.

Still.

Breathing.

Existing.

Then, as always, it hit me.

The ache.

The second I was fully awake, it rushed in, pain, weakness, and hunger. Starvation, my silent alarm clock, reminding me my body was still fighting to stay alive.

The sun streamed through the window. Birds chirped softly outside. And all I could think about was my mom.

Her face.

Her tears.

Her voice.

This morning was different. I still felt the ache, the weight of everything I'd been carrying. But something else was there too.

That spark.

And in that moment, it burned brighter than ED.

Relentless.

Fierce.

Small, but powerful.

I closed my eyes.

Clenched my fists.

And for the first time in so long, I felt something.

Anger.

Rage.

Life.

I had gained an ounce of real control.

And even that tiny bit?

It gave me power.

Not ED's power.

But mine.

The real me, the girl buried beneath the disorder, was begging to be released.

It was like something had been unleashed. A surge of energy rushing through my veins. I threw my arms into the air, fists tight, and slammed them into the mattress.

And I screamed.

"Fuck this."

Again, louder: "Fuck this."

One more time: "Fuck this."

Within seconds, the guilt came crashing in.

Shame.

Exhaustion.

ED's tidal wave, furious it had lost control, even for a moment. And what ED didn't know was that it would only get weaker from here. Because in that single moment of rage, something in me changed.

ED still had its grip.

But I had fire.

And I was just getting started.

I rolled out of bed.

Terrified and shaking.

But standing.

My body was still weak.

But I stood a little taller.

And I decided… Today would be different.

Not drastically.

Not dramatically.

But different.

No grand declarations.

No over-the-top promises.

Just one choice.

To live.

Instead of wishing to die.

It wouldn't be easy. It wouldn't be linear. But forward is forward. And I had to do it.

For her.

For my mom.

That's the thing about rock bottom.

There's only one way out of the darkness.

Up.

It could've swallowed me whole.

Or I could climb.

Not fast. Not gracefully. Maybe not even steadily.

I was ready to take that first step. I didn't know what recovery looked like. I didn't know how I'd get there. But I was ready for help.

And if it got too hard? If I couldn't do it? ED would still be there, waiting. That's what I told myself. But first, I had to try.

That morning, I started my fight.

I chose to live.

For my mom.

And since that day?

I've never stopped fighting.

Because now…

I'm not just living for her.

I'm living for me.

CHAPTER 15

Where Recovery Took Roots

"Healing begins when we let hope grow in the cracks where pain once lived."

— *Morgan Harper Nichols*

The day finally came.

June 2008.

I was officially admitted into the local eating disorder program.

The first crack emerged in 2006 with my stepdad's fat-shaming words, seared into memory. That was the initial trigger. But my disorder didn't explode on impact.

It crept in quietly.

Lurking.

Watching.

Waiting for the perfect moment to strike.

And sometimes I wonder…

If I hadn't gone on that trip.

If I hadn't come home shattered, desperate to reclaim control.

Would things have been different?

Would I have remained a girl with disordered eating habits? Or was I always destined to become the girl with a full-blown, aggressive eating disorder?

I spiraled down the rabbit hole of weight obsession.

But would I have fallen so far without those triggers?

I'll never know.

Life doesn't always offer answers.

It doesn't always reveal the silver lining.

All I know is the universe chose this path for me.

That's the thing about disordered eating and body image issues, so many people live with them silently. But not everyone crashes. Not everyone hits rock bottom.

And sometimes, I think those people have it the hardest.

Because without a collapse, there's no reckoning.

No defining moment.

No catalyst for change.

Rock bottom forces you to wake up.

If you want out, you have to fight.

Name the darkness.

Untangle the lies.

Rewrite the story.

Freedom doesn't come easy, it demands transformation.

Requiring raw, relentless, uncomfortable work.

But the only way out… is straight through.

What about the ones who live in the grey area?

The ones I call functional disordered eaters.

They don't ask for help because they don't believe they're "sick enough." They're not collapsing. Not underweight enough. Not what society imagines when it hears the word disorder.

But they're still obsessed with the scale and still tie their worth to a reflection. They still see restriction as good discipline and food anxiety as simply being cautious.

And the scariest part…

They could live that way forever.

Their bodies still function. They show up to work. Go to social events. Laugh, smile and blend in.

But are they really living?

To truly live, your worth can't be shackled to a number. Your joy can't depend on your pant size. And your reflection should never be your enemy. The problem is society only validates pain when it's extreme. Only treats illness when it's visible.

But these functional disordered eaters?

They still need help.

They still deserve support.

Even if they never ask.

Even if no one notices.

Sometimes, being seen, truly seen, is what saves them.

I started that way. Just a girl with disordered eating habits. It didn't seem dangerous. Just a few rules. A little restriction. It looked harmless, almost normal. But for me, it didn't stay that way.

Because that's who I am.

All or nothing.

At that point in my life everything else felt out of control. So, I clung to the one thing I could control. And once I grabbed hold, I didn't let go. I went full speed into the abyss. Not because I wanted to be sick. But because I needed something to hold onto. This became my anchor. Even if it was dragging me under.

By this point, ED had been with me for about two and a half years.

It crept in quietly, then consumed everything.

And now, finally, I was seeking help.

Taking my first steps into the eating disorder treatment program.

I wasn't the same girl who once walked into high school, bubbly and bright, rainbow tube top and overalls, hope in her eyes and a nervous smile on her face.

That girl had faded.

Piece by piece.

But thankfully, this time, there wasn't a rumor waiting at the door. No whispered humiliation. No shame etched into the walls. Just a quiet place to begin again. A place where maybe I could find my way back to her. Or, better yet, become someone even stronger.

I was considered a critical patient. Technically, I should have been admitted full-time as an inpatient. But there wasn't a bed. The system was overflowing with people like me, people who had waited far too long.

Luckily, my psychiatric nurse, Debbie, saw something in me. She trusted me enough to start as an outpatient. It was a risk, but one she was willing to take.

It meant I could begin treatment, without becoming a resident of the ward. It also meant I'd be facing the hardest parts, meals, nights, and thoughts on my own.

It wasn't ideal, but it was a start.

And between the day my mom found me on the bathroom floor and my first day in the program, something unexpected happened.

Something I didn't see coming…

I started putting in the work. I was eating more. I wasn't purging. I wasn't abusing laxatives.

I was actually eating.

Don't get me wrong, I was still restricting.

But for me, that was progress.

A step forward, a step toward healing, toward recovery.

In that short window of time, I gained seven pounds.

Seven.

That's why Debbie trusted me to begin as an outpatient. I had shown her, I could try.

But seven pounds?

For someone with ED, even half a pound feels like a tidal wave. Seven feels like the world is caving beneath you. It feels loud and terrifying, like failure.

But it wasn't.

It was proof.

Proof that I hadn't given up.

Proof that maybe I could fight my way back.

Here's the tricky part about being an outpatient…

It's easy to follow the rules when you're in group. When structure holds you up and when eyes are watching. But the second you walk out those doors, you're on your own.

When you're outside those walls, it's easy to cheat, skip meals, fake smiles, and hide behaviors.

I wanted to.

I truly did.

But something had changed.

ED still had its tight and unforgiving grip.

But I had a flicker of hope.

That flicker lit a fire.

Then there was my mom.

Her love, her pain.

Her unwavering presence.

She found me at my worst and stayed.

That love.

It was strong enough to ground me.

Strong enough to make me try.

To do my part.

To come back to life.

As an outpatient, I attended the program Monday through Thursday, 9 AM to 4 PM. Four days of structure. Four days of support. Four days of accountability. But Friday, Saturday, and Sunday were all mine. Three full days without check-ins. No one watching. Every choice was mine to make.

So, I had to ask myself…

Was I going to fight for my life?

Or let ED win?

Ultimately, that's all it was, repeatedly.

Every meal.

Every mirror.

Every moment.

Recovery wasn't a straight line. It was a question I had to keep answering. Every weekend felt like a test, of will, and of strength.

Of whether I was ready to live, or still afraid to.

I still remember my first day in the program.

The moment my two worlds collided.

ED had built a town inside my mind. Ruled by fear and control. Streets paved with lies. Homes built on shame. It was familiar and it was mine. But that day, something was different, an invader arrived.

For the first time, ED's stronghold was under attack. A new force had entered. Trained, tactical, and unafraid. It had seen ED's kind before. Knew the tricks, the weapons, even the hiding spots. It wasn't looking for compromise; it was ready for battle. To expose the cracks in ED's armor. To remind me there was another way.

There was a new sheriff in town, and it had one mission.

To save another life.

Only problem, I wasn't sure I was ready to be rescued. ED wasn't just my illness, it was my best friend, my only friend. Yet somehow, my worst enemy.

How do you let go of something that's been with you through everything, even as it's been slowly destroying you?

I didn't have the answer, but it didn't matter.

It was my time.

My mom dropped me off at the treatment program. She gave me that look, the one that said she believed in me, even when I didn't believe in myself.

As the doors swung open, I stepped inside.

Onto the battlefield.

Just like that, the sheriff and ED prepared for a showdown.

To my surprise, the psychiatric ward wasn't cold or clinical like I'd imagined. It was welcoming and warm. There was a softness to it. Everyone moved with purpose like they were there to help, to heal, and to hold space for people like me.

The lobby had tall ceilings that stretched upward, making the space feel open, breathable, like maybe I could finally exhale. Green furniture lined the waiting area, cozy touches softening the sterile edges.

Our group therapy room was smaller, more intimate, about the size of a conference room with a large oval table where we sat side by side. The white walls were covered in positive affirmations and old medical posters trying to say, "you'll make it through this," without using those exact words.

The chairs swiveled gently and were surprisingly comfortable. Like someone thought, if they're going to sit here and share their pain, the least we can do is make it easier to sink in.

And in that space, for the first time in a long while, I felt like I belonged.

I felt safe.

I didn't know what the next steps would look like, or how long it would take to feel okay again.

But I knew one thing for sure.

This was where I was meant to be.

I was nervous when the nurse introduced me to the other girls.

Would they be cold?

Guarded?

Judgmental?

I was the new girl, stepping into an unspoken sisterhood I hadn't earned my place in yet, and sometimes, girls can be catty. I knew that all too well.

But this wasn't high school. This wasn't a lunchroom, or a hallway lined with lockers.

This was survival.

There was no room for mean girls here. No energy for drama or competition. We were all fighting the same monster, just wearing different armor.

And to my surprise, they welcomed me. No side-eyes, no mean chatter, just quiet understanding.

They let me in.

And just like that…

My new journey began.

The ED program used Cognitive Behavioral Therapy—CBT.

A method that doesn't just scratch the surface. It dives deep into the mind, emotion, and behavior. It rewires thought patterns, untangles long-held lies, and teaches you how to cope in ways that don't destroy you.

I had learned about CBT while studying psychology in university. Even then, I admired it. It's practical and powerful. It's not just about managing symptoms; it goes deeper. It targets the root, the real pain. The beliefs beneath the behaviors. It's whole-body recovery: mind, body, and soul.

Here's the truth I had to face…

Even the most effective therapy in the world can only take you so far. Healing isn't handed to you. You have to reach for it. You have to want it. No one else can make that decision for you.

So, there I was, sitting in group therapy, surrounded by a small circle of girls.

Eating disorders don't discriminate.

They can affect anyone. Any gender, age, or background.

But in this room, it was just us.

Some were bulimic.

Some anorexic.

Some struggled with self-harm.

Some had been suicidal.

All of us lived with depression.

After all, here's the part no one talks about enough. When you develop an eating disorder, you almost always develop depression, too. They go hand in hand, shadows chasing each other in circles. One feeds the other, pulling you deeper into a cycle that feels impossible to break. You stop eating to feel in control. Then you feel empty. So, you binge. Then you purge. Then you hate yourself. Then depression settles in, casting lies.

In that room, we didn't have to explain it.

We all knew.

Even in silence, we understood each other's pain.

We were at different stages in our recovery.

Some girls were nearing the end of the program, thriving, eating, healing, and laughing again. They had walked through the fire and refused to turn back. They were the inspiration. The proof that recovery wasn't just a dream. It was real.

Others weren't ready, not even close. They never chose to be there. Doctors, parents, and hospital beds had decided for them. They weren't angry, just numb. Trapped in denial, with a long road ahead before healing could even begin to spark.

Then there was me.

Somewhere in the middle.

Maybe leaning closer to not ready but starting to try. I had gained some weight. I was showing up, I was trying, but I had no tools yet.

No idea how to cope with the noise in my head.

I was a beginner, a therapy virgin.

But I was open.

I wasn't fighting it.

I was there.

And for now, that was enough.

We talked a lot about our thoughts, our feelings, and the ways we could push back against the negative voices in our heads. Recovery wasn't just about food; it was about unlearning the toxic thought patterns that had held us hostage for so long.

My nurse, Debbie, once described the disorder in a way that stuck with me forever.

She said:

"It's like a tape recorder in your head that never fully stops."

It's always playing.

Sometimes it's loud, screeching, blaring, drowning out everything else. Other times, it's quieter, still spinning in the background, but not as all-consuming. But no matter the volume, it never really goes away.

That was the goal of recovery.

Not to erase ED's voice entirely, because perhaps that's not possible.

But to mute it.

To turn the volume down until it loosens its grip.

When the tape recorder is screaming, that's when relapse creeps in. That's when the spiral starts. But when you're in control, not the disorder, that's when it quiets. That's when you can breathe.

That's when you can live, truly live, without your weight or your reflection defining your worth.

That's what we were all fighting for.

To hear our own voices again.

To keep our tape recorders on mute, as often and for as long as possible.

Group therapy had heavy moments.

Tears.

Struggle.

Raw honesty.

We talked about our triggers, our family dynamics, our trauma. The hidden parts, the painful parts, the ones we tried so hard to forget. Anything we were holding on to, anything weighing us down, had to be brought to light. Only then could we start to take back control. Only then could we begin to heal.

I wasn't ready to bring everything to light. Some things were buried for a reason, locked up tight, far below the surface, and I wasn't ready to face them. Some wounds were still too raw. Some truths, too heavy. Even in a room full of people who understood pain, there were pieces of mine I couldn't let out. Not yet.

As part of the program, we each had to write our autobiography. Every day, someone took a turn reading theirs aloud.

One day, it was Emily's turn. She began with her childhood, her upbringing. She had clearly done the work, digging into the parts of herself most people spend a lifetime avoiding.

At first, I was listening.

Present.

Grounded.

Safe.

But then… I felt it.

Her aura darkened.

The way her hands trembled. The hesitation in her voice. The way she fidgeted in her seat. The air became thick. It was like I had a sixth sense. I could feel something dark moving into the room. It was like a shadow, a presence, something uninvited was pressing on my chest.

Her heart was pounding. So was mine. My body started to shake. Heat spread like a fever. Sweat crawled down my skin.

I wasn't ready to hear it.

I already knew what was coming.

Then she said it.

Her voice cracked. Her body folded beneath the weight of what she was about to release. Then with one breath, she told us.

She told us about the time she was raped.

The room fell silent.

Not empty silence, but sacred.

Still.

Paralyzed by pain, we listened. Her words shattered the air. It wasn't that we didn't know that kind of trauma existed. It was that now it had a name, a face, a voice.

Emily kept going through the tears. She didn't run, didn't hide. She faced it. And in that moment, as broken as she was, she was the strongest person in the room.

I tried to listen. I wanted to hold space for her pain, to honor her courage. But suddenly, I couldn't breathe. The atmosphere thickened. The walls closed in. And there she was, speaking her truth while I ran from mine.

Before I could stop myself, my body took over.

Fight, flight, freeze.

I chose flight.

The guilt hit instantly. She was brave. She said the words I hadn't even whispered to myself. And I walked away. But it wasn't because I didn't care. It was because I cared too much.

It was too close.

Too familiar.

Too real.

I wasn't ready to hear that it had happened to another girl.

I wasn't ready to go back to that dark corner of my memory I'd sealed shut.

I wasn't ready to face it.

A week later, it was my turn.

Still the newbie, still learning the ropes, still unsure how much of myself I was ready to reveal. I sat at that oval table, hands trembling, pounding rhythm in my chest, unsure how deep I'd go.

I talked about growing up with a single mom, who was strong, stretched thin and full of love. I opened up about my dad, about the absence that echoed louder than a presence ever could. I mentioned Grant. I brought up the trip from hell.

But my own sexual abuse?

Hell no.

I couldn't bring that to light.

A part of me still believed it was my fault. That I'd let it happen. That going back meant I deserved it. That I should've fought harder, screamed louder, ran faster. I clung to that story as a shield. If it was my fault, maybe I had control. Maybe it wasn't rape. Maybe it never happened. Maybe it was just a nightmare I couldn't wake from.

Because the truth?

The truth was too heavy.

Too dark.

Too real.

And if I named it, I'd have to accept that it happened.

To me.

I was afraid people would look at me differently.

That they'd see shame instead of strength.

That they'd judge me, not for what happened, but for how I handled it.

So, I left it out.

Buried it deeper.

Locked it away for another day.

Healing is complex, and sometimes, survival means not saying everything.

Not all at once.

Speaking of my stepdad. Grant's no longer in my life. He wanted a wife all to himself. And when my mom chose to take care of me at my lowest, he finally left. This time, it wasn't only a threat. And for once, I didn't feel guilty.

Finally, my mom saw it too. She saw how toxic he was. She realized she wasn't happy. This time, his absence didn't feel like a loss. It felt like relief.

I remember the day he left. My mom and I went for a drive, no destination, just the need to get away. Then when we came home, his things were gone. His presence had vanished. But instead of feeling hollow, for the first time in years, it felt like home.

There was space to exhale.

There was light.

My mom always describes that day as if a cloud of darkness has been lifted from our home.

She was right.

It was like the mood of every room lifted and the walls could finally breathe.

And so could we.

Every day in the program was heavy. The therapy was taxing. The eating overwhelming.

As an outpatient, I had to eat two snacks and lunch during the program. Breakfast, dinner, and evening snacks were up to me. That meant three meals and three to four snacks a day.

Some days, it felt like all I did was eat. No sooner had I finished lunch then it was time for another snack. My body wasn't used to this much food. My mind definitely wasn't. I had spent so long fearing food, avoiding it, controlling it, and now I was being asked to embrace it.

It felt unnatural.

Some days, impossible.

But I was trying.

And for now, trying was all I had.

We sat around yet another large oval table and ate together.

Part of our lunch routine was mindful eating. For so many of us, meals had always been something that needed an escape. Reading, scrolling, or watching TV, anything to distract from what we were putting in our bodies. Anything to avoid feeling it.

Not in therapy. There was no escaping. No phones. No small talk. Just us, our food, and the clink of forks against plates. Each bite demanded our attention. The sweetness of strawberries. The graininess of bread. The way peanut butter clung to the roof of your mouth.

It was inescapable.

No multitasking. No numbing.

Just presence.

Just discomfort.

We had to taste everything.

Feel everything.

Sit with it.

Eating with presence rather than avoidance was one of the hardest adjustments. It was like staring into a mirror, forced to see everything we tried to hide.

In the beginning, I wasn't allowed to pick my meals. I was still considered critical, my body needed to stabilize. So, I sat there, tray in front of me, watching the other girls, further along in recovery, choose their own food. Some even had smaller portions.

More freedom.

More say.

More control.

But not me.

I ate what I was given.

Didn't matter if I was a picky eater. If the food made me gag. If it turned my stomach. I had to eat it anyway.

And lunch felt endless.

We couldn't move on to group until every tray was cleared.

No one left behind.

No one excused.

We waited.

Together.

That was one of recovery's first lessons…

You don't rush healing.

You sit with it.

You chew it.

You finish it.

Together.

There we were, fighting our ED minds. Rewriting habits. Rebuilding our relationship with food, one painful bite at a time.

All of it under watchful eyes.

Every bite was monitored.

Every behavior noted.

No tricks.

No food in napkins.

No pushing it around the plate.

They saw everything.

That was the point. It was hard, uncomfortable, and exhausting. But recovery wasn't meant to be easy. It was meant to rebuild us, piece by piece.

The staff didn't just watch, they ate with us. Like a familiar gathering around the table. But it wasn't like a typical family meal. No stories, no laughter, just silence. Heavy silence. Broken only by the sound of our struggle.

They modeled what normal eating looked like, biting with ease. No fear, no guilt. They ate because they were hungry. Because food was fuel. Because eating wasn't something to apologize for.

And even though ED screamed at me… a quiet part of me noticed. They weren't just telling us food wasn't the enemy; they were showing us. And whether I realized it or not, those moments mattered. They helped me believe, just a little, that recovery was possible. That maybe one day, I could eat like that too.

Over time, things got better. Slowly and steadily.

Then came a turning point, I was allowed to choose my meals. It seemed small but it meant everything. It meant I was trusted. It meant I had earned it. And for the first time, I had a little control that didn't feel toxic. I felt empowered.

Of course, I was still watched closely, I didn't have full control. If ED behaviors crept back in, I was gently, yet firmly, called out.

Uncomfortable?

Yes.

Necessary?

Absolutely.

I hadn't realized some of my habits were disordered until I was in the program. Like breaking my food into microscopic pieces before eating. I wasn't alone, others did it too. Smaller bites felt safer. More manageable. I'd done it for years.

But now I saw it for what it was. ED, and all its tricks.

Awareness was the first step.

Then there was mustard.

Yes… mustard.

Apparently, we all had a discreet obsession with it. It was the perfect "safe" food. Low in calories, no fat, and full of flavor.

We put it on everything.

Mustard on cereal?

Done it.

Mustard on bananas?

Been there.

Gross?

Absolutely.

But back then, it made sense. It was flavor without fear. Comfort without consequence. Or so we thought. Another illusion of control. Another trick. And once I saw it for what it was, I couldn't unsee it.

Every day, someone was triggered at lunch. Someone would break down, sometimes quietly, sometimes not. Forks paused mid-air. We'd sit in silence, talk it out, or hold space.

Because we understood. And somehow, through all that pain and struggle, we became a little family.

Not bound by blood but forged in fire. Not the kind who grew up together, but the kind who recognized each other's scars.

At home, my mom followed me after meals.

In treatment, it was the staff.

No one went to the bathroom alone.

They stood outside the door.

Listened.

Zero privacy.

But I respected it.

Because it kept us honest.

Kept us safe.

Recovery required boundaries, even when those boundaries felt intrusive.

And little by little…

They helped us heal.

If the food itself wasn't triggering enough, we also had to write about it after every single meal. Log everything, every item, every portion. Then we had to write how we felt about it.

There was no avoiding our emotions.

No pushing them aside.

No pretending we were fine.

Everything was laid bare.

The fear.

The guilt.

The shame.

The anger.

The sadness.

All of it.

It was hard.

Therapy was hard.

Healing was hard.

There was nothing easy about any of it.

Even though with time I was finally ready, ready to change and ready to fight, I still had to do the work. Still had to show up, day after day, and push through.

Because readiness doesn't make it easier. It just means you're willing to walk through the fire instead of running from it.

I remember when some of the girls got the green light to join the yoga class on the ward. I was never allowed. Physical activity was like kryptonite for my recovery. My weight was too low, and I was too fragile. I wasn't even allowed to take the stairs. Every time we moved between floors, I had to use the elevator. It felt ridiculous, like I was being enclosed in bubble wrap. Like they didn't trust me to climb a few steps.

But I knew why. They were doing everything they could to make sure every pound I gained stayed put. Still, I was annoyed. Jealously, I watched the other girls head off to yoga. I wanted that freedom. That movement. That little piece of normal.

But I told myself, "It's all good. You have stairs at home. When you leave here, you can go up and down the damn stairs as much as you want."

And I did, within reason. By then, I was putting in the work and I wasn't about to sabotage my progress just to feel in control again. That, in itself... was growth.

I had begun spending more of my off time at the lake.

My grandma lived there in her camper during the summer. Tucked in a seasonal campground my family has now been going to for over sixty years.

It was my happy place. My second home. The place I felt safe enough to just... be. No expectations, no pressure. Just the sound of water, the hum of dragonflies, and the rhythm of simple living.

Without even realizing it, the lake became a part of my therapy.

A big part of my recovery.

Healing doesn't only happen in treatment rooms.

Sometimes, it happens in the stillness.

In sunlight on your skin.

In the way your grandma makes your favorite meal without asking.

In the safety of a place that's always been yours.

Every Thursday after group therapy, I'd race home and pack a bag with whatever clothes fit me best in that moment. Some hung off my frame, but they were all I trusted. The idea of slipping into my smaller clothes, the ones from before weight gain, was enough to send me spiraling. I wouldn't see strength,

I'd see failure. Recovery isn't just about food. It's about the war we wage with our reflection, and sometimes, that war starts in the closet.

I grabbed a quick snack, another checkpoint in my eating routine. It still felt strange, forcing food down when my mind, when ED, screamed in horror. But I did it anyway because I had to.

Then I'd jump in my little blue car, heart racing, and head straight for the lake. The second my tires hit the road; I felt free. Same country playlist, every time. Singing at the top of my lungs until the noise in my head resolved into melody.

With each familiar landmark, it got easier to breathe. The weight in my chest lightened. And for the first time all week, I felt like me again.

On those drives, I wasn't the girl with ED.

No calorie counting.

No guilt.

No obsession.

I was just a girl, driving toward the place that made her feel alive.

Trying to remember who she was without ED.

And even though the drive always ended, those miles were a beacon of hope. They reminded me that freedom was possible. That maybe one day, I wouldn't just borrow it from the road, I'd carry it with me.

Out there, I had no agenda. Just time in nature, away from the noise. But even in that peace, the work didn't stop. I still had to log my meals. Still had to journal. Still had to eat. Because if I skipped a meal or missed a log, they'd pull me from outpatient. The second a bed opened; it would be mine. That was the deal.

Healing followed me everywhere, and this time, I wasn't running from it.

I was showing up.

Doing the work.

If I relapsed, I'd lose the freedom of the lake, my second therapy space. And I wasn't willing to let that go.

I had been a perfectionist with ED.

Followed every rule, no breaks.

So now I had to be just as committed to rebuilding.

No shortcuts.

No excuses.

No turning back.

This time, my obsession wasn't with shrinking.

It was with surviving.

Despite my commitment to mastering the art of recovery, my eating journal remained a warzone, each page a silent tug-of-war between me and ED. Each entry a clash between what I ate and how I felt about it. Every word peeled something back. Every sentence revealed more than I was ready to see.

I started to recognize the patterns. The strict requirements. The rituals. The characteristics I thought made me feel safe, but really, just made me feel trapped. And beneath it all, I found something deeper.

Rage.

Rage at how much power ED had.

At how easily I let it take the wheel.

At how long I mistook its voice for mine.

But now, I was fighting back.

Its grip was loosening.

Mine was strengthening.

Mealtimes were our biggest battleground. That's when ED fought hardest. It knew when to strike, right after I ate. Right when my body started to feel something like peace. That's when it would whisper loudest.

My breath would freeze.

My hands would shake.

It was ED and me, face to face.

Battling for control.

My body, finally remembering nourishment, started responding with life. Tiny sparks of energy. Fleeting moments of peace. But in my mind, there was still a fight between good and evil, sickness and health, ED and me. It stood in the shadows, revealing guilt, and shoveling fear. Telling me I had failed. Telling me to turn back. Luring me home, back to restriction, back to the silence that comes with emptiness.

But this time…

I was learning to stay.

Stay with the discomfort.

Stay in the fight.

Stay alive.

It felt like I was walking a tightrope. A delicate, terrifying balance between recovery and relapse. Behind me stood ED, the circus ringmaster. Waving its cane, tipping its hat, taunting me. It would tap the rope ever so slightly, just enough to send a swirling wave beneath my feet, forcing me to grip tighter, to balance and fight harder to stay upright.

If I fell, it would be there, arms wide open, smiling. Welcoming me back home. If I could just make it to the other side, maybe life would get easier. I imagined the other side as a landmark of recovery, a place where the survivors live. It was calling my name. Faintly, but steadily. But the tightrope played tricks on me. It spun me around for its own amusement. Wobbled beneath me like it had a mind of its own.

ED was determined to hold me back. It didn't need to pull me down, it just had to keep me stuck. Because until one side overpowered the other, I was trapped. Balancing in the middle. Suspended between healing and breaking. Terrified of both.

It wasn't just the eating journal. The CBT activities we did in therapy often sparked the fiercest battles between ED and me.

One in particular, I'll never forget. Recovery wasn't just about food; we had to confront our distorted body image too.

Here's the thing about living with an eating disorder…

The way you see yourself in the mirror. It's almost never what your body actually looks like. Your eyes begin the lie then your brain distorts the reflection. Your body becomes the frontlines of illusion, and you're stuck in the crossfire.

No matter how thin you get, ED always whispers:

Not enough.

Not small enough.

Not good enough.

It's not about vanity.

It's about control.

Fear.

Punishment.

And in this exercise, we had to face that distortion head-on.

We were asked to draw our bodies, head to toe. No face, no hair. Just the shape of how we saw ourselves. It was uncomfortable, but I took it seriously. I thought I had done okay, I tried to be realistic. Honest, even. I knew my perception was off, but I thought I'd landed close to reality.

Then came the reveal.

We lay down on giant sheets of paper while staff traced our actual outlines, our real size. Then both versions, ours and the traced ones, were hung side by side.

And... Holy shit.

The difference was staggering.

In my drawing, I had curves, a wide stomach, and thick arms. But the tracing looked like a twig. My stomach was sunken. My limbs looked like they could snap. And still, ED had me convinced I was too fat.

Now I had proof.

Proof that ED had been lying.

That my eyes couldn't be trusted.

That my thoughts weren't facts.

It was a wake-up call.

Yes, I was eating again.

Yes, I had gained a few pounds.

But seeing those outlines side by side?

I realized just how far I still had to go.

ED was still screaming.

Telling me I was expanding out of control.

That I was going to lose everything.

The truth was right there on the wall...

I was still skin and bones.

The five additional pounds I'd gained in the program felt like thirty in my head.

But in reality, they were barely visible.

And I wasn't alone.

Not a single girl in that room had drawn herself accurately. Every self-portrait was bigger, fatter, wider, and distorted.

It was terrifying how deeply ED had infiltrated us all. How loud the deceptions had become. How easily we believed them.

But it also meant something else.

Maybe those lies could be unlearned.

I took both outlines home and taped them to my living room wall. I needed to see them. Every time I felt chubby, every time ED told me I was too much, I'd look at those drawings. And it helped, not perfectly, not instantly, but it helped.

It reminded me that what I saw wasn't always real.

That what I felt wasn't always true.

That ED's voice could be challenged.

It didn't silence it completely, but it planted doubt.

And that was a start.

It's wild how distorted our self-perception can become.

Even people without eating disorders struggle to see their bodies clearly.

So many live with body dysmorphia, seeing flaws that aren't there, fixating on imperfections no one else notices.

Then in that moment, I realized something big...

Just because I was finally eating food didn't mean I was done fighting.

Because eating is only half the battle.

The other half...

Is learning how to look at yourself, to really look, and not flinch.

I would have to learn how to accept my reflection.

To quiet the cruel inner monologue.

To love the girl in the mirror.

And that.

That was going to be a whole new war.

One that didn't live in my stomach.

But in my mind.

In the mirror.

In the silence of my own thoughts.

And I knew, I'd have to face that one next.

Just like the draw-yourself CBT activity, getting rid of the scale was another huge step for me.

In the program, they said, "Just get rid of your scale. Maybe give it away or hide it in a closet."

But that wasn't enough for me.

I didn't just need to remove it.

I needed to destroy it.

So, I took it to my backyard and smashed it into a million pieces. I didn't want to just throw it out. I wanted it to be unrecognizable. I wanted to erase its power over me once and for all.

It was a bit of a mess to clean up, I won't lie. Tiny springs, shards of plastic, little gears scattered across the grass. But I didn't care. Because I'll never forget how incredible it felt to feel that thing break beneath my feet. The object that had ruled my emotions for years.

Let's pause for a second.

Before you keep reading, ask yourself:

How often do you use your scale?

Does it control how you live your life?

Does it dictate how you see your body?

Does that number affect your confidence?

Your worth?

If the answer is yes to any of those questions, do me a favor.

Go get your scale.

Right now.

Pick it up.

Take it outside.

And smash it.

I'm not kidding.

Be safe, wear goggles or gloves if you need to. I'm asking you to break free, not break a finger.

But seriously go break it.

Because the second you start stepping on that scale every day, or worse, multiple times a day, that number starts to own you.

It controls your thoughts.

Your mood.

Your identity.

And you deserve more than that.

If you stash it in a cupboard, you'll dig it out. Hide it behind the toilet or in the back of a closet?

You'll find your way back.

So don't just hide it.

Destroy it.

Shatter it.

Throw it away.

Or give it away if that feels safer.

But if you can feel that moment...

That delicious, liberating crack of the glass breaking and the grip it has on you disappears with it.

Pure freedom.

And if smashing it isn't an option today?

That's okay.

Pick it up.

Toss it in the trash.

Take the trash out.

Walk away.

Leave it somewhere you can't get it back.

Go do it.

Right now.

And don't look back.

I'll wait...

The day I smashed mine was one of the most therapeutic feelings I've ever had.

All the power it held over me.

The control.

The anxiety.

The obsession.

Gone.

Just like that.

For the first time in years, I felt lighter.

If I didn't have a scale to stand on every day, I didn't know my weight.

And if I didn't know my weight…

That number couldn't consume me anymore.

Couldn't dictate my day.

Couldn't define my worth.

Couldn't whisper that I wasn't good enough.

A few days passed after I said goodbye to my scale, and I thought for sure I was going to cave. I kept expecting this urge to win, to run to the store and buy a new one.

Because stepping on the scale had been a ritual. It was a routine I clung to like a lifeline. But the longer I went without it, the easier it became.

Then eventually, the silence where that number used to scream…

Felt like peace.

Felt like clarity.

Felt like breathing for the first time.

Since that day, I've never owned a scale.

Not once.

And I don't miss it.

My worth was never meant to be measured.

Not in pounds.

Not in inches.

Not in numbers.

I was never created to be weighed.

I was created to live.

To breathe.

To feel.

To take up space.

And choosing to let go of the scale wasn't just about breaking a habit. It was about breaking a belief. One that told me I had to shrink to be loved.

Now, I know better.

Now, I choose freedom.

CHAPTER 16

The Courage to Continue

"Sometimes the bravest thing you can do is decide to keep going."
— *Shaina Leis*

There are moments in recovery that force you to look deeper.

Beyond the surface behaviors, beyond the diagnosis, beyond the labels.

Moments where you stop asking what you're doing and start asking why.

It was during one of those stretches that a quiet shift happened inside me.

I stopped seeing my eating disorder as just a disorder.

I started seeing it for what it truly was.

Something that had wrapped itself around my life the same way addiction wraps around its victims. The more I learned, the harder it became to ignore the undeniable parallels between ED and addiction. The obsession, the fixation, and the willingness to sacrifice everything just to feel the illusion of power, a sensation of joy.

It mirrored the way an addict chases their high.

And suddenly, my thoughts turned to my dad.

For so long, I saw his absence as exactly that. A choice. A conscious decision. I believed he could've stopped. Could've quit the drugs. Could've chosen us.

But now, I see it differently.

If I couldn't just quit ED…

If I couldn't stop, even knowing the damage it was doing…

Then maybe it wasn't that simple for him either.

Maybe he wasn't choosing drugs over us.

Maybe he was trapped.

Just like I had been.

It doesn't erase the pain, but it softens the edges. It helps me see him not just as a father who left, but as a human being who was suffering, too.

Maybe his choices weren't black-and-white.

Maybe there were forces stronger than willpower.

I know what it's like to feel powerless. To want out and still feel stuck. To be buried so deep, you're not sure you'll ever claw your way back.

Maybe he felt that, too.

Maybe it wasn't about chasing a high.

Maybe it wasn't about self-destruction.

Maybe it was about survival.

A way to cope. A way to manage pain he hadn't made peace with.

Just like ED was for me.

I spent years angry, believing he didn't care. That he walked away without a second thought. But now, for the first time, I saw something else.

He lost something, too.

I always thought it was only us who were broken by his absence. My mom, my brother, and me.

But maybe he was broken, too.

Maybe he lost his family.

His connection.

Maybe he lost a part of himself along the way.

My childhood wasn't as simple as just saying my dad left.

There was more to his story.

So much more…

To him.

Every week in treatment, I grew, physically and mentally.

I discovered new coping mechanisms, new ways to challenge my body dysmorphia, new strategies to quiet the lies ED fed me. And every single day, I was learning how to fight back.

But the lake?

The lake had just as big an impact on my recovery.

I truly believe it was the combination, structured support from the ED program and the soul-soothing escape of the lake that brought me back to life.

The program gave me the tools.

The lake gave me the space.

Together, they created balance.

The lake softened my relapses.

It gave me peace when my mind was at war.

It reminded me that healing isn't always found in clinics or journals.

Sometimes it's tucked into quiet mornings, hidden in the hush of the trees where your soul finally exhales.

Everyone's recovery looks different.

And this was exactly what I needed for mine.

At first, the program and the lake felt like two equal pillars holding me up. But slowly, the lake began to take the lead.

It felt lighter, less clinical, and less heavy. It didn't carry the same emotional weight as the therapy room.

At the lake, I wasn't just recovering.

I was living.

I knew, it was time to move forward.

Time to leave the program.

To spend the summer at the lake.

To give myself a chance to heal in a different way.

For once, it wasn't ED telling me to change.

It was me.

And I was ready.

Ready to trust myself.

Ready to take the next step.

Not with fear, but with faith.

At first, my mom refused.

"Absolutely not. Not happening."

I understood her reaction.

I had only been in the program for a month. I wasn't close to my goal weight. There was still so much work to do.

I was expected to stay in the program for the entire summer. Therapy takes time, and I had just begun.

But when I was at the lake, I felt normal.

I wasn't a diagnosis.

I wasn't a meal plan.

I was Jody.

Just Jody.

The girl who laughed with her grandma. The girl who sang with the windows down. The girl who skipped rocks and breathed in fresh air.

That feeling, that return to self, was something the program couldn't give me. Not in the same way.

I was learning how to be me again.

Then every Monday, I'd head back to the city. Back to therapy. It felt like I was being dragged under again. I still needed therapy; I knew that. I also needed a break.

A break from constantly talking about ED. From being defined by it. From the suffocating cycle of it being my entire existence.

In treatment, the talk of it was inescapable.

Always ED, ED, ED.

Which made sense, that was the point of the program, I respected it.

But I'd reached a new place.

I had tools.

Insight.

Awareness.

And for the first time, I felt ready to take the next step on my own terms.

Not in defiance.

Not in rebellion.

But in trust.

Trust in myself.

In my healing.

In the quiet voice inside me.

The one that wasn't ED.

It was me.

And she was ready.

It was a huge risk. I was leaving behind the professional support, the structure, the safety net. And once I left, my spot would be gone. No second chances. I knew all of that. Yet still, I was ready.

Something inside me was different.

Something was stronger now.

Even though the program saved me, even though I'll always be grateful for that chapter, I was determined to do the rest of the heavy lifting on my own. Not because I didn't need help anymore. But because I was starting to believe I could help myself.

So, there I was, having this gut-deep realization. This inner certainty that it was time for me to leave.

"Absolutely not," mom said again.

Then Debbie, my psychiatric nurse, also said "No."

They thought I was giving up on myself. What they didn't understand was this wasn't giving up. If anything, it was me choosing to gain more strength.

When I told Debbie, she was stunned. She insisted I needed to stay.

She listed every risk.

The relapses.

The setbacks.

The chance ED would pull me back under.

She looked me dead in the eye and said:

"If you relapse, this disorder could kill you."

She wasn't wrong.

That was the reality.

However, I also knew something she didn't.

I knew where I felt most alive.

Most free.

Most me.

And I wasn't backing down.

Eventually, I think Debbie realized as an outpatient, she couldn't stop me. She could warn me. Worry about me. But she couldn't make the decision for me. And I had already made it.

I sat in her office for hours that day. Not crying. Not yelling. Just talking about the progress I had made, the battles I had fought, and the work still ahead.

It was honest.

It was calm.

It became clear, I wasn't running.

I was choosing to move forward.

And somehow... I convinced her.

Maybe it was the conviction in my eyes. Maybe it was because, for the first time, she saw me choosing life on my own terms.

By the end of our conversation, she agreed.

It was time.

Time to heal beyond the walls of the program.

When hearing that "yes," it didn't feel like permission. It felt liberating.

I wasn't being cut off completely. I'd still be a patient, only in a different way. Instead of coming four days a week, I'd check in once a month. For therapy and for support. A safety net from the sidelines.

It wasn't much, but I told myself...

It's going to be enough.

It has to be enough.

I've got this.

And in the end, it was.

For me, it was enough.

Flash forward to one of my final check-ins with Debbie.

She looked at me, and with a soft, loving smile, said something I'll never forget. She told me she was proud of me. Despite all her concerns in the beginning. Despite how strongly she had urged me to stay. She admitted something that stopped me in my tracks.

She said there was always something special about me.

That she had truly believed in me from the start.

Debbie was nearing the end of her career, overdue for retirement, really.

But she hadn't left, not yet.

She needed one more win. One more reminder of why she did what she did. Why she had spent a lifetime fighting for people like me. Why she had poured her heart and soul into helping others find their way back to life.

Then, before I left her office, she hugged me.

And whispered:

"You are my final success story. And because of you... I'm finally retiring."

I stood there, letting her words wash over me. Letting them settle in my bones.

This woman.

Who had seen me at my lowest.

Who had walked beside me through my darkest chapter.

Who had been my voice when I couldn't speak.

My fight when I couldn't fight.

Was now closing her career on a win.

On me.

She was an incredible nurse.

And I will be forever grateful for her.

When I announced I was leaving, saying goodbye to everyone else in the program was so much harder than I expected.

The shock was immediate. Some were sad. Some were confused. Some didn't understand at all. Even though I had convinced Debbie, many of the other nurses, even the doctors, still weren't convinced. They thought for sure I'd be back one day. They believed I was leaving too soon. That I wasn't ready.

But what they didn't realize was, I wasn't ready to fail either.

This wasn't me walking away from recovery.

This was me stepping into the next phase of it.

This was part of my process. Something I had to follow through on my own. I needed to prove to myself that I could do this outside the therapy walls. And even if doubt still lingered in the room, even if they weren't entirely sure...

Eventually, they accepted it.

The ED program had saved me from drowning, handed me a life raft, and gave me directions. Now, it was up to me to paddle to shore.

I am deeply grateful for that ED treatment program.

It was my starting point.

My lifeline.

My chance at survival.

I know, without a doubt, I would have never been able to recover if I hadn't been a patient there.

They gave me the tools I needed. They helped me find confidence. They helped me believe in myself again.

For the first time, I could actually picture a future Jody.

The one who listens to "I Will Remember You" and thinks, I'm not that girl anymore.

Because of that place, I had hope.

I had fight in me.

I wasn't just staying alive for my mom anymore.

I wanted to live, for myself.

I wanted a real life.

A life where I could mute the tape recorder.

A life where I could finally breathe.

A life where I could truly live again.

I wanted options.

To go back to school.

To follow my dreams.

To build a career.

To fall in love.

And maybe, just maybe if my body wasn't too far gone, I could still have kids someday.

For the first time, my future wasn't just a fantasy.

It wasn't a wishful thought kept deep within my imagination.

It was real.

It was possible.

And it was waiting for me.

I felt reborn.

I was finally getting my second chance at life.

After a hard week of tying up loose ends. Finishing my final therapy sessions. Scheduling future appointments with Debbie. And more goodbyes.

Goodbye to my family. Goodbye to the girls who had become my sisters. Goodbye to the staff who showed me compassion and support without judgment. That team taught me how to stand on my own two feet again. Walking away from them was a goodbye that weighed heavy on my heart.

I finally left.

This time, I wasn't coming back on Monday.

My bags were packed.

My car was full.

And I was heading out to the lake for the rest of the summer.

I was starting phase two of my recovery.

No more program.

No more structured safety net.

Just me.

My fight.

The open road ahead.

I was determined, but also terrified.

If you've ever questioned eating disorder therapy, wondered whether it really helps, or whether it would be the right fit for you, please learn from my experience.

It helps.

It provides the support, the guidance, and the tools that can enable your recovery.

I can't speak for every treatment program, only the one I was a part of.

But I can tell you this… help is out there.

If you're ready, or at least close to readiness.

Do it.

You deserve to have your life back.

You deserve to feel free again.

You deserve to live a life where the tape recorder is muted, instead of screaming at you every second of every day.

You are worth the fight.

You are worth the commitment.

You are worth the effort.

Help is available.

Seek it.

Be open to it.

There is life on the other side of this.

It is waiting for you.

Most importantly, please know…

You are not alone.

CHAPTER 17

He Saw Me For Me

"To be loved by someone who sees all of you, not despite your cracks, but because of them—is a kind of healing no mirror can offer."

— JmStorm

Phase Two: Lake Therapy. Let's Go.

The sun danced across the water, shimmering like a thousand tiny mirrors. Waves clapped against the shore, carrying quiet promises of healing.

I know what you're thinking.

Was this an epic fail?

Did I actually manage to keep going?

Realistically, it could've gone either way.

But there's something about the lake.

Something magic in the way the air feels fresher, the world quiets, and time slows just enough for clarity to creep in.

The lake didn't erase my pain.

It didn't cure me.

But it gave me space.

Stillness.

A chance to find out who I was without ED constantly in my ear.

Lake life has always been my place. Not just soothing, but stirring, igniting something deeper. Maybe it's the weightlessness of floating. The grounding of toes in sand. The way the water holds you without question or judgment.

If you're a lake person, you get it. It's not just a place. It's a feeling.

That one spot at the end of the dock holds a piece of my soul. I could sit there for hours listening to the waves, the loons, the breeze brushing my skin. There, I am at peace. Time disappears. Chaos fades. And all that's left is me, the water, and my thoughts.

I've always needed to express what I feel. Keeping it in only leads to an explosion. And sometimes I don't need someone to listen, I just need to speak. That dock became my sacred space. My therapy room. Where I could say everything, whether to myself, the air, or the people I've lost.

I like to think of them as my angels. On quiet nights, I look to the stars and speak to them. They don't answer. But I believe in signs. A sudden shift in wind. The rustling of trees. That one light across the lake that's never on yet flickering to life just when I need it.

Maybe it's coincidence.

Or maybe, it's something more.

Either way, I choose to believe they're still here.

I've spent countless nights on that dock, pouring my heart out to the water, to the stars, to whatever or whoever might be listening. Because the lake didn't just give me an escape. It gave me a place to find myself again.

I've always been someone who welcomes support, who leans into love and guidance. I truly believe we're stronger together. No one is meant to walk this world alone.

I had that support.

My mom, my anchor.

My brother, my quiet constant.

Family cheering from afar.

And a team of lake friends, walking beside me through my next phase of recovery.

They showed up.

They listened and encouraged.

They reminded me who I was when I forgot.

They say healing is a journey, not a destination.

I've learned it's who walks beside you that makes all the difference.

I wasn't just finding myself again.

I was remembering I never had to do it alone.

My brother, Michael, was already living out at the lake, and by the time I arrived, he was like a whole new person.

Growing up, he was always reserved, thoughtful, comfortable in his own company. If anyone was sneaking out or pushing curfews, it was me. He followed the rules, and I tested them at times.

But at the lake, a tide turned. He found his own kind of freedom, and it was beautiful to watch him come out of his shell.

There's something special about lake life. It strips away the noise and lets people just be themselves. Friendships aren't based on cliques or status. No one cares what school you go to or where you're from. If you're a lake person, you're friends with the other lake people. Simple as that.

No hierarchy.

No social games.

Just connection.

Just community.

Just real human support.

And at that point in my life, that's exactly what I needed.

Not something forced.

Not clinical.

Not prescribed.

Just... enough.

I was excited, genuinely excited to be part of that kind of social life again. After everything I'd been through, it felt like stepping into the sun after a long, relentless winter.

If my life had a forecast, the past year was filled with gray skies and bitter cold. Storms that never lifted. Downpours that drained every ounce of strength. Some loud, some silent, but all of them dark.

Until now.

The clouds were parting. The air felt different. The sun, warmer. And for the first time in a long time, I was ready to fully step in.

This lake life was my change in seasons.

The heaviness was lifting.

The frost was melting.

And inside me, something was beginning to bloom.

So, there I was, in my little worn-down trailer, starting fresh.

It wasn't much. Just a small, weathered place tucked among the trees.

But it was mine.

A blank slate.

A new chapter.

Originally, it had been my grandma, Mary's. But as Alzheimer's slowly made independent living harder, she moved back to the city. It broke my heart to see her go. I missed her warmth, her stories, the way she made any space feel like home.

But in many ways, the timing was right.

For the first time, I had real independence.

And even though I've never loved being in solitude, I wasn't scared in that little trailer. Because I was never really alone.

The campground was full of familiar faces. Friends, neighbors, people who looked out for each other. You didn't have to ask for help. It just showed up when you needed it.

We were a community.

And we still are.

Even now, when I sit beneath the stars, I know I'm watched over.

My grandma has since passed, but she's still with me, one of my angels. Listening when I talk to her in the quiet of the night.

The lake has a way of making you feel connected to the people around you.

To those you've lost.

To something greater than yourself.

And in that little trailer, on the edge of a new beginning, I felt that connection stronger than ever.

The eating itself wasn't necessarily the main enemy anymore. I was hungry, really hungry, and for the first time in what felt like forever, I truly gave in to my cravings.

Then something unfamiliar happened.

I felt satisfied.

I felt full.

That deep, contented feeling after a meal, one I'd long forgotten, washed over me.

But it didn't last.

Within an hour or two, the hunger returned. Intense and insistent. My body, after years of deprivation, had flipped into autopilot with one command.

Keep going. Keep going. Keep going.

I can only imagine how excited my organs must've been, dancing with joy, celebrating their long-awaited nourishment. After being starved for so long, they finally had something to work with. Flavors, nutrients, energy. Food wasn't just being swallowed; it was being used.

Mechanically, I had the eating part mastered. I followed the plan. I ate. I chewed. I swallowed. But the fear lingered. The voice in my head still divided food into "safe" and "scary." When I faced a "scary" food, my body tensed. My thoughts spiraled and anxiety swelled in my chest like a pressure cooker.

But I was determined. I wanted to reach my goal weight. I wanted to prove I could do this. So, I choked it down. Even when it felt like poison. Even when my whole body screamed no. Because this wasn't just about gaining weight, it was about reclaiming power.

Speaking of my goal weight, it was technically considered "healthy," but not the number the program had set for me. Theirs was higher. Too high. Too scary. I wasn't ready to completely let go of ED's control.

So, I drew a line in the sand.

A quiet, invisible rule.

Once I hit my number, I'd stop.
Not because it was safe.
But because it felt safer.
It wasn't about health.
It was about fear.

My worst setback during this still-early phase of recovery wasn't food.
It was my fixation on my stomach.
In therapy, they warned me weight gain would show up in the midsection first. A survival response. A protective mechanism. My organs, damaged from years of starvation, needed padding. Fluid, fat, anything to shield them.
Logically, I understood.
I understood the science.
But emotionally, I still hated my stomach.
It felt bloated. Foreign, like I was carrying something that didn't belong. Sometimes, it even looked like a baby bump. Ironic, considering I couldn't remember the last time I'd had sex.
Each glance in the mirror triggered something deep. The tape recorder wasn't screaming anymore, but it still hummed in the background, whispering old fears, old doubts.
My greatest enemy became my own perception of my body.
My image was completely distorted.
Some days, I could accept the changes.
Other days, I wanted to crawl out of my own skin.
I couldn't mute the tape recorder.
But I could fight it.
I would breathe deep into the corners of my chest where anxiety liked to hide, and coach myself through it.
My body is doing what it needs to survive. Each pound isn't failure, it's life returning. Your organs are healing, let them. Everything will balance out. Just keep going.
Most days, those pep talks helped. They didn't erase the thoughts, they softened them. They reminded me why I chose recovery in the first place.

I remember the first day I could pinch my skin again, there was something there. I wasn't just flesh and bones anymore.

And when I felt "fat" I'd remind myself…

It's not fat.

It's health.

It's life.

My body does not define my worth.

The more I fueled it, the clearer my mind became.

I could laugh again.

Think again.

Feel again.

Those things mattered more than a number or a reflection.

But beyond body image, something else was surfacing.

Something I hadn't expected.

Something bigger.

Something that needed to be rebuilt.

My sense of self.

It's been missing for so long now.

I had spent years in survival mode. So long detached, that now, fully awake, I didn't even recognize the girl staring back at me.

I wasn't numb anymore.

But I wasn't me either.

I was lost.

ED had consumed everything. My time, my thoughts, my identity. And now, in healing, I didn't know how to rebuild. How to find the girl I used to be.

The confident, outgoing, bubbly girl.

I missed her.

Sometimes, just for a moment, I'd catch a glimpse of her. Around the table with friends playing a game of cards, mid-laugh, deep in conversation.

Present.

Light.

Alive.

And just like that, there she was.

The girl who felt good in her skin.
Who didn't second-guess every word, every bite.
But she never stayed long.
I couldn't figure out how to keep her around.
That is…
Until he came along.

I made a lot of friends at the lake, but one stood out, someone I wanted as more than a friend.
From the moment I met Aidan, I felt drawn to him.
Like gravity.
There was something about his energy, carefree, wild, and unfiltered. He lived without hesitation. And that was exactly what I needed.
Adventure.
Spontaneity.
Laughter.
He was all of that, wrapped in one captivating soul.
With him, I wasn't stuck in my head.
I was living.
He pulled me out of my shell, coaxed me back into the world, reminded me what it felt like to be young, reckless, and free.
He was magnetic. I convinced myself he was the key, the missing piece to help me become the girl I used to be.
Up until now, ED had been my only real relationship. There was no room for a man when my mind was fully consumed.
I'd had a boyfriend at the start of my disorder. Like I said, I never really knew how to be single, even when I was sick.
But the relationship didn't last.
The deeper I sank, the less space I had for anyone else.
It wasn't like I ran when it got too real. This time, it never held a chance. He was the one who left, not out of cruelty, but clarity. He wasn't equipped to go on that journey with me and I never expected him to be.
We started off romantic. Intimate. Hopeful. But somewhere along the way, it switched. By the end, he wasn't my boyfriend

anymore, just a friend checking in. Making sure I was still breathing. Still surviving. He cared but he wasn't mine.

As I lost weight, I lost visibility. Pound by pound, I didn't just shrink, I disappeared. Even a longtime friend, someone who had once been an on-and-off fling, showed no interest when I was at my worst.

I don't blame them.

My body was brittle.

Fragile in a way that wasn't exactly a turn-on.

Maybe they were scared they'd break me. Maybe they feared the disorder itself, like it was contagious. Regardless, it didn't faze me. Intimacy wasn't on my mind.

When ED was in control, everything shut down, including my sex drive. There was no desire for closeness. Only the pursuit of discipline, control, and shrinking. It was just me and ED, locked in a twisted, dysfunctional relationship.

The only satisfaction I craved was an empty stomach.

The rush of a "successful" restrictive day.

The false power in watching the scale drop.

That was what kept me going.

At least, for a while.

Now, I was in recovery.

Slowly, I was starting to feel like me again. Like a woman again. And for the first time in a long time, I found myself interested in someone.

It felt good to have a crush. To feel that flutter, that spark, that nervous anticipation. It was like waking up from a long, numbing sleep and realizing the world is still here. It's been waiting for me.

I wasn't just surviving anymore.

I was living.

Doing the things a twenty-one-year-old girl should be doing.

What started as a little harmless flirting turned into something more. A summer fling that didn't fade when the season ended. Aidan and I kept dating for another year. And he fit perfectly into my usual pattern.

You remember my type, right?

That bad boy energy.

Yeah... that was him.

Not an asshole. Just that mysterious, outgoing, slightly edgy guy with a big heart. The kind of guy who had just enough wildness to keep life interesting. But beneath it all, there was something soft. Something good.

Naturally, I was drawn to him.

Aidan had those deep, unreadable eyes that pulled me in before I even realized it. He looked at me like he saw past everything. Like he could see into my soul.

And that smile...

It was disarming.

The kind that made it impossible to stay mad, no matter how hard you tried.

He wasn't just my type emotionally, he checked every physical box, too.

Tall. Confident. Just the right amount of rugged. It was easy to get lost in the idea of him. Easy to believe he was exactly what I needed.

He was the first guy who didn't see me as the sick, skinny girl. Even when his friends joked and called me Skeletor.

Harsh, but not entirely wrong, he never joined in.

He didn't look at me that way.

He saw past the frailty.

Past the damage.

Past the shell of who I'd become.

And somehow... he saw me.

The girl I used to be.

The girl I could be again.

He never met her, but he believed in her anyway. And moment by moment, all summer long, he helped bring her back to life.

Aidan knew where I had just come from. He knew I was fresh out of treatment, still piecing myself together.

He didn't care.

Most guys would've run.

But not him.

He didn't just accept it; he carried it with me. He made me feel seen, special, and cared for in a way I had long forgotten.

It had been so long since I let myself receive that kind of love.

And having it again…

It was everything.

If I had never gotten up off that floor, I would've never known what it felt like to be loved again.

To finally fall in love.

Up until then, every time something real started to form, I'd run. Fear always won, but Aidan was different.

Maybe it was timing, where I was in my life. Raw and vulnerable. Open in a way I'd never been before. Or maybe it was the way he made me feel safe, without ever trying to cage me in.

Whatever it was, for the first time, I didn't want to run.

I wanted to stay.

To feel it.

To know love.

Not just brush up against it and bolt.

My guard was still there.

But with him, I learned how to fall.

I wasn't defenseless.

I wasn't hiding, either.

The shield I always carried, still there but lowered.

So yes, I can fall in love.

I just don't know if that guard will ever fully come down with it.

When Aidan entered my life, he became the most beautiful distraction from ED. Not a cure, not a fix. But a light in the middle of everything I was still trying to untangle.

Recovery was still messy. ED didn't vanish overnight. But with Aidan by my side, it all felt a little easier.

The relentless tape recorder in my head, the one that had played for years, finally began to fade. Food wasn't as terrifying. I wasn't overthinking every bite. And for the first time in forever…

I had moments where I actually saw my body as beautiful.

Not perfect.

But mine.

Strong.

Capable.

Alive.

Then something happened I never thought I'd experience again. I got my period back.

It was surreal. Like going through puberty again, except this time as a twenty-one-year-old woman. My body, once frozen in survival mode, was waking up. And though part of me felt uneasy, another part of me knew.

This was proof.

Proof that I was healing.

That I was coming back.

Aidan gave me something I didn't know I needed.

The ability to see myself through his eyes.

Where I once saw flaws, he saw beauty.

He looked at my growing curves like they were art.

To him, every change in my body was sacred.

My skin glowed again.

My eyes sparkled with something new.

My face, no longer sunken, held light and life.

Slowly, I started to believe him.

I started to love myself again.

To accept myself again.

Then came the moment I had worked so hard for. The day I was told I had reached a healthy weight. It was end of that summer, and for the first time, the fight was starting to feel worth it.

I was still doing monthly check-ins with Debbie, my nurse.

Since I didn't own a scale, I had no idea where I was until that weigh-in. And this moment could've gone in so many directions.

Remember, my personal goal weight had always been lower than the program's ideal. And now, I had surpassed that number. Instead, I landed on the one I once swore I'd never reach.

I could have panicked.

I could have spiraled.

But instead of spiraling, I celebrated.

I was shocked by how fine I felt. No meltdown, no urge to undo the progress. Just calm. Pride, even.

A week later, I wanted to mark the moment.

So, I called around the city, searching for a tattoo studio that could take me that day. I jumped in my car and hit the highway, country music blaring through the speakers.

This time leaving the lake and heading back to the city.

Funny enough, the drive didn't feel as heavy.

This time, I wasn't returning to the program as the girl drowning in her eating disorder.

I was going back to honor something. To celebrate the hard work, the resilience, the fight I had found within myself. To acknowledge the courage it took to walk away from treatment before anyone thought I was ready, and to keep going anyway.

I knew exactly what I wanted.

My mom and I share the same middle name: Ann.

To honor our bond, and everything we had survived together, I got Ann tattooed on my wrist.

Surrounding it were angel wings.

Wings to represent how close I came to becoming one.

Wings to honor her, my angel.

The one who washed my hair when I was too weak.

The one who stood by me through every terrifying, gut-wrenching moment.

That tattoo wasn't just ink.

It was proof.

Proof that I chose life.

Proof that, because of my mom…

I didn't give up on myself.

The first year of my recovery was a year of rediscovery. It felt like being reborn, piece by piece, breath by breath. And through it all, there was Aidan, by my side, steady and sure, seeing the beauty in me when I couldn't see it myself.

Despite how deeply we loved each other, we were very different. And in some ways, a little dysfunctional. His energy, his spontaneity, his free spirit. It was magnetic, but I liked structure, predictability, and control. I needed balance and he thrived in chaos.

They say opposites attract, and that was us.

We complemented each other's best traits. He taught me how to let go. I grounded him, often without him realizing it. But just as easily, we triggered each other's worst.

Our fights were intense.

Raw.

Consuming.

We were a lot.

Aidan was fighting his own battles, carrying invisible weight. He let me in, trusted me with the heaviness he carried, and I did the same. We leaned on each other. Needed each other. When we were together, it felt like we could survive anything.

It was passionate.

It was consuming.

It was the kind of love that makes you feel alive.

But passion doesn't mean perfect.

And we were far from that.

It sounds like a movie. How he entered my life during recovery. How I finally let my guard down, just enough to fall.

But sometimes, even the most beautiful things aren't meant to last.

We were still young. Still becoming who we were meant to be. And for me, that meant asking a hard question:

What was I going to do with this second chance?

I had clawed my way out of the darkest place I'd ever been.

And now, for the first time, the future didn't feel like something slipping through my fingers, it felt like something I could build.

Before everything spiraled, I was in my second year of university, studying to become a teacher and hopefully one day a guidance counselor. But after the surgery and my admission to the program, I had to take a medical leave.

Dropping out felt like another thing ED had stolen from me.

But now, I had the chance to take it back.

I re-enrolled. I got my job back.

And slowly, my life started falling into place again.

I was more motivated than ever. I wanted to help people, especially teenagers. I knew how easy it was to get lost. I just wanted to be someone they could turn to. Someone who could help them find their way before they ever felt as lost as I once did.

I felt like I could breathe again.

I could dream again.

I was chasing my goals without ED dragging me backward.

And with all the new beginnings came something unexpected...

A new version of perfection.

At first, I thought I was rebuilding myself. That if I worked hard enough, I could return to the girl I once was. But eventually, I had to face the truth.

That girl was gone.

She was effortless in her joy.

Confident and carefree.

She didn't care what anyone thought.

She marched to her own beat, unapologetically herself.

But this version of me?

She cared.

Too much.

She saw herself only through other people's eyes.

And so, she became obsessed with being perfect.

Everyone had to like her, because if they didn't, how could she like herself?

Somewhere along the way, my self-worth became dependent on approval.

I had reached my goal weight.

I finally fell in love.

I had done everything "right."

Yet still, my body dysmorphia had the upper hand.

So, I came to a new conclusion…

If my body couldn't define my worth, everything else had to.

How I looked.

How I performed.

How I was perceived.

There was no room for "good enough."

It was all or nothing.

And if you weren't keeping up, you were in my way.

Which brings me to the breakup.

Eventually, our summer-fling-turned-love-story began to fade. And just like I've done so many times before… I ran.

But this time was different. It wasn't instant. We kept trying. Trying to fix what was slipping, to hold on to something that no longer quite fit. And every time I left, I came running back.

Because I loved him.

Saying goodbye was hard.

Still, I was stuck in my head. No matter how beautiful Aidan made me feel, I couldn't see what he saw. Unless I was also achieving, succeeding and proving my worth.

I told myself we both had to grow immediately.

I was becoming the perfect teacher. Proper, professional, and polished. I needed discipline, structure, and control. Then in that moment, Aidan's wild spirit, the very thing that once pulled me in, suddenly didn't fit.

He was still living for the party. At first, I was right there with him. But alcohol and antidepressants never mixed well. It wasn't always about fun; it was about numbing. And I hated who I was becoming.

So, I made a decision.

Everything had to change.

I didn't just hold myself to that standard, I put Aidan on that podium too.

I expected him to evolve at my pace.

To shift.

To plan.

To catch up.

And when he didn't, when he stayed in the moment while I sprinted into the future, I started planning my escape.

Realistically, we were young. That's what young people do, they party, they figure it out slowly. But I didn't want slow. I had no patience for slow.

I gave him a few chances, but not much room. Because in my mind, I had already drawn the line.

This is the new Jody.

This is who I have to be.

If he can't keep up... he can't come.

Looking back, I see it clearly now. I was focused. Determined, selfish, even. I was chasing an identity I thought would make me whole. Seeking approval from people who looked like they had it all together. We were both still figuring it out and that was normal. But I wanted perfect, I wanted forward.

So, I ran.

At first, a little space.

A little distance.

Then a jog.

Then a sprint.

Until I was gone.

That was the hardest relationship I had ever walked away from.

Because this time, I was actually in love.

I saw a life with him.

A future.

But I convinced myself I couldn't have both.

I couldn't love him and become who I needed to be.

I asked him to change. And the hardest part was, he had started to. But I didn't stick around to see it through.

I broke his heart.

He didn't see it coming.

He was devastated.

Don't get me wrong, I'm not the only villain in this story.

Aidan had a tendency to act before thinking. To follow impulses without considering the fallout. Sometimes, the consequences of his actions really hurt.

He wasn't cruel, he never intended to cause me pain. But there were moments. Moments when his recklessness, his inability to pause and think things through, left me feeling unconsidered.

Unimportant.

Hurt.

I spent more nights than I'd like to admit crying because of him. Crying over things he said, things he didn't say. Things he did, and things he didn't do.

A part of me always feared he would never grow up.

Then again, I'll never know.

Because I never gave him the chance.

Despite everything, he never stopped showing me love. Never let me forget how special I was to him. It was the hardest breakup of my life. I didn't walk away relieved. I walked away just as heartbroken.

But I was on a mission.

So, I did what I'd learned to do best…

I buried it.

All the heartbreak.

The pain.

The what ifs.

I shoved it down and threw myself into becoming the version of me I thought the world would love.

I drowned in structure.

In discipline.

In the pursuit of success.

Because if I just kept going, then maybe I wouldn't have to feel it.

Sadly, we never got closure.

There are still unanswered questions. No matter how much time has passed, one thing remains the same.

Aidan was my first real love.

The first person who broke through my walls just enough to let in something real. The first one who made me feel safe enough to feel.

My recovery began with my mom.

She pushed me toward help.

Then came therapy.

Lake life.

I was already on the right path before Aidan entered. But a part of me will always feel like he saved me.

Aidan brought me back to life faster than I ever expected.

People come into our lives for a reason. And that summer, he was meant to come into mine.

I will always be grateful for Aidan.

For his presence, his love, and his impact on my recovery.

On my life.

So, there I was, over a year into recovery, with only a few minor relapses in my rearview.

The food rules had loosened.

The rituals had faded.

Then just like that, the obsession transformed.

From food… to approval.

I became a people pleaser.

If others liked me, praised me, admired me, maybe then I could like myself.

Maybe then I'd feel enough.

I was lost.

Desperate to be found.

Desperate to build an identity I could be proud of; one I could finally love.

Desperate to look in the mirror and see someone worth loving.

That's the thing about life, about living.

I was finally doing it.

But I didn't know how to love the person who was living it.
I didn't know if I ever truly could.
And that terrified me.

What if this was it?
What if I was always just a body.
Breathing.
Moving.
Functioning.
But never fully accepting.
Never fully embracing.
Never fully being.

That was my greatest fear.
The day I finally feel whole…
Might never come.

CHAPTER 18

The Girl in the Mirror: Who Is She?

"I lost myself trying to please everyone else. Now I'm trying to remember who I was before the world told me who to be."

— *Anonymous*

I was back in the city after a second summer spent at the lake, soaking up the sun and chasing every moment of open sky.

Cue the cinematic re-entry. Like Carrie Bradshaw in heels, wide-eyed and ready to take on the world. Okay, maybe without the sex and the NYC skyline, but you get the vibe.

I was standing on the edge of something new. A little nervous, a little empowered, and totally determined to rewrite my story. I was ready to create the new Jody, the healed version.

Jody 2.0.

What I wasn't ready for, what completely blindsided me, was this… my body found its plateau. And it stayed there. No drastic weight swings. No defeat. No creeping climb into the unknown. Just stillness.

It was like my body exhaled and said, "We're good now."

For the first time, I realized my body wasn't the enemy, it never was.

It had just been trying to survive.

Now that it was safe, it could finally rest.

So could I.

That moment, the plateau, is one of the most terrifying in recovery. It triggers panic. What if I go too far? What if I lose control? And just like that, old habits start whispering. Come back, we'll fix this.

But they never fix it. They just prolong the war. The bravest part of recovery isn't starting, it's staying. It's choosing to let your body settle.

To trust it.

To let it breathe.

To let it be.

That kind of surrender takes strength I didn't know I had.

But I do.

And if you're here fighting, trembling, and choosing recovery. You have that strength too.

When I hit my goal weight, I celebrated instead of spiraling. I got the tattoo. I marked the moment. I felt proud. But beneath the surface, I was holding my breath, waiting for the other shoe to drop. Afraid my body would keep growing and stretch beyond control.

That's when ED started whispering again.

Recovery isn't clean, it's layered, messy, loud and quiet at once. ED lurks, waiting for the smallest cracks to bleed itself through. And if I gave into fear, even for a second, it would come back.

But that spiral never came. My body reached a healthy, functioning weight, and stayed there.

And if I'm being completely candid, I helped it a bit.

Yes, my body had plateaued. It had learned how to function again, how to survive. For the first time in a long time, it felt safe.

It was finally happy.

But quietly, almost imperceptibly at first, a few small rules around food and restriction began to creep back in. Nothing drastic. Nothing that screamed relapse.

But they were there.

I ate balanced meals, repeated my mantras…

There's no good or bad food.

Just food.

The truth?

I was slightly restricting.

Not loudly.

Quietly.

A few bites left on the plate. A smaller scoop. Just enough to be "fine." Enough to fuel me, to look healthy, to pass as recovered. But maybe not enough to fully thrive.

That was all I was willing to give.

I served myself smaller portions of foods I shouldn't be calling scary, but sometimes still did. If I wanted ice cream, I let myself have it, but only a baby cone. Just enough to say I did, but never enough to indulge.

Snickers, my favorite, I'd have one. But eat the whole thing? Never. Half is plenty, or so I convinced myself. It's not deprivation. But it's not true freedom either.

I was following the rules, but quietly writing new ones no one else could see.

Then there was exercise. That old companion came back fast when I moved home. Back into routine. Back into control.

So, between the workouts, the balanced eating, and the subtle restriction, my weight stayed right where I wanted it.

And yes…

That's still where I am today.

Writing this now, I realized something big.

It sounds like I went from disordered eating to a full-blown eating disorder, then slowly circled back again to disordered eating.

But there is a difference.

I still allow myself to indulge.

To enjoy food.

All food.

Both the safe and the scary.

It's not so much what I eat anymore.

It's the quantity that crept its way back in.
The urge to slightly reduce.
To limit, just a little.
I still savor flavors.
I still let food nourish my body.
The same body that's still here to enjoy it.
Over time, I've built a toolbox. One filled with strategies and small, but powerful, techniques to help me fight back against the guilt.
I don't measure food.
I don't count calories.
I'm just a little more disciplined.
These days, I'd say that 75% of the time, my eating wouldn't be classified as disordered.
To me, that's winning.
I may not be flawless in recovery.
But I've made progress I never thought possible.
Is it perfect?
No.
But to me, it's a win.
This is what people don't always understand about eating disorders.
They don't just disappear.
You don't recover and, poof, it's gone.
Like any addiction, it's managed, not cured.
It's a lifelong journey.
I'm someone with an eating disorder in recovery.
ED isn't in control anymore.
My behaviors aren't fully active.
They're not running the show or ruining my life.
It doesn't consume me the way it once did.
However, it's still there.
Quiet, distant, and lingering in the background.
A shadow I've learned to live with.
Not obey.

My good days far outweigh the bad ones.

And that is something I take pride in.

So, there I was. Back in the city, back in university, back to reinventing myself.

I still had a few small rules around food, but my body sat at a healthy weight. On the outside, it looked like I was stepping into a new chapter. But inside, I had no idea who I really was. I'd crafted this image: polished, perfect, put-together. I thought I was rebuilding, maturing, stepping into my future. But what I was really doing was performing.

Before ED, I wanted to be liked, but that wasn't my identity. Now, everything hinged on it. How I acted. What I said. How I looked. All filtered through the question… Do they approve?

Every night, I replayed the day like a movie. Scrutinizing every scene, every line, every look. Did I say the right thing? Did I smile enough? Was I enough?

It was exhausting and yet, I couldn't stop. I was now a people pleaser, chasing validation like oxygen. It wasn't just about being beautiful. It was about being appreciated.

Impressive.

The girl everyone wanted to know.

If I wasn't that girl, who was I?

Being alone still terrified me. So, of course I found a new boyfriend, fast. But this time, I locked my heart away. Love had proven to be too painful, and I couldn't afford another broken heart.

School.

Career.

Control.

Those were my new priorities.

I thought I had my life together.

But the reality was…

I was lost.

Wandering through a fog, chasing a finish line I couldn't even see. The girl I used to be, she was gone. A ghost in the shadows, replaying reminders of a time I couldn't get back. Some people find comfort in their shadow. Mine haunted me.

As much as I chased the memory of her, I wasn't her anymore. I was never enough. I had to push harder, be better, go beyond the limits holding me back.

So, I tried.

If I couldn't get her back, the carefree, fearless girl I once was.

I would build someone new.

Stronger.

Sharper.

Unstoppable.

No cracks.

No mercy.

No flaws.

Weakness wasn't allowed to breathe.

If you asked me now, I'd tell you something different. I'd tell you flaws aren't failures. That our messiness makes us beautiful. That strength isn't found in perfection, it's found in honesty.

But back then, weakness was the enemy, and I was on a mission to eliminate it.

I told myself I was maturing, and in some ways, I was. More responsible, more driven. More focused on the future.

The party scene slowed down, but my obsession with appearing picture-perfect only intensified. It looked admirable. Yet it wasn't rooted in confidence, it was born from fear.

The tape recorder in my head had quieted, but it still tried. Triggered by a bad grade, an offhand comment, a disapproving look.

Then when it spoke, I didn't rest.

I pushed harder.

There was no such thing as "enough."

Just the next milestone.

The next version of me I needed to become.

I pictured myself crossing the finish line, arms raised, drenched in pride. I told myself I'll arrive. That I'll finally be whole. Let's just say, that fantasy didn't hold up.

Life doesn't come with one final finish line. It's not linear. It bends, twists, doubles back. Even Google Maps loses its way sometimes, so why wouldn't we?

That's the beauty of it.

Every twist, every detour, every unexpected chapter, gives us a new opportunity to level-up. We have those hell yes moments. Those days we look in the mirror and think, damn, I made it through that. We also have the moments that knock us down. That make us question everything. While asking yourself, who are you now? Who will you be next?

Yet we elevate.

Again, and again.

Because forward is forward, no matter the speed.

Whether you sprint, jog, or crawl.

What matters is that you keep going.

That is strength.

That is growth.

That is transformation.

And eventually, you realize, the finish line isn't the end.

It's just another beginning.

It took me forever to realize this.

People-pleasing is never the path to the finish line you're chasing.

In fact, people-pleasing is a bitch.

It drains you. It reshapes you, carving out pieces of who you are until one day, you no longer recognize the version of yourself buried beneath the need to be liked.

You monitor every word, every expression.

Did I upset them?

Did they misunderstand?

Do they still like me?

Even when you've done nothing wrong, you question everything. You entangle yourself into their comfort zone, until you vanish altogether.

The moment you stop chasing approval.

The second you stop molding yourself into someone else's idea of perfection.

That's the moment you begin becoming your true self.

Comparison is suffocating.

Individuality…

That's your superpower.

You weren't created to fade away.

You were born to stand out.

To be a presence.

To shine.

So, turn up your volume.

March to your own damn beat.

Reclaim your voice, your choices, your worth.

Because this isn't about becoming someone new.

It's about coming home to who you've always been.

You don't need applause to love yourself.

You don't need perfection to be powerful.

You just need to be true to yourself.

I wish I had known all of this back then. I wish I had broken my people-pleasing habits in my twenties. Not standing here on the edge of forty.

Maybe everything had to fall apart exactly the way it did, so I could fall into alignment with the woman I was always meant to become.

I still don't know the true silver lining. But I do know this…

The perfection I chased.

The approval I craved.

The ache of never feeling good enough.

It all led me here.

Here is powerful.

Here is confident.

Here is me.

Unfiltered.

Unapologetic.

And yeah…

I'm kind of a badass woman now. Because when you've lived most of your life buried under insecurity, and you finally rise…

You celebrate.

You own it.

I do.

I'm not perfect.

I still have work to do.

But I'm more Jody than I've ever been.

As for that younger version of me…

The girl in this chapter.

Buckle up, sweetheart.

You've got one hell of a journey ahead.

You're going to fall.

You're going to doubt everything.

You'll question your dreams, your worth, your strength.

But you'll keep going.

One shaky step at a time, you'll climb.

Your voice will grow louder.

Your light, brighter.

Then one day, without even realizing it, you'll feel it.

That shift.

That moment when you realize…

You're not who you used to be.

And it's beautiful.

Because healing doesn't look like perfection.

It looks like resilience.

It looks like rising.

It looks like becoming.

And girl…

You're just getting started.

CHAPTER 19

Pencils, Passion, Purpose

"They didn't choose their circumstances. But every day they choose to rise."
— *Jessica Stephens*

Just like that, another cap.

Another gown.

Another walk across the stage.

Another moment not only to accept a diploma, but to honor the blood, sweat, and self-doubt it took to get there.

I didn't coast through university; I clawed my way through it. I didn't just graduate, I thrived.

I earned every mark, every credit, every late-night study session that bled into dawn. I graduated with a high GPA. I wasn't gifted; I worked for every damn decimal point.

I graduated with a double major in Psychology and English, then went on to earn my Bachelor of Education. With my full teaching certificate in hand and a fire burning in my chest, I was ready to walk into the classroom. Not just as a teacher, but as someone determined to make a difference.

I wasn't only there to facilitate lessons. I was there to shape minds, create safe spaces, and remind kids that resilience lives inside them. Even if no one's ever had the words to say it out loud.

So, why teaching?

Ever since I was a little girl, I didn't just dream of helping people. I felt it in my bones. A calling, a purpose. I didn't want to stand on the sidelines; I wanted to help change the game. So teaching, more specifically the path to becoming a counselor, felt like the way in.

But before that, there was another dream.

I imagined becoming a therapist and opening my own practice. A cozy office filled with trust, safety, and openness. A place where people could come to feel heard and held. That vision felt purely like me. Entirely me.

Until someone close to me, someone whose opinion I valued, told me not to dream so big. Instead of encouraging me, they planted seeds. Seeds that began to sprout roots of doubt in my mind.

Maybe you're not capable of that, I thought. So, I let go of that dream. Not because I didn't want it. Because, for a moment, I believed in the doubt more than I believed in myself.

I won't say teaching was my second choice, but it definitely felt like the safer path. There would always be schools. Always students. Always a need for teachers. I'd still be helping people, in a different way. One that offered more stability, more certainty. A steady track with job security, unlike the risk of running a private practice that might never succeed.

Teaching became the more secure route.

A reliable one.

A legacy.

Even my grandmother was a teacher, so were my great-grandparents and great-uncle. Education ran in my blood. So, when I chose it, it didn't feel like a detour. It felt like a redirection. One that still aligned with my heart's mission. To help, to heal, to make a difference.

But that doesn't mean I didn't doubt myself.

There were days I walked into schools and felt like I was stepping into a grand castle, one I didn't quite belong in. It was like attending a masquerade ball, where everyone wore a mask, and mine became my shield. With it on, I had a disguise. And with a disguise, I had confidence. Everyone else seemed to be wearing one too. At least I wasn't alone. I fit in; my flaws stayed hidden. My insecurities, safe.

The mask let me conceal the voice that whispered, you're not enough.

The one that asked, who do you think you are to be here?

Still, I pressed forward.

Most of the standard education courses in university didn't exactly light a fire in me.

Sure, classroom management, assessment strategies, and lesson planning were important. I engaged, I did well, and I respected the foundation they laid. Literacy, numeracy, global citizenship, I understood why it mattered.

But something was missing. I didn't go into teaching just to deliver curriculum. I went in to reach hearts. To guide, to connect.

Then came the course that changed everything.

Alternative Classrooms.

I'll never forget one class in particular: Teaching At-Risk Youth. That was the moment it all clicked. It was like a door I hadn't even realized I'd been knocking on finally swung open. Every story of struggle, every theory grounded in compassion, every conversation.

It all felt like home.

This wasn't just about behavior management. It was about seeing the child behind the misery. Reaching the ones who fall through the cracks. Not labeling them for their struggles but recognizing them for their strength. That course didn't just inspire me, it defined me. It introduced me to the teacher I was meant to become.

Of course, the doubts crept in. Learning came with challenges. I needed more time to absorb new concepts, to bridge theory with practice. And because of that, I carried a quiet fear. A fear that someone like me, who had to work twice as hard, didn't belong at the front of a classroom.

On the flip side, one-on-one with the so-called troublemaker, the kid everyone warned me about...

That's when I came alive.

During my practicums, those were the students I gravitated toward. Not because I had all the answers but because I understood them. I knew what it felt like to not belong. To question your worth. To carry wounds no one else could see.

These weren't bad kids. They were kids fighting battles the world didn't notice. Trauma, abuse, poverty, abandonment. Most of their stories were written in survival, not safety.

Where others saw disruption, I saw desperation.

They weren't broken.

They were trying.

And I was drawn to that flicker of fight inside them.

They'd seen more, felt more, and survived more than most adults ever will. And that didn't make them hopeless, it made them heroic.

From day one, I knew, I wanted to be the teacher who never gave up on them. Who looked past behavior and saw humanity. Who recognized their strength, even when they didn't.

The stories I've heard from these kids have stopped me in my tracks. You can't make this shit up. And yet, somehow, they still show up. Shoulders heavy with invisible burdens, just trying to make it through the day.

They never asked for this life. These were the cards they were dealt. And still, they keep going.

That's bravery.

Raw, unfiltered, heartbreaking bravery.

But here's the reality.

Sometimes, even that's not enough.

Some don't make it.

Some never see their eighteenth birthday.

That haunts me.

I've seen the fight in their eyes. Heard the tremble in their voices. Watched them try to hold on while the world kept letting go. That's why I do this work. Because maybe, just maybe if one adult truly sees them, truly believes in them…

It might be enough to change their story.

I think of my friend Jared. He would have been labeled one of those kids. His childhood was unstable, but you wouldn't know it from his smile. He lit up every room. He made everyone feel loved.

But behind that light, he was drowning. The depression finally became too much.

He took his life in high school.

That loss gutted me.

I've been to funerals before, but this was different.

This was devastation.

Not just for the boy we lost, but for the life he should've lived.

Then came the guilt.

Why didn't I see the signs?

Why didn't I fight harder to show up for him?

I always said I wanted to help people.

So why couldn't I help him?

That's the thing about depression. It deceives you with lies. It isolates. It convinces you that nothing will ever change, even when love surrounds you. Sometimes, love isn't the powerful remedy we hope it will be.

Jared's death broke me.

But it also shaped me.

I never want another kid to feel unseen. If I can be the one who notices the pain behind the smile, who stays and who listens, then maybe I can help someone else find their way back.

I got lucky with my eating disorder.

I survived.

But many don't.

Many never get the chance to tell their story.

Our stories may be different, but pain is pain. I know what it takes to survive something that nearly kills you. I know how hard it is to wear a smile when you're unraveling inside. I know the courage it takes to claw your way back, one breath, one step at a time.

That's why I don't see problems when I look at my students.

I see perseverance.

I see resilience.

The moment that cemented it for me, the one that lit a fire so bright I could never look back, came during my practicum at a youth detention center.

I was teaching a media literacy unit. One day, on a gut instinct, I decided to share a personal poem I had written. One I'd never shared publicly. It came from the raw aftermath of my eating disorder, during the earliest days of recovery.

It told the story of a girl drowning. Consumed by her disorder, fading away piece by piece. But the second half was different. In it, she found help. She survived; she chose to live. I didn't tell them it was my story.

As I read, it aloud, I paused and I asked them what they thought would happen to the girl.

"She's gonna die."

"She won't come back from that."

Their answers weren't cruel. They were honest. Not a single one believed she'd make it. Because hope, for them, wasn't a language they spoke.

These were boys who had learned that survival was rare. That good things don't happen. That people don't change. So, when they heard a story of someone sinking, they didn't imagine a rescue. They braced for the inevitable.

Then I read part two. The girl in the poem lived. She got help and she made it.

Silence…

You could feel the room lighten.

You could hear a pin drop.

For a brief, fragile moment they let themselves believe that maybe people can change, that maybe pain doesn't get the final word.

But hope is a dangerous feeling when you've been taught not to trust it and they shut it down just as quickly.

"She probably relapsed."

"She's probably dead now."

I hadn't planned on telling them it was me.

But I knew I had to.

I looked up.

Locked eyes.

And said, "That girl… was me."

Another silence.

But this one was different.

Not disbelief.

Not dismissal.

But awe.

They saw it.

I was proof.

That rock bottom wasn't always the end.

That redemption wasn't just fiction. That someone who once almost didn't make it was now standing in front of them.

Alive.

Healing.

Teaching.

Their reaction was electric.

They exploded.

Shouting, cheering, wide-eyed and completely lit up. The security guard even came running in, thinking something had gone wrong.

But for once, nothing was wrong.

Everything was right.

Because in that moment, they weren't inmates.

They weren't criminals.

They were kids again.

Laughing.

Believing.

Hopeful.

And maybe, for the first time in a long time, they saw something different.

Possibility.

For a minute, we weren't teacher and student. We were simply people. Souls stitched together by survival, by sorrow, by truth. No titles, no roles. Just raw humanity, sitting quietly in the same flicker of light.

I don't know where a lot of my students are now.
Maybe they stayed the course.
Maybe they didn't.
But I know what I gave them, a seed.
A sliver, a breath of faith.
And sometimes… that's sufficient.
I'm not here to rescue anyone.
I'm not here to rewrite their whole story.
But if I can help them believe, if even for a heartbeat, that they are more than their mistakes. That they are worth saving, worth becoming.
Then that moment is everything.
That's why I stay.
That's why I teach.
Even when systems fail.
Even when hearts break.
Even when it feels like I'm shouting into the wind.
If I reach just one…
If one chooses hope over hurt, life over numbness, then all of it, every hard day, every cracked-open heart, is worth it.
I've worn many hats in this life. Through every chapter, every wreck, every moment of grace, I've learned this…
All I can do is the best I can.
Not perfection.
Not performance.
Just presence.
And you…
You're doing better than you think.
We won't always be on our A-game.
We won't always get it right.
But if you showed up today with love, with effort, with truth, then that is enough.
Let go of the pressure.
Let go of the chase.
Let go of the lie that says you have to be more to be worthy.

Say it with me confidently, firmly, fully:
"I'm doing the best I can. And that is good enough."
Because it is.
Because you are.

And when you start to believe that.
You begin to unlock a kind of power the world can't take from you.
The kind that roots deep and blooms wildly.
The kind that declares:
"Not when I get there. But I am becoming."

That is everything.

CHAPTER 20

Motherhood: No Manual, Just Love

"There's no way to be a perfect mother and a million ways to be a good one."

— *Jill Churchill*

Beyond the role of teacher, what other hats have I worn?

Thirteen years spent shaping minds. That's not even counting the seasons I weathered in university, fighting to earn my place at the front of the room.

Teaching was just one thread in the fabric of who I was becoming.

So, what filled those thirteen years?

Let's just say the past decade was stitched with self-reflection, untamed growth, and wisdom that didn't come easy.

Another romance.

Another goodbye.

One more relationship I ran from before it could unravel me first.

I told myself it was for the best. In my mind, the only way to be the best was to win everyone else's approval, even if it meant sacrificing pieces of myself along the way.

My eating disorder had loosened its grip. Its chokehold no longer strangling my every move. My behaviors weren't an issue.

But body dysmorphia?

That was a whole new battlefield.

I was knee-deep in the wreckage, piecing myself back together.

Bone by bone, thought by thought, rebuilding from the inside out.

Clinging to possibility like a lifeline, quietly telling myself that maybe, just maybe I could learn to love the girl in the mirror again.

There were roadblocks.

Setbacks.

Moments that nearly broke me.

But also, some beautiful things bloomed along the way, bursts of joy and unexpected surprises that reminded me life still had magic to offer.

Did I fall in love again?

Did I get married?

Yes.

I finally found him.

My best friend, Kris.

The one who, very quickly, became my husband. And when I say quickly, I mean fast. We eloped after just five weeks of dating. And surprisingly, it was my idea.

So much for being the girl with no spontaneity, huh?

We actually met during our teenage years, but he wasn't on my radar back then.

I had him labeled.

The nice guy.

Quiet, calm, collected.

I had no idea he had a secret rebel side; he could have been my type. But I wasn't curious enough to find out. He came from a good home, a stable family, and looked like he had his whole life lined up.

And teenager me?

I figured, why would a guy like him be interested in a girl like me? A girl from a small home with a single mom, a girl who carried a little baggage. I assumed guys like him were judging me. That I wasn't the kind of girl they'd go for.

But I was wrong.

All along, I was the girl he noticed. He never cared about where I came from or what my family dynamics looked like. That was a lesson I had to learn the hard way. That sometimes, the biggest lies are the ones we tell ourselves. Things aren't always what they seem.

The guy I thought had it all figured out? He had his own demons. Kris had battled addiction. And, just like me, he had spent time in rehab, his journey echoing mine in the ED program. When we reconnected at twenty-six, we were both deep in recovery. Living life again, not perfectly, but as healing human beings.

The moment our paths reconnected, something clicked.

He understood me in a way no one else ever had.

He understood my disorder.

My thought patterns.

My inner chaos.

Because he'd lived it too, just in a different form.

Addiction and eating disorders aren't so different.

And yes, this is coming from the same girl who once blamed her dad for his addiction. Who was angry he couldn't just "choose better." Let me be proof, you can't judge a path you've never walked.

With Kris, I found a connection deeper than anything I'd known.

He didn't just love me, he understood me.

He knew my ED, like his addiction, wasn't something that would magically disappear. It was something we'd both face, again and again. A daily battle we were willing to face, together.

In him, I found safety.

Safety to be seen.

To be soft.

To let love in again.

The connection we made was incredible. Deep, emotional, reawakening. But I would be lying if I said I wasn't also physically drawn to him. Because yep… another tall guy. I guess I really have a thing for height.

There's something about being with someone bigger than me, someone who towers over me, that makes me feel smaller. And in a way, my ED brain preferred that. It's not something I consciously thought about at the time, but looking back, I can see how it played a role.

It wasn't just his height. He was strong, and being wrapped in his arms made me feel protected, like nothing in the outside world could touch me, as long as he was by my side.

There was this effortless charm to his appearance, something that caught people's attention wherever we went. People always said the same thing: "He looks just like Ryan Gosling."

They still do to this day. And hey, I'm not complaining. Gosling is one gorgeous man.

But what mattered most was this. For once, I didn't feel like I had to fix him. He'd already done the work. And for the first time, I realized it's not my job to fix anyone.

Funny enough, it took writing this book to fully see that pattern. The urge to heal, to carry, to be the one holding it all together, over and over again.

Kris isn't perfect.

We've been married for twelve years, and we've had our fair share of challenges. I've shed plenty of tears, some because of him. And there were moments I had one foot out the door, ready to bolt.

Old habits die hard, right?

But I stayed.

We put in the work.

We grew together.

We pushed through the hard stuff.

And honestly, I don't regret marrying him after only five weeks, standing barefoot on that beach.

Because that day?

It's still one of the best decisions I've ever made.

Yes, we eloped on the beach at the lake, right next to that little campground where we first met. The same place that later became my therapy.

That place is more than a memory; it's a part of my soul.

And here's a fun twist, he proposed a few months later.

Yep, after we were already married.

On that same beach.

I know, it's backwards.

Married first, then engaged.

But that was us.

We didn't tell anyone when we eloped.

It was our little secret, sealed in spontaneity.

Why keep it quiet? Because I didn't want opinions clouding the moment. I didn't want to hear, "It's too soon," or "Are you sure?"

It was our choice.

We made it, just the two of us.

Yet… I still wanted the big wedding.

Call it diva energy.

I wanted the long white dress, the flowing veil, the flowers, the moment surrounded by everyone we loved.

That had always been my dream.

So, he saved up.

Bought a ring.

Got down on one knee.

And I said yes, to my husband.

It might sound silly, but I love our story.

It's different.

Imperfect.

Ours.

After sharing vows the first time, life moved fast. We bought a cozy little condo tucked into a new neighborhood. Sunlight streamed through the windows. And true to my nature, I made it my own within weeks.

My energy practically spilled onto the walls: bold, expressive, alive. Sunny yellow in the kitchen like a permanent smile. Rich red in the living room, loud and vibrant. Even the bathroom was orange. Every wall had its own personality. Just like me.

Looking back, it was chaotic and colorful, but it was us.

It was home.

These days, my style's a little softer. Muted tones, cozy textures, rustic charm. But that creative spark never left. Now it's warm woods, flickering lights, and spaces that feel lived in and loved.

Our home tells a story of comfort, commotion, and charm.

One still unfolding.

The following summer, we got married again.

This time, my dream wedding.

A rustic venue with barn-like charm. Wooden beams. Twinkling string lights. Romance met comfort. It was soulful, everything I had imagined.

Well, almost. The florist botched the centerpieces with wrong flowers, and wrong colors. But I really didn't care. I wasn't about to be a bridezilla over flowers. Besides, we were already secretly married.

That day wasn't about perfection; it was about celebration.

Joy.

Connection.

Love.

In all the ways that mattered, it was perfect.

The maid of honor speech was legendary. My best friend, Megan, and our emcee, Chelsey, rewrote "Don't Stop Believin'" to tell the story of my life up to marrying Kris. Tone-deaf and drunk. Belting it out like Broadway stars. Pure havoc, and absolutely unforgettable.

Our wedding was one of the biggest highlights of my life.

The dance floor never emptied.

The energy was electric.

The love in that room?

You could feel it.

We even had the same person who married us on the beach officiate again so we could keep our secret.

Very Mission Impossible of us.

And we actually kept it for ten full years.

It wasn't until our tenth anniversary that we spilled the beans.

Then we renewed our vows.

That's right.

I've officially married my husband three times.

Will we do it again?

Absolutely.

At this point, it's kind of our thing.

Our family jokes about it now.

But I wouldn't have it any other way.

Because every time, in every version of our story…

I'd still choose him.

Kris loves me, for me.

He's been there through all of it. The highs, the lows, the quiet moments, the storms. He's my biggest fan. No matter what wild dream I throw into the world, he believes in it, because he believes in me.

He's the one who pushed me to write this book.

I didn't think I was good enough.

"I'm not an author," I told him.

"I don't have the skills."

"Who am I to tell a story?"

But he reminded me that I have a voice. That my story matters. That my willingness to be honest and vulnerable could help someone else feel less alone.

Because of him, I pushed through the doubt.

And finally, I did it.

I'm so grateful Kris never gives up on me. That he keeps cheering me on through every chapter, every breakdown, every comeback. Helping me change the world, one word, one student, one life at a time.

So, first comes love, then comes marriage, then comes a baby in the baby carriage...

At least, that's how the saying goes.

Being a mom had always been a dream of mine.

Not just any mom. I wanted to be like my mom. Full of love, overflowing with kindness, and unshakably present. I wanted to give my children what she gave me. Her time, her heart, her whole self.

But I wasn't sure if that dream would come true for me.

Yes, my body had healed. My cycle had returned. My organs were functioning again.

But deep down, one fear lingered...

Had I done too much damage?

I couldn't forget what that doctor once told me at my lowest point.

"There's a chance you might not be able to have kids."

So, I started preparing myself for that possibility. I reminded myself there are many ways to become a mother. That even if I couldn't carry a child, I would still find a way and be happy. Because one way or another, I was meant to be someone's mom.

Still, deep down, I wanted to experience it all.

I wanted to feel pregnancy.

To carry life.

To grow a baby inside me.

But with my ED brain still lurking in the shadows, that dream felt equally terrifying.

Pregnancy meant change.

It meant weight gain.

It meant my stomach, my hips, my thighs, my face, everything would grow.

And yes, I knew that was natural.

I knew it was part of the miracle.

But to my eating disorder brain, it was petrifying.

Would I gain more than just baby weight?

Would I get fat?

Would I lose myself in the mirror?

Would I see strength, or something I'd despise?

I didn't feel ready. As much as I wanted the baby, I didn't know how to make peace with what it might do to my body.

The war between my heart and my head had only just begun.

So, I re-entered another ED program.

Once again, an outpatient.

But this time was different.

This program wasn't for those in crisis, it was for those of us in recovery. Our tape recorders weren't screaming anymore. They were whispering. Subtle, but still there. We were functioning and living. But we still needed help.

We met weekly in group therapy. And just like before, I found myself sitting around a table with people who got it. People still learning to quiet the voice and live fully.

But unlike before, there were no food journals.

No calorie charts.

No rigid meal plans.

This program wasn't as focused on controlling food, it was about learning to accept ourselves. It was about confronting our haunting and cruel body dysmorphia. It was about recognizing the negative beliefs we carried and challenging the quiet lies we told ourselves for far too long.

Week after week, we sat in that circle, sharing our truths, our struggles, and the stories that shaped us.

I felt transported back to my first program, sitting in a similar wobbly chair around the oval table.

But something was different.

The people around me had changed.

I had changed.

I wasn't just surviving anymore.

I wasn't clinging to life.

I was living it.

Choosing to heal.

Choosing to seek support.

Preparing myself for what lay ahead.

I wasn't just holding on.

I was reaching for something bigger.

Something beautiful.

I was chasing the hope of motherhood.

Throughout this program, I grew more confident in the possibility of pregnancy. Once again, that place helped me in ways I can't fully explain. It will forever hold a special place in my heart.

This program showed me that if I became pregnant, my eating disorder didn't have to take over. It was possible that it wouldn't come back in full effect.

But I was still scared.

Scared of the control.

Who would have it, me or ED?

What if pregnancy became a trigger?

What if my ED brain roared back to life?

What if I restricted again?

What if I couldn't protect my baby from my disorder?

That fear was real.

Loud.

Persistent.

Because even in recovery, I knew the voice hadn't disappeared. It was quieter, yes, but still there waiting for a moment of weakness to take the wheel.

With eating disorders, there's never full certainty.

They hide in silence, lingering beneath the surface.

Sometimes, all it takes is one trigger to undo everything.

That's what scared me most.

Still, over time, I felt stronger.

More grounded.

More ready.

Then... it happened.

After months of trying.

Two bold lines on the test.

My body.

The same body that had once been on the brink of collapse, the one I had abused, starved, and doubted, was pregnant.

That was the most beautiful gift it had ever given me.

I was overwhelmed with gratitude.

And to my surprise… I cherished my pregnant body.

The curves.

The softness.

The stretch and swell of life growing inside me.

I didn't just tolerate it.

I loved it.

And ED?

It didn't stand a chance.

For the first time in my life, I saw my body not as something to shrink or control, but as something powerful.

Something capable of creating life.

And for the first time in so long…

I felt beautiful.

I didn't hate my reflection.

I didn't avoid mirrors.

The more my belly grew, the more confident I felt.

Not because I needed approval.

Not because I was trying to please the world.

But because I was finally accepting myself.

Finally understanding myself again.

In those moments, I caught a glimpse of the girl I thought I had lost.

The one who used to believe in magic.

The one who had almost disappeared.

But she was still there.

She was smiling.

She was proud.

And so was I.

The more I grew, the more beautiful I felt.

Not just physically, but emotionally.

I was healing.

I was becoming me again.

For the first time in years, I stepped on a scale. Not by choice, but because it was part of my prenatal visits. I couldn't resist. But I did it on my terms. I turned my back to the numbers, refusing to give them power.

I wouldn't let my doctor tell me my starting weight.

Then curiosity got the best of me.

I asked how much I'd gained throughout the pregnancy.

And the number?

It wasn't small.

It was a lot.

Shockingly... that didn't scare me.

Every pound felt like a badge of honor.

With every pound, I was becoming a mother.

With every pound, I was bringing life into the world.

My body, the same body that was once dying, was growing life.

Even when it came to cravings, ED didn't stand a chance. When my body wanted something, it got it. And let's be real, those cravings were no joke.

My biggest one?

Bacon.

I'd wake up in the middle of the night, wander into the kitchen, and fry a plate of crispy, salty, greasy bacon.

Just for me.

No guilt.

No hesitation.

Just satisfaction.

Just joy.

Then I'd crawl back into bed, belly full, heart content.

No tape recorder in my head.

Just me.

My hand resting on my beautiful belly.

Feeling my baby squirm.

Feeling it take in the nourishment.

Knowing, deep in my soul, that I was going to be a good mom.

I had been given a second chance.

This time, not even ED was going to get in my way.

My children are older now.

Yes, plural.

I have two adorable kids, Nolan and Maddy, who I love to pieces. Kris and I aren't planning to have more, but I must say… I miss the way I loved my pregnant body.

Looking back, those months were when I felt the most radiant. It was the heaviest my body had ever been, and yet, I felt stunning. I'd look in the mirror and, for the first time, truly love every inch of myself.

And ED?

It had no voice while I was expecting.

For those sacred months, I was completely confident.

Completely at peace.

Then came childbirth, another incredible gift my body gave me. There's no feeling like bringing a child into the world. Even now, I'm still in awe that my body did that. Childbirth is sacred. A moment where strength, vulnerability, and love collide in the most powerful way.

Mom life is 24/7. A wild, ever-shifting ride of peaks and valleys, with curveballs you never see coming. Just when you think you've cracked the code, your kids flip the script.

One night they're sleeping like angels, the next they're screaming for hours. Their favorite stuffed bunny goes missing, you tear the house apart, buy three backups, and the next day, they're over it. One day, they ask for seconds of broccoli. The next, they act like it's poison.

It's the unpredictable chaos of parenting. Just when you think you got this, your kids remind you: Nope. Try again.

But here's the thing…

We forget the lows because of the highs.

They're that high.

Those moments of pure joy and connection.

They're everything.

Like bedtime. Singing our special song, "You Are My Sunshine," watching them drift off to sleep. Or when they try something new and succeed, seeing the pride in their eyes.

Riding a bike.

Building LEGO worlds.

Turning couch cushions into castles.

But the sweetest game my kids play?

When they pretend to be Mommy and Daddy. Imitating our voices. Repeating our phrases. Acting out our lives with wide-eyed joy. It's hilarious, and humbling.

A reminder that they're always watching.

To them, we are their world.

And then come the bear hugs. Arms around my neck. Legs clinging to my waist. The way their tiny hands fit perfectly in mine, reminders of how small they still are, and how fast they're growing. One day, those little hands won't reach for mine out of instinct, but intention.

While that truth tugs at my heart, for now, I hold on tighter. I soak in every hug, every handhold, every silly game and bedtime snuggle.

Because in this moment, they never want to let go.

And neither do I.

I love being a mom.

With every challenge, every sleepless night, every twist, I wouldn't trade it for the world.

Even now, I sometimes stand and watch my children sleep.

Peaceful.

Safe.

Their steady breaths, their chests rising and falling, each movement a quiet reminder of life. In those moments, I drift, caught between overwhelming gratitude and a flood of what-ifs.

What if I hadn't gotten up off that floor?

What if I hadn't got help?

What if ED had still been there tightening its grip, pulling the strings?

That thought is paralyzing…

Until I come back to the present. Back to the soft glow of their room. Back to the most beautiful thing I've ever seen. Them sleeping soundly, existing.

Because I chose to fight.

Yes, I thank the universe.

More importantly…

I thank myself.

The universe wasn't the only force at play.

I made the choice.

I chose to fight for my life.

I chose to rise when it would've been easier to stay down.

Sometimes I forget just how strong I am.

This body, once broken, naked, and shivering on a bathroom floor, is the same body that carried and birthed two beautiful children.

That still stuns me.

I'm in awe of my body.

Its strength, its resilience, its ability to heal.

I'm grateful.

So incredibly grateful.

To be alive.

To be a mom.

To have this life.

And yet, I'll be real, sometimes I lose sight of that. Life gets busy. The days blur. The to-do list grows. I slip into go-go-go mode, always chasing the next task.

But over the years, I've learned to pause. To slow down, to zoom out. Because when I do, when I really let myself take it all in, I feel it.

The gift of being alive.

People who've danced with death often see life differently. I was one of them. Now, I try to soak in everything. Every heartbeat, every breath, every fleeting moment.

Because the truth is, we never know how much time we have.

So don't waste it.

Don't wait for a near-death wake-up call to start truly living.

Start now.

And I don't mean just existing.

I mean really living.

Do the things that bring you joy.

That make you laugh until you can't breathe. Until you pee your pants and trust me, I've birthed babies, that happens.

Here's the thing, I can always change my pants. What I won't do is miss out on the kind of laughter that feeds the soul.

Laughter is healing.

It's contagious.

It feels good and it spreads that goodness to others. So let it out, loud and proud.

I get it, this advice is easier said than done.

Life is unpredictable.

Things go wrong.

Sometimes really wrong.

We can't control the uncertainty.

But we can control our mindset.

We get to choose how we respond.

We can choose to lead with joy instead of letting negativity take the lead.

But for some reason, we let the bad energy take up all the space.

Why?

Why do we give the hard moments the loudest voice?

I refuse to live that way.

I've worked too hard on my mindset to hand the wheel back to darkness.

Now, I choose to find joy. Even in the unraveling.

To wake up and say, "Today's going to be a good day."

If I start miserable and negative, that's exactly what I'll project, exactly what I'll receive. I truly believe the energy you put out is what comes back to you.

Since I've been living that way, I can honestly say, it works.

Living with a positive mindset isn't just about optimism.
It's about survival.
It's about freedom.
So don't waste your time drowning in what ifs.
Don't wait for opportunities to show up.
Go make them happen.
Even if you're not ready, do it anyway.
That's when the magic happens.
Stop focusing solely on the outcome.
Start embracing the becoming.
The real growth lives in the process, the stretch, the climb.

Not every day is a good day.
But there is good in every day.
And it's up to you to find it.

Of all the lessons motherhood has given me, this one stands out most. Find light in the shadows and live each day with purpose, presence, and an open heart.

CHAPTER 21

Stretch Marks & Strength: Postpartum Body

"Your body is not ruined. You're a goddamn landscape of love and survival."

— *Nikita Gill*

A woman's body during pregnancy is nothing short of extraordinary. It's a masterpiece of transformation, strength, and grace.

Her skin stretches gently over the swell of her belly, creating a sacred space where life begins. Each day, she watches in awe as her body shifts, expands, and evolves. Cradling the tiny soul within.

Every time her hands rest on her stomach, a quiet connection forms, an unspoken bond between mother and child. The soft flutters, the playful squirms beneath her fingertips, hums of new beginnings. Silent promises of the love soon to bloom in her arms.

With every kick, she's reminded of the miracle she carries. Her body isn't just changing, it's thriving. Glowing with purpose. Radiating power. A cocoon of warmth, safety, and strength.

She stands before the mirror, tracing the gentle curve of her belly, marveling at the beauty in every line and mark. Each one telling the story of creation. She feels powerful, stunning, and deeply, indescribably incredible.

During pregnancy, this is exactly how I felt about my growing body.

I embraced every change with awe and admiration.

I loved it.

Accepted it.

Praised it for the incredible work it was doing.

My body wasn't just mine, it was a home, a vessel.

I felt strong, beautiful, and full of purpose.

But after giving birth, that mindset began to transition.

The extra weight that once held meaning suddenly felt different.

While pregnant, those pounds were justified, they were essential.

But once it was just me again, no longer carrying life, I struggled with the lingering softness.

The excuse had vanished.

All that remained was me.

Standing in a body that didn't quite feel like mine.

I tried to remind myself of what my body had just done. Grown a human, given birth, created life. That alone was something to be proud of. But still, the self-acceptance I had embraced so easily during pregnancy began to slip. I found myself caught in contradiction, grateful for what my body had done yet haunted by the pressure to look like I hadn't just created a miracle.

I remember one afternoon in particular, when I finally carved out a moment for myself. Nolan was napping and Kris was home, so I decided to go for a walk. Just me, the fresh air, and the steady rhythm of my footsteps. A rare, peaceful pause.

As I strolled through the neighborhood, I ran into our neighbor. She smiled warmly, then glanced at my stomach.

"Oh! Any day now! When are you due?"

My heart pounded.

I managed to say, "There's no baby left in me. I already gave birth a few weeks ago."

Her face turned pale.

She stammered an apology, clearly mortified.

But it didn't matter.

The damage was done.

Her words, though unintentional, cut deep. Slicing through the fragile confidence I'd been clinging to.

Suddenly, that peaceful walk wasn't about fresh air anymore. My body spun into fight mode. My pace quickened. My mind spiraled.

Move faster.

Sweat more.

Burn it off.

Shrink back down.

I wasn't walking anymore, I was running. Running from the shame. From the fear that my body would never be what it once was.

That one comment flipped a switch. Old habits stirred. Old punishments resurfaced.

I knew I shouldn't let it get to me.

I knew she didn't mean harm.

Yet in that moment, I couldn't stop the flood of emotion.

That walk stopped being about self-care. It became about fixing what I thought was broken.

I reminded myself, it took nine months to grow this body. To stretch. To make space for life. Of course it would take time to heal.

Logically, I knew that.

Emotionally, I was impatient.

I didn't expect perfection, but I craved recognition.

I wanted to look in the mirror and see me again.

Or at least, someone I recognized.

That's when ED crept in.

Whispering old lies.

My body image twisted.

The baby weight.

The softness.

Now felt magnified under my critical gaze.

I knew my perception was distorted. But that didn't stop the feelings from taking hold. It became a tug-of-war between reason and fear. Between truth and a voice that never really left.

I had done something incredible. I had brought life into the world. And still, I stood in front of the mirror, unable to see that power. All I could focus on was how much my body had changed, and how long it might take to change back.

Despite the haunting reflection in the mirror, I didn't relapse. Not because the thoughts weren't there, but because I knew I couldn't.

I was breastfeeding. My body needed fuel. I needed strength to hold, rock, and soothe my baby. I needed energy to survive sleepless nights, and the resilience to show up, again and again.

Being a mom is an around-the-clock job. No pause button. No room for weakness. No space to deprive myself just to keep going.

My body was nourishment.

It was comfort.

It was home.

So, I ate.

Not because it was easy, but because it was necessary.

Motherhood demanded more from me than my eating disorder ever had.

In those early months, the love I had for my child spoke louder than my self-doubt. I ate regular, balanced meals, with my typical sprinkle of restriction. Nothing extreme. No red flags. Just quiet rules. Small limits that felt safe.

The only time I truly let go was during pregnancy. When my body wasn't just mine, and I honored that.

But postpartum, when it was just me again, the control crept back in.

Not starving.

Not punishing.

Simply managing.

It was just enough to feel like I was doing something about the body I still struggled to accept. My habits stayed within a "healthy" range. My body was structured, but still nourished.

Eventually, Kris became the cook in our home. Not just because he's good at it, though he is now, but because I needed distance.

When I cooked, I slightly tweaked the recipe. Less butter. Less oil. A "safer" substitute here, a swap there. And before I knew it, we were eating bland, unsatisfying meals that neither of us enjoyed.

So, Kris stepped up, and I let go.

I got to eat mindfully and peacefully, without overthinking every step. It was a small shift, but a powerful one. Sometimes, the only way to loosen your grip is to place it in someone else's hands.

The real struggle wasn't physical.

It was internal.

A quiet war between acceptance and criticism.

Still, every time I saw my reflection, I felt torn.

Some days, I looked at my stomach, the stretch marks, the soft folds, and felt pride. This body had grown life. These marks were proof.

Other days, self-loathing took the lead. Every dimpled line, every wrinkle, every sign that my body was different, all felt like something to fix.

It was a constant coin flip...

Would I wake up feeling strong and grateful?

Or defeated, longing for the version of me that no longer existed?

It was the classic battle of angel on one shoulder, devil on the other.

The angel whispered:

You're beautiful.

You're enough.

Look at what your body did.

But the devil fought louder:

Be smaller.

Be tighter.

Be better.

Every day, I waited to see which voice would triumph.

Days when I was sleep-deprived and empty, the devil's voice nearly always won. Those were the hardest days. I'd avoid mirrors. I'd reach for my safe clothes. Baggy, shapeless, forgiving. Anything fitted felt like a risk. If something hugged my waist too tightly it became proof, in my mind, that I needed to shrink.

So, I hid.

Not just from the mirror, not just from the world, but from myself.

I wrapped my body in fabric, trying to disappear.

Trying to feel safe when my own skin felt like the enemy.

Luckily, caring for a newborn left less time to spiral. Less time to obsess, overanalyze, or get lost in thought.

Yes, the negativity still crept in.

But it didn't consume me like it used to.

Motherhood became my anchor.

My days were filled with feedings, diaper changes, soothing cries, and beautiful, sacred moments that reminded me…

This is what matters.

This new role.

It saved me from myself.

That being said, my postpartum recovery was much harder after my son, Nolan.

He was my first. I was navigating uncharted territory. I was figuring out motherhood, adjusting to the overwhelming shift in identity, and trying to balance it all.

I was vulnerable and raw.

The ED brain now had more power. I didn't yet have the tools to fight it.

However, when my daughter, Maddy, was born, my mindset was heightened.

I wasn't a first-time mom anymore.

I knew what to expect.

I had more coping mechanisms, more insight, more strength. I'd already fought some of those battles. Already learned how to push back against the toxic thoughts.

They still showed up, but they didn't grip me the same way.

I was more prepared.

More equipped.

The second time around, I gave myself more grace.

I knew the weight didn't have to disappear overnight.

My body wasn't ruined.

It had simply changed.

While I still had hard days, I had more power over them.

I was stronger.

Not just as a mother, but as a woman learning to rewrite the narrative in her own mind.

Two months into my postpartum journey with Nolan, I felt myself slipping.

The beautiful summer weather was fading, replaced by the crisp bite of autumn. Leaves turned from green to red and orange, swirling at my feet as I walked.

With colder days came shorter walks. I found myself retreating indoors more often. With each passing day, as the sunlight faded, so did a part of me.

The chill seeped into my bones. A familiar heaviness settled in. The more I stayed inside, the more I felt trapped. Not just physically, but mentally. The walls closed in. The silence grew heavier.

Isolation, which had been subtly creeping in since birth, now pressed down harder, like an unwanted guest settling in.

I knew, if I didn't act, I'd spiral.

There were moments, late at night, when Nolan was asleep on my chest, his breath soft against my skin.

The house was silent.

In those still moments, my mind would drift…

Suddenly, I wasn't in my living room anymore.

I was standing in the middle of the woods.

Alone.

The grass brushed my legs. The earth was soft and damp beneath me. A cold wind wrapped around my body like an unwelcomed spirit. The sun was shining, but its warmth wasn't enough to stop the chill.

I slowly spun, scanning my surroundings.

Paths stretched in every direction but none of them felt right.

I had no map.

No guide.

No sign pointing me home.

I was a new mom.

I was grateful.

I was doing my best to nurture and protect this tiny life.

But part of me felt lost.

Drowned out by the towering trees.

Swallowed by the stillness pressing in from all sides.

It was as if the trees were watching me.

Giant sentinels seeding doubt.

I was a good mom, I knew that.

But the loneliness settled in anyway, heavy on my chest.

And I knew if I let it, I would be consumed.

I needed to find my own way out of those woods.

Not just as a mother.

But as me.

I needed to make peace with my body before the dark thoughts gained too much power.

Before they became more than whispers.

I had a choice to make...

Stand still, lost in the trees.

Or start walking and carve out a new way forward.

Support has always played a profound role in my life, and I knew if I wanted to keep from slipping further, I needed to find my people.

I needed connection.

A community of other moms who could lift me up and remind me I wasn't alone.

So, I made the conscious decision to seek it out.

That decision changed everything.

There were plenty of options. Library story times, baby music groups, walking meet-ups.

But I knew myself.

I didn't just need a stroll or small talk.

I needed movement.

I needed to feel strong in my skin again.

Fitness had always been a part of me.

A place where I could feel powerful, grounded, and present in my body, no matter what phase of life I was in.

So, I leaned back into that part of myself.

I joined a mom-and-baby fitness group, and it was, hands down, the best thing I could've done for my mental health and postpartum body image.

With every class, every rep, every shared laugh with other moms, I felt myself pulling further away from the darkness.

I followed the sunshine, step by step.

Slowly, I found my way out of the woods.

The lingering chill of loneliness began to lift.

It was replaced by something warm and steady, radiating from within, telling me...

You're exactly where you're meant to be.

You're going to be okay.

ED still lurked, waiting for weakness.

But the light of motherhood.

Its joy, its love, its purpose was stronger.

ED knew it didn't stand a chance.

Motherhood had given me something far more powerful than the voice in my head ever could...

Purpose.

Love.

An unshakable will to fight for myself.

Yes, the fitness helped shed some of the baby weight, but that wasn't the victory.

The real progress was deeper.

I wasn't obsessing over every inch or pound.

I was moving, and that movement gave me something far more valuable than weight loss.

It gave me strength.

Physically and mentally.

It gave me energy.

And as a new mom, energy is everything.

The sleepless nights.

The constant feedings.

The emotional toll.

All wears you down.

But movement gave back what motherhood tried to drain.

I felt stronger.

More capable.

More alive.

Along with that strength, I gained more to offer.

More laughter.

More patience.

More play.

More presence.

I wasn't just surviving.

I was embracing motherhood.

And for the first time in a long time, I felt like I was winning the battle against the thoughts that once held me hostage.

It started with one class a week.

Then two.

Then three.

I was hooked.

These classes became more than just fitness. They became my safety net. A group of moms in the same phase of life. Sharing the same worries. Navigating the same whirlwind of commotion. Loving their babies with the same all-consuming fierceness.

We swapped stories.

They were raw, hilarious, and messy.

From diaper explosions that required full outfit changes... for both mom and baby. To late-night ER visits for harmless rashes. To panic over our babies' skin looking yellow, only to realize it was just from carrot baby food the day before.

We cried over teething nights that robbed us of sleep.

We laughed through exhaustion.

We reassured each other we weren't alone.

These women understood me in a way no one else could at the time. We built genuine connections, and I'm so grateful that some of those moms are still in my life today.

What started as a simple decision to move my body became something so much greater.

I found my community.

Through them, I found a clearer identity of myself again.

I think a lot of brand-new moms go through a tough transition in the beginning. Everything is new and overwhelming. Even, at times, completely terrifying.

Simple outings, things we once did without a second thought, suddenly felt like massive undertakings. There's hesitation to leave the house, creeping anxiety about car rides or navigating grocery stores and crowded malls. The idea of exposing our baby to the outside world feels risky.

Unpredictable.

What if they cry in public?

What if they get sick?

What if something goes wrong?

Many of us retreat to the safety of our homes. Social distancing becomes less of a recommendation and more of a choice. Our four walls feel controlled, secure. A place where we can protect our babies from everything.

While that instinct is natural, biological even, it can become isolating. The longer we stay indoors, the harder it becomes to go out. Loneliness creeps in quietly, disguising itself as comfort.

Eventually, we realize we need connection. Because while our babies may be our whole world... we still need the world beyond them. Finding that balance is one of the hardest parts of early motherhood; it's about learning how to protect our babies without losing ourselves in the process.

For me, getting out of the house during that stage was exactly what I needed.

I've always thrived on social interaction, on movement and on connection. Motherhood didn't change that. It simply added another layer to who I was. While I adored being a mom, I also knew I couldn't lose myself in the process. I needed to socialize, to connect, and to remember that I was still me, just in a new role to carry alongside my others.

So, I made it a point to get out nearly every day, just like I did before becoming a mom.

The only difference...

Now I had a baby in tow.

Even a simple grocery run felt like an expedition. Lugging the car seat. Navigating narrow aisles. Juggling a growing to-do list while soothing my little one.

It was exhausting.

But it also gave me purpose.

It broke up the long days, brought structure to the chaos, and reminded me that I still existed beyond diaper changes and nap schedules. While those outings were tiring, they were also incredibly fulfilling. They gave me a sense of normalcy in a life that had changed overnight. In those early months, that small sense of normalcy made all the difference.

I had a stationary bike at home for the days I didn't feel like going out.

As much as I loved my little outings with the babies, some days I just craved stillness. No plans. No socializing. Just the comfort of home. As extroverted as I am, I need those quiet, reflective moments to reset and recenter.

Those days were simple.

A quick ride while the baby napped, followed by cozy couch cuddles and marathon sessions of cooking shows.

Slow.

Easy.

Needed.

But my time on that bike was more than just exercise. It wasn't just about breaking a sweat, it was therapy. A space to process the hard stuff I didn't always have time to acknowledge in the busyness of motherhood.

When I rode, I wasn't just moving. I was feeling, letting go, breathing deep, and sifting through emotions. Funny how an exercise bike is designed to go nowhere. Yet for my soul, it went everywhere.

Exercise found its way back into my life naturally.

Yet, it didn't look the same as it did before kids.

I wasn't in the gym following strict routines. My mom-and-baby fitness classes, and my bike at home, became my anchor. They gave me space to move, to breathe, to reconnect with myself. A way to prioritize my mental health and sense of identity, all while keeping my little ones close.

With two babies close together, Nolan only nine months old when I found out I was pregnant again, movement became my release.

People thought I was ridiculous for having them so close in age. But I wouldn't change a thing. My kids are best friends. They hit milestones together. We tackled diapers, big kid beds, and tantrums in sync.

And moms?

We love easy.

In a life that's full-on, those overlapping stages felt like a gift. I was constantly pulled in every direction, but exercise gave me something of my own.

A space to breathe.

To reflect.

To reset.

It wasn't about fitness anymore. It was about showing up for me, so I could keep showing up for them.

Eventually, I turned my love for fitness into something more. During my second maternity leave, I became a certified fitness instructor.

It felt like a natural fit. I've always loved public speaking, thrived on connection, and believed in the power of movement. Not just physically, but mentally and emotionally. Becoming an instructor blended everything I was passionate about, teaching, inspiring, and building community.

On the other end, I also craved balance. I wasn't ready to let go of my role as a teacher.

So, I adjusted, switched to part-time, creating a lifestyle that honored every part of who I am: an instructor, educator, and most importantly, mom.

This wasn't just about fitness anymore.

It was about building a life that felt whole.

Fitness became a pillar.

My non-negotiable.

It offered structure and kept me grounded.

While I embraced it for the right reasons. Strength, energy, and joy. I'd be lying if I said ED didn't try to hitch a ride.

When insecurities spike and the mirror distorts, my ED brain clings to the weakness. It feeds on the burn. On the illusion of control.

Despite my best efforts, it creeps in, tightening its grip, persuading old demands.

Go faster.

Push harder.

Burn more.

Then just like that, movement doesn't feel so pure.

The bliss fades, replaced by pressure.

Still, even when ED lurks in the background, most days, I rise above it.

I return to my mantra.

I remind myself why I move...

For strength.

For clarity.

For joy.

Most days, I hold that truth close. I stay rooted in purpose.

Because while ED may still attempt to convince, it no longer leads.

Coaching gives me something to fight for, a reason to rise, to lead by example. Not just for my clients, but for myself.

It keeps me accountable, not just in movement, but in mindset. It reminds me to protect the intention behind my workouts, to ensure exercise never becomes punishment again.

Instead, I step into every class with one purpose.

Movement is strength.

Movement is self-care.

I am so much more than the body that moves.

I'm the soul behind it.

And so are you.

I started with mom-and-baby bootcamps and cycling classes. My favorite ways to move. It felt natural to teach what I loved. Also, being surrounded by other moms in the same stage of life made it even more fulfilling.

But as my kids grew, that chapter began to grow alongside them. They weren't babies anymore. So, I was ready to expand my reach. And my role.

Naturally, I branched out. Stepping into new studios, taking on fresh challenges, and growing as an instructor.

What began as a passion became something more. A career. A community. A space where I could challenge myself and others to feel strong, capable, and empowered.

I landed a gig as a spin instructor at one of my favorite studios, one I had admired from afar. A space known for being the best of the best.

I still remember the audition like it was yesterday. Bright red sports bra. High ponytail. Head held high. On the outside, I looked ready. But inside, I felt like I didn't belong.

No matter how hard I've worked, no matter how many skills I've mastered, that deep-seated feeling of not being enough has always lingered.

A voice that says, you're not good enough, you don't belong here.

That voice can eat you alive. It can hold you back, limit your potential, it could even make you question your greatest accomplishments.

I know it.

I'm aware of it.

Yet awareness doesn't always silence the struggle.
So, there I was…
A new mom, older than everyone in the room.
Competing for a coveted spot.
The doubts were screaming…
What am I doing here?
Who do I think I am?
Just because I want this doesn't mean I'll get it.
But despite the noise, I showed up.
I walked to that bike, cranked up "Larger Than Life" by the Backstreet Boys, and made an entrance.
Loud, unapologetic, and iconic.
I wanted to stand out.
I needed to prove I brought more than just technical skill.
I had presence.
Energy.
Passion.
I clipped in.
Forty people watched as I took the podium.
In that moment, I blocked them out and let go.
The second I get on that bike, something in me wakes up.
It's not just movement.
It's soul.
And that passion.
It's contagious.
When I surrender to the music, to the ride, others feel it too.
They connect.
They grow.
They find their strength.
And despite the self-doubt clawing at my insides…
I was one of the first selected.
Chosen to be part of their elite team.
I had walked in feeling like an outsider.
But I left that ride having proven I belonged.

I'll always be grateful I found my home in that studio. It wasn't just about becoming an instructor, it was about becoming a motivator.

And that's exactly what we do.

If you've never been to a spin class, let me paint a picture:

You walk into a dark room lit by candles and spotlights. The air hums with energy. The music pulses deep in your chest. You clip in, and before you know it, you're drenched in sweat. Your body moves in rhythm with the beat.

Except it's more than just pedaling.

We ride with purpose. Choreographed movement to the beat of the music, fused with athletic power. Like dancing, but with intention behind every motion.

That's the physical side.

But spin is so much more.

There's an emotional layer. A mental release.

And that's where we, the motivators, come in.

We don't just cue moves, we speak to something deeper.

We speak to the part of you that craves change.

That aches to grow.

That's desperate to believe in its worth.

Spin isn't just a workout.

It's a therapy session on a bike.

Every ride, we talk about life.

Not just fitness.

Not just movement.

Life.

We encourage our riders to chase their dreams, to take risks, to forgive, to let go, to love themselves through the mess.

And that's where I found my voice.

I always knew I wanted to help people.

I did it through teaching, through personal connection, through giving.

But it was spin that showed me I could help with my words.

I never realized how powerful my voice could be until I stepped on that podium and started speaking from the heart.
By being open, honest, and vulnerable, I created space for others to grow.
To heal.
To let go of shame.
It wasn't only about getting stronger; it was also about becoming whole.
Spin became more than movement for me.
It became connection. It became empowerment.
That's why I fell in love with it.
That's how I knew I belonged.
Because this isn't just spin.
This is transformation.

Has my body changed significantly since having kids?
Hell yes.
No matter how much I exercise, no matter how many times I've flirted with restriction...
I will never have the same body I had before.
My stomach will never be as flat, not after stretching and expanding to grow life.
My breasts will never be as full or perky, not after feeding and nourishing the babies who made me a mother.

So, I work on flipping the narrative.
It's not easy, and it takes commitment, but it's worth it.
I tell myself...
The softer stomach.
The smaller breasts.
The extra bit of flabby skin.
These aren't flaws.
They're my badges of honor.
Etched into me like a map of where I've been.
Of what I've survived.

These are the marks of motherhood.
Of resilience.
Of strength.
Of love.
This body.
It tells the story of everything I've overcome.
And that story…
Is one worth celebrating.

CHAPTER 22

War With My Reflection

"The mirror is just glass. The war is behind your eyes."
— *Beau Taplin*

My kids are now six and eight.
The postpartum chapter is long behind me.
So, what's different now?
Do I love my body unconditionally?
Do I see my true reflection when I look in the mirror?
Am I fully healed?
Do I have a perfectly healthy relationship with exercise?
The truth?
The answers aren't black and white.
Healing isn't linear.
Self-acceptance doesn't come with a finish line.
Some days, I feel strong, grounded, and grateful.
Other days, the old habits still murmur.
The insecurities still creep in.
It's not a yes or no.
It's a journey.
One I continue to walk, step by step.

So much has changed. I've grown in ways I never imagined. I've gained wisdom, self-awareness, and strength.

But my reflection?

It still haunts me sometimes.

Shaped by years of self-criticism and impossible standards, I see wider hips and a stomach that doesn't lie flat.

And deep down, I know, I'm the only one picking myself apart. The flaws I obsess over, most people don't even notice them.

I don't look in the mirror and think… Holy shit, I am gorgeous!

Not every time, anyway.

But then come the magic days.

The ones where I feel radiant.

Strong.

Alive.

Unstoppable.

And those moments?

They matter.

They may not show up every day, but when they do, I hold onto them like gold.

I don't hate my reflection. It's not a monster staring back. But I do have to work at what I see.

I have to challenge the thoughts that try to tear me down. I have to choose, again and again to see beauty in my imperfections.

It's a daily battle.

Me and the mirror.

Some days, I win with ease.

Other days, it takes everything I've got.

I want to see myself as beautiful.

I deserve to.

So, I show up for that fight.

With compassion.

With gratitude.

With the kind of love I'm still learning to offer myself.

Sometimes, I wish I could step outside of myself, just for a day. To see my body through the eyes of someone who loves me unconditionally. Someone who isn't scanning for flaws, just seeing me.

My perception has shifted. I've worked hard to rewrite the narrative and honor what my body has carried.

But it's not perfect.

And some days, I still wonder…

What do they see that I can't?

So… am I healed?

No.

And in reality, I don't think I ever will be.

Not fully.

This disorder is lifelong. Not just the eating disorder, but the body dysmorphia, too.

But here's the difference.

I have the upper hand now.

Most days, I'm in control.

Most days, I win.

And for that, I am proud.

It took two decades, but I finally flipped the narrative.

When I look in the mirror and feel the urge to criticize my stomach, I pause. I shift.

Instead of zeroing in on what I was taught to hate, I remind myself:

There are organs working hard beneath the surface.

A body that has never stopped showing up for me.

A body that brought life into this world.

A body that carries me, every single day.

And for that, I am deeply grateful.

When I notice the wrinkles around my eyes, I try not to see fading youth. I see lifelines. Smile lines. Evidence that I've laughed, cried, loved, and lived deeply. They tell the story of a life that has mattered.

This shift didn't happen overnight.

It took years of fighting my own mind.

Years of choosing to focus on what's good.

What's real.

What's worthy.

Now, instead of obsessing over what I'd change, I practice gratitude.

Because my body is not the enemy.

It's my home.

Every single day, I'm learning how to honor it.

Not hate it.

What about my relationship with exercise?

Is it healthy?

Yes… and no.

I'm still working on it.

Exercise has always been therapeutic for me. It's fun. It challenges me. It makes me feel strong, energized, and confident. When I move, it's for joy, not punishment. That's something I've fought hard to reclaim.

But the issue isn't quality.

It's quantity.

That's where the struggle still remains.

What happens when I don't move?

When I miss a day?

When I don't hit my goal?

That's the part I'm still healing.

Because how I feel about my body when I do exercise?

That's healthy.

Empowering, even.

But how I feel when I don't?

That's the battle.

For years, I followed a strict, non-negotiable routine. Every day, whether sick, exhausted, or drained, movement came first.

Rest didn't exist.

I called it discipline.

But truthfully, it was fear.

Fear of losing progress.

Fear of gaining weight.

Fear of not being enough.

I held myself to impossible standards. Missing a workout felt like failure. Even my mantra, move for joy, not punishment… started to blur at times. It wasn't until these past few years that I finally started taking rest days.

And that shift didn't come easy. It took time, intention, and endless self-talk to remind myself that rest isn't weakness. Rest is part of the work.

I'm still learning balance.

Still unlearning old rules.

But I'm making progress, and that's what matters.

For years, I couldn't enjoy vacations until I'd exercised. Those carefree, relaxing days, sitting on the beach with the family, soaking in the sun, feet in the water, they happened. But only after I had my workout.

But now?

Now I take rest days.

And most of the time, I'm okay with them.

I don't spiral.

I don't feel gross.

I don't rip myself apart with guilt.

A few years ago, if you had asked me to skip a workout, I would've laughed and said, hell no. But I get it now, movement should never come from fear. And rest doesn't mean failure. It means rebuilding.

Still, I'm not all the way there yet.

Exercise still consumes a large portion of my day.

Twice a day, occasionally three times. Monday through Friday.

There are only twenty-four hours in a day, and if we're asleep for eight, that leaves sixteen waking hours.

And for me, a significant chunk of that time still goes to movement.

When I don't exercise, I feel it.

My pants feel tighter.

My reflection becomes distorted.

I feel like I fell short.

It doesn't ruin my day, not anymore.

But the thoughts still come.

The feelings of self-hate.

The lingering belief that if I didn't move, I didn't measure up.

I know this isn't healthy.

I know these are old beliefs.

Outdated rules I don't want to live by.

But old habits don't vanish overnight.

They cling.

They resurface.

And this is still my struggle.

A lot of my self-love is still tied to the amount of exercise I get. On the days I hit my goals, I feel strong, beautiful, and worthy. But if I don't, everything's different.

Suddenly, I see pudgy arms.

Thick thighs.

A swollen stomach.

A face I barely recognize.

It's as if overnight, my body changed.

Even though I know it didn't.

Then, what happens next…

Slight restriction creeps in.

I skip the pizza.

Settle for the salad.

The sprinkle of restraint turns into a scoop.

It's never extreme enough to make me physically unwell.

Though mentally, it's damaging.

My body doesn't change overnight.

But my mind does.

That's where the real battle lies.

I've struggled with this since my eating disorder began. My body image is still tied directly to how much I move.

But I am getting better.

I judge myself less.

I take more rest days.

I remind myself that doing less doesn't mean I've failed.

ED still slithers into my thoughts at times.

Still pushes.

Still lingers.

But here's what matters most...

I'm alive.

I'm here.

And I'm doing the work.

I've finally separated my self-worth from what others think of me.

Something that used to control me entirely.

And now, it doesn't.

That's progress.

That's power.

And I'm proud of how far I've come.

So where do I still struggle?

Separating my worth from exercise.

That's the one divide I haven't fully bridged yet.

But I know I will.

Maybe not today.

Maybe not tomorrow.

But someday.

Because if there's one thing I've learned about myself...

I don't stop fighting.

The hardest times for me are always the lead-up weeks to a big event. A wedding. A birthday. Any social gathering where I know I'll be surrounded by people.

Don't get me wrong, I love social functions. I'm an extrovert through and through. Crowds don't faze me. But you know what does? The fear of what people will think if I don't look "in shape" enough.

In my head, I imagine the hushed tones.

"Oh wow, have you seen Jody tonight? Looks like she put on some weight."

I know it's irrational.

I know people are focused on the celebration. On the bride, the happy couple, or the birthday party, exactly as they should be. Not on my body.

But that doesn't stop the thoughts from creeping in. Then once they do, the behaviors follow.

Even though I can logically recognize the distortion, I still fall into the patterns of restriction, over-exercising, and compulsions that tighten their grip the closer the date gets. So, the only way I don't make up an excuse to stay home is by doubling down.

It becomes a deal I make with myself. If I just eat less and move more, I'll earn my place in the room.

That's the lie I still wrestle with.

The fear of wearing a form-fitting dress can be paralyzing. The anxiety builds. I get angry, frustrated, hungry, and utterly exhausted.

During those weeks… I become someone else entirely.

Then there's the dress dilemma.

I always buy the perfect one. The dream dress. The one that hugs me in all the right places. The one I imagine myself wearing when walking into the room. Feeling confident, glowing, and proud.

But I also buy safety dresses.

Floral.

Patterned.

A size up.

Flowy.

Forgiving.

Just in case I feel too fat the day of the event. Because canceling last minute has happened before.

The safety dress is my backup plan. My lifeline. It's how I stay in the game when my mind is screaming at me to bow out.

And the number of times I've worn the safety dress instead of the dream dress… Far too many.

There's one dress I always dreamed of wearing. A fitted, silk, yellow dress. Like the one from *How to Lose a Guy in 10 Days*.

First of all, Hudson and McConaughey… I mean, come on. That movie is adorable, easily one of my all-time favorites. And that scene, when she steps out of her apartment in that stunning, silky, perfectly draped yellow dress. Breathtaking.

I wanted my yellow dress moment. I craved it.

Yellow is my favorite color. It symbolizes light, joy, warmth. Everything I want to embody.

Throughout the years, I've bought and returned at least twenty yellow dresses.

Not because they didn't fit.

Not because I didn't love them.

But because I didn't love me in them.

Until this past summer.

I found the one.

Beautiful, silk.

Stunning.

My dream dress.

I bought it in two sizes, just in case. And yes, I picked up two more safety dresses, in case I backed out.

But I told myself… Not this time. You're not going to chicken out. You're going to wear the yellow dress. This is your moment.

But of course, the behaviors kicked in.

I over-exercised. I became hyper-focused on food. What I ate, how much I ate, when I ate.

I was irritable, and difficult to be around.

I reassured myself… As soon as the wedding is over, you'll go back to normal.

And I did.

I always do.

My behaviors return to inactive, only a sprinkle.

But is that something to be proud of?

Yes, I know how to stop myself from spiraling too far. Yes, I have the tools, awareness, and control.

But I shouldn't have to white-knuckle my way to an event. I shouldn't have to morph into someone else just to wear a dress. I shouldn't turn into a monster throughout the process.

Truthfully, "Monster" feels like the right word.

Because in those lead-up weeks, I'm not me.

I'm anxious.

I'm short-tempered.

I'm a loose cannon, quick to snap, impossible to soothe, hard to love.

The worst part?

It's not even about the dress or the body image anymore.

Everything starts to unravel.

I begin to doubt everything about myself.

My body, my worth, my work, my relationships.

Suddenly, I'm not a good mom.

Not a good wife.

Not a good instructor.

Not enough.

Anywhere.

It's like the fear seeps into every crack and contaminates it all. The self-doubt becomes all-consuming. It swallows everything. It's an awful, heavy feeling.

Then, once the event is over, it's gone.

Just like that.

The darkness lifts.

The self-doubt fades.

It disappears.

So… why can't I stop this lead-up behavior?

Why do I still fall into the cycle?

I know it's body dysmorphia and ED at its loudest.

I know it's unhealthy.

This isn't something I have advice for.

Because I haven't figured it out yet.

Not yet.

Maybe one day, I won't feel the need to buy twenty dresses. Maybe I won't put myself through two weeks of hell just to show up to a room full of people.

I'm hopeful, I have to be.

Because if there's one thing I know, it's that change is always possible. I've grown so much already.

While I don't have all the answers yet, I can tell you this...

Despite all the noise in my head. Despite changing in and out of dresses a hundred times before the wedding even started...

I wore the damn dress.

The yellow dress.

I finally had my yellow dress moment.

Not only did I wear it, I went downtown to a building that looked just like her apartment in the movie. And yes, I took a ton of pictures.

I had my *How to Lose a Guy in 10 Days* moment.

And I felt beautiful.

The second I stepped into that Uber, there was no turning back.

So, I wore it like a boss.

And I was proud.

So damn proud.

Maybe I couldn't stop the lead-up behaviors this time.

But wearing that dress?

That was a battle won.

A bold step toward self-love.

A middle finger to the voice that told me I wasn't good enough.

For one night, I squashed ED's voice down to merely a faint hiss.

I felt free.

It was incredible.

I know my eating disorder will never fully disappear.

But I've found so many ways to cope.

I'm managing.

I'm awakening.

I'm learning to give myself more grace, especially when it comes to exercise. My body certainly appreciates the moments of relaxation and rest.

The growth I've made in how I see myself is nothing short of a quiet revolution. I've spent years rewiring the narrative, gently replacing the cruel thoughts that used to creep in with kinder words.

Words of love.

Of encouragement.

Of truth.

Slowly, I began to see my body for more than its reflection.

I started to appreciate it, not for how it looked, but for how it carried me through this life.

I didn't just wear the yellow dress…

I claimed it.

Over the past two years at social events, I've whipped off a pair of body-shaping Spanx in the middle of the evening, tossed them into a bathroom garbage can, and ran barefoot onto the dance floor.

For the first time, I could breathe.

I didn't shame myself for the big wedding meal.

I didn't punish myself for a stomach that curved instead of flattened.

I ditched the corset, and in doing so, I found freedom.

I stopped saying no to events just because my body didn't feel "ready."

Now, I show up.

That's the difference.

That's the breakthrough.

I show up more fully, freer, and unapologetically me.

Something I couldn't do not so long ago.

I'm human.

But I'm putting in the work.

And the fact that my days aren't completely consumed by my distorted perception of my body anymore. That I can still live, laugh, and show up for my life, even on the days I hate my reflection?

That makes me feel like I'm winning.

A quiet victory.

I've learned how to fight back.

To stop my dysmorphia from hijacking my entire day.

I can still smile. Still bring joy into a room. I can still run around and play with my children, even when my mind whispers that my thighs are clapping, or my stomach is bouncing with every step.

This is something I live with.
Something I'll probably battle forever.
And that's okay.
There are good days.
And there are hard ones.
But most of the time, I have the upper hand.
I'm still learning how to love myself unconditionally.
Still learning how to see myself the way others do.

And every year?
It gets a little easier.

With every new year, I feel a little less lost…
And a little more found.

CHAPTER 23

Resurrecting the Darkness

"Trauma is not the story of something that happened back then. It's the current imprint of that pain on your body, mind, and heart."

— *Bessel van der Kolk*

Writing this book demanded a kind of soul-searching I wasn't sure I was ready for.

I knew certain chapters would be heavy. But nothing could have prepared me for the weight of returning to that basement bathroom.

This wasn't just memory.

It was resurrection.

I wasn't simply recalling what happened.

I was inside it.

Reliving every breath, every tremble, every silence that screamed.

Every word clenched my chest, slicing through old wounds, tearing open scars I'd spent years trying to seal.

There was no more pushing it down.

Pandora's box had been flung open, and with it came a tidal wave of pain. Crushing, consuming, and relentless pain.

I was drowning in the very memories I had spent a lifetime trying to bury.

I had no choice but to sit in the discomfort.

To let the pain emerge, break the surface, and be released.

It was like staring into a mirror of the past, watching my younger self crumble under the weight of something she never asked for, never deserved.

The shame.

The humiliation.

The powerlessness.

It came back in full force, raw and unfiltered, flooding every corner of my being.

But as excruciating as it was, I kept going.

I owed it to her.

To the girl I used to be.

The girl broken from this experience.

So, I kept writing.

Letting the truth spill onto the page, one painful sentence at a time.

I unearthed it.

Dragged it into the light.

Forced myself to face what I had buried for so long.

With every word, my senses sharpened.

It was like being hurled back in time, ripped from the present through a warped orbit, and dropped, against my will, right back in that basement.

I saw every inch of the room.

The narrow staircase creaked beneath my weight, each groan a warning I never listened to.

The air was thick and unmoving.

Dampness clung to my skin like a second suffocating layer.

Smoke curled like transparent vines, twisting through the room.

Blurring edges, warping sound.

Breathing became a struggle.

Seeing, a blur.

Running?

Impossible.

I felt everything.

The cold bite of the metal futon frame.

The sharp springs of a broken mattress against my back.

My body. Frozen, trapped, helpless.

And then... his look.

One glance.

That was all it took.

His eyes seized control.

Made me feel small.

Powerless.

That look, silent and commanding, left no room for resistance.

It stripped me of the invincibility I once believed I had.

My heart pounded against my ribs, each frantic beat echoing a scream for help that never came.

I was back there.

I was her again.

And in that moment...

It felt like I was being raped all over again.

Every good book breathes through its imagery. And the only way I could write those chapters was to step inside them.

To fully relive them.

But in doing so, I unearthed something I had buried so deeply, I almost forgot it was there.

I've been living with post-traumatic stress disorder for over twenty years.

For two decades, I carried the weight unknowingly. Never realizing how deeply it had shaped me. How it seeped into the foundation of who I am.

With every word I exposed, I finally faced the beast.

Trauma warps the mind. It stunts growth. It cages you in survival. For years, I lived in a loop of silence and suppression, gripping my pain like a lifeline.

Guilt and shame kept me small.

Kept me voiceless.

Kept me hidden.

The day I finally wrote those chapters, Kris and I were at the cabin our family had been staying at that summer. Our kids stayed back in the city with Grandma so I could focus on my writing.

I woke to the sharp crackle of thunder, so loud it shook the walls and stirred something inside me.

I hadn't yet found the courage to write about my assault.

I couldn't even talk about it. I'd been circling it for weeks. Avoiding it. Afraid to put it into words. I knew how much it would hurt.

I had buried it so deeply, pressed it down so far, it had started to feel like a dream. A dark, distant blur I could pretend hadn't happened.

So why go back?

Why burst the bubble?

That morning, wrapped in gray skies and storm light, felt like the time had come.

The cabin was still cloaked in shadows. Rain tapped steadily against the windows like a clock ticking down.

My husband lay beside me, asleep, unaware of the battle I was about to face.

I stared at the ceiling.

Something whispered inside of me... Now.

Do it now.

So, I did.

At first, the words came slow. Jagged, heavy, reluctant. But as the storm outside collided with the trees, something in me broke open. And just like that, the flood came.

Eventually, I moved to the window seat in the living room, curled into the chair overlooking the lake.

Rain dissolved into the water below, like it had always belonged there. Lightning split the sky, illuminating the storm's violent beauty.

The trees moved like dancers, chaotically graceful and wild. Thunder rolled, yet inside the cabin, it was quiet enough to hear my racing heartbeat.

Time suspended itself. The universe holding still.

I reached for my phone, exhaled slowly, and started speaking.

Not typing, speaking.

The words poured out in that vulnerable space between sleep and waking.

If I had been fully present, I might have stopped myself. But in that half-dream state, I surrendered.

I didn't have the strength to see the words on a screen.

But I could say them.

I could hear them.

I could finally let them go.

My body went numb.

The words moved through me like shadows, there but untouchable.

I felt sadness.

Rage.

Exposed.

And then, the memory surged.

Not trickled.

Not crept.

Surged.

It clawed to the surface.

It flooded my senses.

I suddenly remembered everything.

His touch was not just a violation, but a brand.

Invisible to the world.

Impossible to wash away.

I remembered the fear.

The kind that wraps around your throat and convinces you no one is coming.

That there is no way out.

My heart pounded louder than the thunder outside.

And still, I kept going.

The memory had lived buried for too long.

And now, it refused to be silenced.

It wanted to be seen.

To be told.

Eventually, I finished the chapters.

The words had poured out, leaving behind a hollow ache.

I sat by the window as the storm raged on. Rain hammered the glass. Wind howled through the trees and the crackle rolled above like an aftershock of all I had just released.

I had written it.

I had spoken it.

I had survived it.

Again.

Kris woke up and found me sitting by the window. His voice was soft, familiar, asking if I wanted coffee, what I felt like for breakfast.

I didn't answer.

I couldn't.

Just minutes earlier, I had been speaking non-stop, pouring two decades of silence into my phone.

Now that it was out, now that the chapters were written, I felt hollow.

Mute.

The words had vanished.

I couldn't shake it.

I was still there, back in that basement.

The memory clung to me. Thick, suffocating, inescapable.

My body felt tainted, like something had been etched into it that couldn't be scrubbed away. Some stains live deeper than the surface.

Outside, the storm began to ease.

For a moment, the world paused.

It was still, hushed, as if the sky was afraid to exhale.

Thunder lingered in the distance, low and threatening, like a memory that refuses to die. Raindrops pierced the lake in rhythmic pulses, each one swallowed by the churning surface below.

The water looked cold, dark, unforgiving.

Just like me.

I knew what I had to do.

I needed to jump in.

To cleanse.

To strip away the weight.

To feel something other than the heaviness.

Without a word, I sprang up from the chair, rushed past Kris, and headed for the closet.

He followed, confused, asking questions I couldn't hear.

I didn't look at him.

I couldn't.

I grabbed my black one-piece, the swimsuit I never wear.

It's not me.

Not bright, not playful, not joyful.

But I wasn't any of those that morning.

I was rage.

I was grief.

I was pain in human form.

I pulled it on with shaking hands, my chest tight with a thousand unsaid words.

Then I stepped outside, barefoot, storm-soaked, and numb.

The air was sharp, bitter against my skin, like tiny needles piercing every inch of exposed flesh.

The dock stretched out before me like a dare, long, narrow, endless.

Each step felt like dragging anchors behind me.

My breath quickened.

My body locked up; my muscles coiled tight like wire.

At the edge, I stopped.

Froze.

Raised my arms and placed my hands on my head.

Fingers twisted in my hair.

Tight, desperate.

I clenched so hard my scalp burned.

I couldn't let go.

Panic crept in fast, ruthless, insistent.

It clawed at my chest.

My lungs begged for air.

My heart pounded like a war drum inside a hollow cave.

I was hyperventilating.

Then, in an instant, I was back there.

In the memory.

In his arms.

Trapped.

Reliving it.

Drowning in it.

I knew, if I didn't move, it would swallow me whole.

So, I jumped.

The water struck like a blade.

Colder than I imagined. Sharp, brutal, shocking. It sliced through me, stole my breath, and clamped down on my chest like a vice. The waves thrashed. Wild, untamed, indifferent.

But I didn't care.

Because the second I hit the water, something shifted.

For the first time in decades, I felt something loosen.

Just a flicker, a tremor, but it was there.

The darkness that had clung to me began to unravel.

With every stroke, every kick, I felt it fall away...

His touch.

His grip.

His power.

His presence.

And for the first time...

My body.

My body started to feel like mine again.

Then the tears came. These weren't quiet tears. Deep, guttural sobs. Sobs that shook through my ribs and spilled out into the freezing lake.

The sky stayed grey. The wind still howled. The waves still pulled.

But I didn't feel them.

All I felt was release.

All I felt was something dangerously close to freedom.

For the first time in over twenty years, I was letting go of his hold on me.

And in that moment, surrounded by water, soaked in pain, and finally staring it in the face…

I wasn't drowning.

I was beginning to rise.

Kris followed me down to the lake, his presence steady, unwavering. He stopped at the edge of the dock, watching. Ready to jump in if I needed him.

He didn't jump, he knew. He understood I needed this moment to myself.

I needed to cry.

Truly cry.

Alone.

Surrounded solely by the echoes of my thoughts and the weight of my feelings. Because I never had before.

The night he raped me, I shut down.

My body went numb.

My mind detached.

I became a hollow shell, drifting through the aftermath with no emotion, no voice, no fire.

I never grieved.

I never got angry.

I never let myself feel it.

Whenever something triggered the memory like an image, a smell, or a word, I'd tense up. Curl inward. Wrap my arms around myself like protection. And then, I'd do what I always did.

Bury it.

Deeper.

Further.

Out of sight.

Out of reach.

But not today.

Today, I didn't shove it down.
I didn't suppress it.
I didn't tuck it away in the cold, dark place where it had lived for so long.
Today, I let it climb back up.
I let the sadness flood in.
The rage burn through me.
The grief press hard against my chest.
And in feeling it, truly feeling it, I began to loosen its grip.
This memory no longer held me hostage.
It was no longer buried.
I was slowly taking my power back.

As I swam through the rain, sobbing into the storm, something deeper surfaced… Rage.
A fire I'd never let burn suddenly ignited, hot, wild, and unrelenting.
My fists clenched.
My throat tensed.
And before I could stop it, the words tore from my mouth.
"I'm so mad! I'M SO MAD!"
I screamed into the sky, my voice swallowed by wind and rain, but I didn't care.
I needed it out.
I needed the world to hear it.
Even if the world didn't answer.
"I'M MAD! I AM FUCKING MAD!"
The fury poured out, raw and real.
I wasn't just screaming for me.
I was screaming for the girl who lost her power.
For the years I stayed silent.
For the weight I carried, alone.
I had been trapped in a maze of pain for so long, circling and searching, never finding a way out.
But now… I saw it.

A light.

Faint.

Distant.

But real.

Kris jumped in. He didn't speak. Didn't reach for me. He just swam beside me, present, steady, solid. A silent anchor in the storm.

Eventually, I returned to the dock, body trembling and heavy, yet somehow lighter than it had been in years.

I climbed out, sank onto the wooden boards, knees pulled to my chest, arms wrapped tight around my legs.

Trying to hold together what was left of me.

Kris sat beside me.

Still quiet.

Still there.

Together, we stared out at the lake.

The storm began to stir again. Clouds curling back into place, reclaiming the sky.

It felt like Mother Nature had opened a brief window of release for me.

I wish this never happened.

Not to me.

Not to anyone.

If I could go back, I would rewrite the story before it ever had the chance to unfold.

I'd silence the curiosity that pulled me toward the new guy with the crush.

I'd stay home.

I'd never step foot in that basement.

I'd never let myself become his prey.

But I can't change the past.

No matter how much I wish I could erase it, undo it, rewrite it, I can't.

What I can do is choose to move forward.

It doesn't matter how fast I'm going, how many steps it takes, or how slow the progress feels. What matters is that I'm no longer standing still, no longer frozen in the same wickedness, circling the same pain.

I'm moving.

And I'm moving toward healing.

I had no idea how much power that night still held over me.

How deeply it shaped my choices, my identity, my view of the world.

Not until I wrote this book.

But now I see it clearly.

This memory didn't just live in the past.

It ruled me in the present.

It kept me small.

It kept me from becoming the woman I was always meant to be.

And I refuse to let it win anymore.

Trauma doesn't just sit quietly inside you.

It festers.

It burrows deep.

It weaves itself into your thoughts, your body, and your voice.

It seeps into your bones like smoke. Subtle, toxic, unshakable.

They say buried pain resurfaces in other ways.

That trauma doesn't disappear, it transforms.

Transforming into anxiety.

Into illness.

Into shame that lives in the cells of your body.

And now… I believe it.

Because when I finally pulled that darkness to the surface, dragged it from the shadows and into the light, I felt it.

Not just emotionally, but physically.

I didn't just feel lighter, I felt healthier.

It was as if every cell in my body had been gripping this secret.

Then once I spoke it out loud, they let go.

The connection between mind and body is deeper than I ever realized.

They're not separate.

They rise together.

Or they crumble together.

For years... mine had been crumbling.

Now, finally, I'm letting myself rebuild.

For the first time in a long, long time, I'm no longer just surviving, I'm slowly healing.

For real.

And this time... I mean it.

Fast forward a few months later.

My PTSD had completely taken over my life.

If you've ever walked through trauma, you're probably thinking "No shit," you saw this coming, even when I didn't.

I truly believed I had done the hard part. I had faced it, spoken it, dragged it from the shadows, and tried to cleanse it from my body.

I thought that was healing.

I thought naming the pain meant I had power over it.

But trauma doesn't work like that.

It doesn't follow a straight line. It doesn't surrender just because you finally found the courage to speak.

The moment I pulled it into the light, I unknowingly cracked open a floodgate I wasn't ready for.

The more I remembered, the more I unraveled.

I wasn't just triggered.

I was spiraling.

I felt unanchored like I was floating above my own life, watching the days pass like scenes from someone else's story.

Disconnected.

Numb.

A shell moving through the motions of motherhood, work, and everyday responsibilities, pretending I was fine.

Telling myself I had to be fine.

I wasn't.

Not even close.

Deep down, a quiet voice I kept trying to silence whispered the truth I didn't want to face...

This storm is just beginning.

I wasn't okay.

And for the first time, I couldn't pretend anymore.

So, I started opening up, slowly and cautiously, to a few close friends and family.

I thought using my voice was the answer. That saying it out loud would finally set me free.

Isn't that how healing works?

But no matter how many conversations I had, no matter how honest or vulnerable I was, the pain didn't lift. The weight didn't disappear.

If anything, it pressed down harder.

I thought I was breaking through.

What I didn't realize was that I was standing at the edge of a cliff, and I was about to fall.

Hard.

Before I could recover, I had to shatter.

And this time, there was no escape.

No distractions.

No pretending.

Just the raw, unfiltered truth.

I had to break completely before I could begin to rebuild.

Panic attacks started creeping in.

First weekly.

Then daily.

At first, I convinced myself it was something physical. An allergy, a reaction, maybe something I ate. My body felt off, like it was rejecting something. But I couldn't see it clearly.

Not until the day I completely broke down at work.

That was the moment I finally woke up to what was actually happening. I had been ignoring my mind, pushing aside my emotions, pretending I was fine.

In reality, every part of me had been screaming for help. And eventually, my body listened. It collapsed under the weight of everything I had refused to deal with.

I was driving to lead a spin class when something inside me snapped.

Out of nowhere, the tears came. Violent, unstoppable sobs that ripped through me like a tidal wave. Not the kind you can blink away or quietly swallow down. These were full-body, soul-level sobs, each one pulling me deeper into a collapse I could no longer outrun.

I had become a confetti cannon. Stuffed with racing thoughts, sadness, fear, and fury. Bursting apart without warning. One snap. One explosion. Pieces of me scattered everywhere.

And just like confetti, once released, I couldn't control where they landed. I couldn't gather them back.

Neither could I gather myself.

My body was screaming for someone, anyone, to hear the silent cries I'd been choking back for years. To tell me what healing actually looked like.

I took a few deep breaths, wiped my face, and stepped out of my vehicle.

My hands still shook.

My head hung low.

I avoided eye contact like it might shatter me completely.

I was on a mission to hold myself together, to shove all the shattered pieces back into the cannon and pretend nothing had happened.

Just keep moving, I told myself.

Power through.

But then, Sharon saw me.

She looked past the mask.

Past the forced breath.

Past the fake calm.

She saw it all... the pain in my eyes, fear in my posture, and asked one simple question:

"Are you okay?"

And just like that, I broke.

My legs buckled, and I collapsed to the floor.
I couldn't fake it anymore.
This wasn't just a hard moment.
This was the moment.
My first true meltdown.
The one I couldn't bury beneath to-do lists and smiles.
I wasn't the strong, powerful woman I had spent years becoming.
I was a broken little girl, completely undone.
And Sharon... she became my lifeline.
Without hesitation, she stepped in.
No questions.
No judgment.
She taught my class for me.
She carried the weight I didn't even know I was still holding.
It was serendipity that she was there.
Or maybe something greater.
Because somehow, she understood.
Trauma knows trauma.
She didn't toss me a life raft.
She jumped in with me.
She saved me in that moment and I'm forever grateful the universe sent her to me, right then, on that very day.

It took a while before I could even think about driving home. I sat behind the wheel, trembling, breath shallow, eyes swollen, holding onto the steering wheel like it was the only thing tethering me to the earth.
When I finally walked through my front door, I didn't even take off my shoes.
I sat at the kitchen table and stared into nothing.
What's happening to me?
Why can't I be strong?
Why do I feel so broken?
The questions spun in my head like a cruel carousel.

I had convinced myself I was already healed.

That dragging my trauma into the light meant it had lost its power.

That speaking it meant I was free.

But now?

It was all-consuming.

I wasn't just struggling.

I was falling apart.

And so, with shaking hands and a voice I barely recognized, I picked up my phone and made the call.

I booked an intake appointment for sexual assault therapy.

For the first time, I admitted the truth I had been avoiding for years…

I wasn't okay.

And I didn't know how to be.

I had exposed my past, but I had no idea what to do with it.

It was here, it was real, and it was staring me in the face, refusing to be buried again.

That day, I finally stopped pretending.

I hit pause.

I took time off work and turned inward.

I didn't leave my house.

It was the only place that felt safe.

The only place I could start facing myself.

And when the intake appointment came, I will never forget it.

The voice on the other end of the line was calm and kind.

Steady.

Warm.

They carried a tone that told me they had walked this road before with others, maybe even themselves, and knew how to hold space without making it feel heavy.

They didn't treat me like I was fragile.

They treated me like I was worthy of healing.

They explained that what I was experiencing was delayed trauma. That my brain had locked it away for years to help me survive. But now that I had cracked it open, it was demanding to be felt.

They didn't sugarcoat it.

They told me healing would be complex.

Not linear.

Not predictable.

Not easy.

There was no checklist.

No magic solution.

No fast-forward button.

Oh, how I wished there was.

But in that moment, I finally understood…

My healing hadn't ended when I found my voice.

It had only just begun.

The next few months of my life weren't marked by peace or clarity. They were consumed by uncontrollable rage and unbearable sadness.

I was grieving.

Angry.

Lost.

And for the first time, I wasn't hiding it.

I still smiled in front of my children. I still showed up. But underneath it all, I was depressed.

Hollow.

Existing, but not living.

My heart kept beating.

My body kept moving.

I was a vessel of life.

But inside, I was empty.

Still, I did everything "right."

I committed to weekly therapy, showing up even on the days I wanted to disappear.

On the days panic crept in, slow and suffocating, when the weight of my trauma felt unbearable, I reached for help.

I called the sexual assault crisis line.

I still remember the first time I dialed. A man answered. Instantly, my body tensed. I froze. The instinct to hang up was immediate, overwhelming. But somewhere deep inside, a quiet voice whispered:

"Stay."

So, I stayed.

I took a breath.

I opened up.

I let him in and I'm so glad I did.

Because as much as my trauma had conditioned me to fear men in my most vulnerable moments, that call reminded me of something important…

Sexual assault doesn't discriminate.

It happens to women.

To men.

To trans and nonbinary people.

To intersex and gender-diverse individuals.

To Two-Spirit people.

To LGBTQIA2S+ communities across all identities.

It happens to those we love.

To those we least expect.

The more I shared my story, the more I realized how many survivors are silently walking among us.

Terrified, ashamed, and invisible.

Some were friends.

Some were family.

People I had laughed with.

Worked beside.

Loved deeply.

And yet, they too had buried their truth.

They carried the same shame.

The same fear.

The same invisible wounds.

It broke my heart.

Through therapy, I began to understand trauma on a deeper level.

I learned about the Internal Family System: the idea that trauma fractures us, splitting us into different parts.

Each one carrying a piece of our pain.

Each one fighting to be heard.

And then, one day, I realized something that changed everything…

It wasn't thirty-eight-year-old Jody, the woman with wisdom, life experience, and hard-earned coping skills, who had been steering the ship.

It was fifteen-year-old me.

The teenage girl frozen in time.

Stuck in fear.

Trapped in pain.

Unable to move forward.

She had been leading my life all along.

Reacting from a place of survival.

Making decisions from a place of deep, unresolved hurt.

And I hadn't even noticed.

I had silenced her.

Ignored her.

Shoved her into the farthest corners of my mind, pretending I had outgrown her.

But she was still there, screaming to be seen.

Screaming for me…to listen.

So, I did.

I turned inward.

I found her.

This time, I didn't push her away.

I didn't try to fix her.

I didn't shame her.

I just sat with her.

She wasn't the enemy.

She was the wounded child who had protected me the only way she knew how.

I gave her a voice.

I let her speak.

And when she did, she hurt loud.

No filters.

No apologies.

She had lived in denial for years, muted, dismissed, and unseen.

Now, she was feeling everything.

Raw.

Unfiltered.

Unforgiving.

The more I listened, the more I began to understand her. The more space I gave her, the more I saw a flicker of light at the end of the tunnel.

It's a long tunnel.

Dark.

Winding.

Lined with the shadows of everything I've spent a lifetime running from.

But now I know, on the other side, the woman I'm meant to be is waiting.

She has always been waiting.

Instead of drowning in confusion, questioning why I couldn't just "get better," instead of blaming my panic, my spirals, my rage on weakness…

I let her speak.

I let her feel.

I let her grieve for the years she lost, for the suffering she carried, for the innocence stolen far too soon.

And for the first time, both of us, her and I, are healing.

Together.

Not by erasing the past.

But by honoring it.

Not by becoming someone new.

But by finally becoming whole.

There were days when she, fifteen-year-old me, felt curious.
Days when the pull crept in.
The urge to find him.
To look.
To know.
And one evening, I let that curiosity win.
I went down the rabbit hole.
Click after click, I searched.
Through the endless abyss of the internet, I dug until I found him.
His face.
His life.
Fragments of who he had become, scattered across social media for the world to see.
I stayed up late that night, staring at his pictures.
And the second I saw him, fear gripped me.
Tight.
Overpowering.
It was like I was fifteen again. Powerless, afraid, frozen in time.
But I didn't look away.
The longer I stared into his eyes, the more something inside me began to shift.
For so long, he had been magnified in my mind.
This all-powerful, untouchable force.
The monster in the shadows.
The nightmare I never escaped.
But now?
Now I see him for what he truly is.
Not a higher power, not an all being.
Not invincible.
Just a man.
A man who no longer deserved the control he once had over me.
Looking at him was like being stung by a bee. Sharp, sudden, and jarring. I flinched. I panicked. But then, like a sting, the pain

347

dulled. The fear began to fade. And in its place, something else started to ascend.

Anger.

Hate.

Power.

Because I was no longer the terrified girl in the basement.

I was a woman reclaiming her voice.

A woman taking her control back.

Still, even with that fire, the pain remained. And sometimes, the pain was so suffocating, so all-consuming, I started to wonder…

Would it be easier if I just wasn't here?

Not in a way that had a plan. Not suicidal in the traditional sense. But I imagined it.

Driving over the train tracks… What if, out of nowhere, a train came crashing into me?

Fast enough to catch me off guard. Fast enough to end the pain before I even knew what hit me.

It wasn't about dying.

It was about disappearing.

About vanishing into nothingness.

Because nothingness sounded easier than this.

Even with the therapy…

Even with the time off work…

Even with the progress…

Just getting out of bed each morning felt like a battle.

On the days I was home alone, I often ended up on the floor.

There's something about depression. Something about feeling this broken that makes the floor feel familiar.

Safe, almost.

When I hit another rock bottom, it only made sense to sink to the lowest place in the room.

So, I lay there.

Helpless.

Motionless.

Listening to the echo of my own heartbeat, pulsing through my body like a cruel reminder that I was still here. Even when part of me wished I wasn't.

But those moments never lasted long. Because my children need their mommy. And that, more than anything, was always the push I needed.

To get up.

To keep going.

To claw my way out of the darkness, no matter how impossible it felt.

When teenage Jody wasn't drowning in depression, she was burning with rage. It surged through my veins like a wave crashing against a cliff.

Ferocious.

Violent.

Explosive.

Some days, the rage crept in slowly, like thunder rumbling in the distance.

Other times, it struck without warning... a tsunami of fury, powerful enough to destroy everything in its path.

When my kids were home and the rage began to rise, I'd clench my fists so tightly my nails would pierce my skin.

The sting grounded me. It gave the fire inside something to grip, something real.

But eventually...

I started losing it.

I couldn't hold it in anymore.

The rage had nowhere to go.

No safe place to land.

And soon, it began to spill out uncontrollably.

This wasn't one of my typical temper tantrums. The kind that builds quietly until it erupts into a flurry of punches against a pillow, ending in breathless exhaustion.

No.

This was something else entirely.

This was the Hulk, unleashed. A force I couldn't tame. A version of myself I didn't recognize.

I had kept it hidden for so long, especially around my kids. Locked it behind clenched fists and shallow breaths.

But then came that night.

The kids had gone for a sleepover at Grandma's. The moment the door clicked shut behind them, I felt it. I don't even know how to explain it, but the chaos I had caged burst free like a dam breaking loose.

Rage.

Confusion.

Fury.

Not just mine.

It was teenage Jody's rage finally unmuted after years of silence.

It was present-day me, furious that I couldn't rewrite the past.

And most of all, it was rage toward him.

The man who broke me.

Then Kris, my husband, the man who had done nothing wrong, asked me a simple question:

"What do you want for dinner?"

And that was it.

To the storm inside me, those words were gasoline on an open flame. I snapped. I screamed wildly and unhinged. The words flew out faster than I could catch them.

Sharp.

Unfair.

Misplaced.

I knew Kris wasn't the enemy. But I couldn't stop. I was cracking.

Overcome with guilt, I stormed to the bathroom, breath heaving. I slammed the door behind me. Hard. I looked in the mirror, searching for something, clarity, grounding, anything.

But all I saw was hate.

Shame.

Disgust.

A reflection I didn't recognize.

I slammed the door again.

And again.

And again.

My fists wailed against it like rage needed a place to land. The door was the only thing I could hurt that wouldn't hurt me back.

When I finally stopped, I saw the dent I'd left.

And I crumbled.

I sank to the floor, breathless, shaking, humiliated.

I'm a grown woman, I thought. And yet I felt like a little girl trapped in a body that was supposed to know better. Wearing a face I didn't recognize.

I decided to go for a hot bath, hoping it would relax me. Hoping I could drown the rage before it consumed me again.

But the rage followed me there.

I started with slow, deep breaths, trying to calm my body, trying to reclaim a sense of control. But the anger didn't settle. It simmered beneath the surface, boiling with every heartbeat.

Then, without warning, I snapped.

My fists slammed into the water, sending waves crashing against the sides of the tub.

It didn't hurt like punching the bathroom door; that thought alone gave me permission to let go even more.

I hit the water again.

Harder.

Faster.

Over and over.

Until it wasn't just splashing, it was flying.

A wave of rage burst from me.

Out of the tub.

Onto the floor.

Up the walls.

I had blacked out in my fury.

And when I finally opened my eyes...

I saw the aftermath. The floor was flooded. Water dripped from the walls like sweat after a brutal fight. I was shaking.

I jumped out, tossing towels on the floor in a frantic, half-hearted attempt at damage control.

My hands fumbled as I pulled on clothes, barely managing to zip up my hoodie, just as Kris appeared in the doorway. Concern etched every line of his face. He didn't need to ask. He saw me. Really saw me.

And he knew exactly what was happening.

I was ready to run.

I needed to scream.

I had to get out of the house before I destroyed anything else. Before I destroyed myself.

And without hesitation, my thoughtful, patient husband threw on a winter jacket, right over a pair of shorts and warm winter boots.

There was no time to change. No time to ask questions. No need for words.

I couldn't drive. I couldn't even think. All I knew was that I needed to get this rage out of me. And Kris? He was right there beside me. Ready to go.

I told Kris I needed to find an open field, somewhere in the middle of nowhere, where I could finally let it all out. I needed to explode in a place where no one could see me. Where no one could hear me. Where the only witnesses to my breakdown would be the earth beneath my feet and the sky above my head.

So, we drove.

Twenty minutes out of the city, far from streetlights, far from noise, far from everything that felt heavy and suffocating.

We found a quiet field, untouched, endless, and swallowed in darkness. Only the soft glow of the moon and a few scattered stars lit my path.

I stepped out of the truck.

My breath hit the winter air like smoke.

My wet hair began to freeze, stiffening against my skin.

But I didn't feel the cold.

All I felt was anger.

All I felt was pain.

I thought the second my feet hit the frozen ground, I'd start screaming. That the rage would erupt like untamed wildfire.

But I didn't.

I just stood there.

Still.

Silent.

Holding a storm that refused to move.

I turned back toward Kris, still in the truck, calm and patient, watching but not interfering. He knew not to push. He would wait. He'd be there when I was ready.

And then, for the first time that night, I felt… embarrassed.

What was I doing?

Standing in a frozen field, lost in my life, yet somehow… more centered than I'd felt in months.

I pulled off my gloves and dropped to my knees, pressing my bare hands against the frozen ground.

I tuned into my body.

Slowed my breath.

Listened to my heartbeat thudding inside my chest.

Felt connected to the silence, to the land, to something greater than myself.

And then the thoughts crept in.

I'm never going to be me again.

I'll never escape this loneliness.

What if I'm trapped like this forever?

Regret crashed over me like a cold wave.

Regret that I ever brought my rape back to life.

Regret that I ever pulled teenage me out of the shadows.

I should've left her there, I thought.

I should've buried her deeper.

Kept her quiet.

And suddenly, I questioned everything.

Why did I write this book?

Who even cares about my story?

My words don't matter.

I don't matter.

I felt like a joke.

Like a failure.

A disappointment to this world.

And then… came the shame.

A tidal wave of it.

Suffocating.

Overwhelming.

Ready to pull me under.

But in that moment, something inside me enlightened.

I realized something I had never fully named before…

It's the shame and guilt I've been carrying that has held me back my entire life.

It's always been there quietly limiting me.

Limiting my potential.

My growth.

My self-worth.

It's the blame I carry that whispers…

"You're not good enough."

"You'll never be good enough."

But then, through the noise, through the storm, a louder voice rose from deep inside me.

A voice I had buried long ago.

This isn't my blame to carry.

This isn't my shame to own.

This is NOT my fault.

And the moment I started to accept that truth, I felt it.

The rage.

The fire.

Building inside me again.

The more shame tried to pull me under, the more my fury fought back.

Until finally, I screamed.

A deep, unstoppable scream.

It tore through me like an earthquake, vibrating from the darkest corners of my soul.

From the place where pain had festered for decades.

Where silence had poisoned me.

Where shame had taken root and grown thorns.

My vocal cords weren't prepared for the force of it.

I gasped for air, cleared my throat, and screamed again.

And again.

And again.

Until every ounce of rage, every ounce of grief, every ounce of power that had been stolen from me... came roaring back into the night.

With each scream, I felt myself getting stronger.

Not healed.

Not whole.

But no longer powerless.

I felt the power returning to my body.

I felt myself breaking free.

And for the first time in so long... I felt like me again.

Eventually, the screaming gave way to tears.

The fire had burned through me, scorching everything in its path, leaving behind only exhaustion.

My chest heaved. My breath came in short, jagged gasps. And the weight of everything I had unleashed settled deep into my bones.

Then, in the silence that followed, I did something I never thought I'd be strong enough to do.

I said his name.

"Devin."

Not a whisper.

Not a breathless, trembling murmur.

I stood there, raw, steady, unflinching, and said his name with power.

Since unearthing this experience, I had thought his name a million times. It echoed in my mind like a curse, a taunt, a loop I couldn't break. I wanted to say it out loud.

But every time I tried, my voice would vanish. An invisible muzzle clamped over my mouth, silencing me. Reducing me to a helpless animal bound by trauma, muzzled by shame, stripped of truth.

But not that night.

That night, I ripped that muzzle off.

And when I spoke his name, when I claimed it, I felt another layer of freedom settle into me.

Small, but seismic.

A victory.

Because I will never be silenced again.

My voice is mine.

Just like my body is mine.

And I will never be voiceless again.

Eventually, I felt ready to turn around and go home.

I knew I wasn't leaving the darkness behind, not entirely.

This shadow... this heavy, haunting shadow, would follow me there.

It would linger in the corners, show up in quiet moments, remind me that trauma doesn't vanish just because you scream into the night.

Healing takes time.

And maybe, just maybe I'll never fully let this go.

Maybe it will always live in me, not as a wound, but as a scar.

A mark of what I've endured.

But I'm ready to try.

I'm ready to stay the course.

To keep showing up for myself, not in spite of the trauma, but because of it.

I'm ready to face the storm head-on instead of running from it.

I'm ready to take my power back.

I'm ready for joy.

For softness.

For peace.

I'm ready to find happiness again.

As we drove home, Kris reached over and took my hand. He didn't say a word and neither did I. I didn't need words. I felt it, his love, his steady presence, his quiet knowing.

It wrapped around me as a promise. An unspoken vow that I wasn't alone in this battle. That he would be there. Through every rise, every fall, and every in-between.

The rage still simmered beneath my skin.

But tonight, for the first time in a long while, I felt more grounded.

Steadier, and maybe, just maybe even a little freer.

There was a glimmer.

A spark.

A fragile flicker of light cutting through the shadows.

I am a survivor.

And I'm going to keep surviving.

I'm not giving up on myself.

I'm not giving up on teenage Jody either.

She's fierce.

She's rising.

And every single day…

She's taking her power back.

CHAPTER 24

Not My Shame

"The shame was never yours. It was forced on you—stitched into your silence. But not anymore."

— *JmStorm*

It's been a few weeks since I stood in that cold, dark, open field. My breath visible in the night air, fists clenched, body trembling as I released the weight of my rage into the vast emptiness around me. My voice, raw and unfiltered, swallowed by the wind.

I haven't gone back since, and I'm closing that door for now. Not locking it, just acknowledging I'm aware it's there. Mine to return to, if I ever need it.

If the fire creeps up again, if the pressure in my chest builds until I feel like I might burst, I'll drive. I'll chase the horizon until the world feels wide enough to brace the storm inside me. And I'll let it go.

Freely.

Fiercely.

My emotions don't make me weak, they make me real.

In the meantime, I've found something softer, something steady. Restorative meditation. Instead of unleashing my fury into the night, I've begun sinking into stillness. Grounding myself. Breathing through the chaos instead of bracing against it. Each inhale pulls me inward. Past the static, past the sharp edges, to the quiet center of me.

And I'm meeting myself there.

My inner child, fragile, yet resilient.

Teenage me, wounded, but unbreakable.

Five minutes.

Ten.

Twenty.

Whatever time I give, I gain even more in return. I feel centered and connected. More in tune with a version of myself I spent years ignoring. Too busy chasing perfection, too buried in to-do lists, too afraid of the darkness to sit with the inner child still living inside.

But now?

I'm slowing down.

I'm tuning in.

Within that stillness, I'm discovering something unexpected...

My true identity.

I still feel on edge most days, like a soldier anticipating ambush. I brace for the next meltdown, the next spiral. But I'm learning, I'm growing, and I'm more equipped now than I've ever been.

Therapy is helping. Coping tools that once felt foreign now feel like lifelines. Anchors when the waves rise.

The shadows still linger. The road is still long. But for the first time in a long while...

I don't feel completely lost.

With every breath, every small step forward, I feel a shift. A crack of light breaking through the darkness. An echo of progress carried on the wind.

And that echo?

It's enough to keep me going.

I've noticed I make the most progress when I face the beast. Not by running. Not by cowering. But by standing tall in my own strength. I'm no longer the damsel in distress, no longer trembling in fear of the big bad wolf like I was just months ago.

I know I'll never confront him directly. I don't want to. That chapter doesn't deserve a reopening.

But something deep inside stirred, it pulled at me, and insisted I return.

Not to him, but to the place.

Where it all began.

Because healing doesn't always mean facing the person who hurt you.

Sometimes, it means reclaiming the spaces they tried to steal.

Taking back the memories.

Redefining the story.

Not to relive the pain, but to reclaim the power.

It was a Wednesday morning. The air was still. The city just beginning to stir. And yet, I felt an undeniable urge. A deep, unshakable impulse to get in my vehicle and face the evil that had bound me in invisible chains for so long.

Since the night he assaulted me, I hadn't let myself drive down his street.

I avoided it with meticulous precision, taking the longest, most inconvenient routes just to keep myself from passing that house.

That cursed, hollow house.

It was more than a place.

It was a wound.

A ghost.

A living nightmare I had spent years pretending didn't exist.

But that morning… something was different.

The fear wasn't gone, but it no longer held the wheel.

I was back at work. Slowly reintegrating, day by day, moment by moment, listening to my body, my heart, my soul. Trying to find a rhythm again. Trying to breathe through the days. And on that morning, I knew… It was time. I couldn't shake the feeling.

So, I didn't.

I surrendered to it.

Let it guide me back to the place where it all began.

Thirty-eight-year-old me knew this was a terrible idea. Every rational thought screamed:

"Don't do this. Turn around. You're not ready."

But it was like something inside me had already decided. And I was just along for the ride.

I took a quick shower, barely registering the water on my skin. Got dressed on autopilot. Grabbed my keys. Stepped outside. The cold slapped my face, sharp, biting. But it didn't snap me out of the trance.

I knew seeing that house could cripple me.

What if I broke down?

What if the panic was so bad I couldn't drive afterward?

How would I get to work?

How would I hold it together?

The questions galloped through my brain like racehorses on their final lap, frantic and breathless. But still, one foot in front of the other, I kept going. I climbed into my car and pulled away.

Logical, grown-up Jody was practically begging me to stop. I even reached out to two close friends, hoping they'd give me a reason to back out. They did, they told me not to go.

But I went anyway.

Because teenage Jody had already decided.

It felt like a war.

A battle between the woman I am now and the girl I used to be.

The girl who lost control.

The girl who was silenced.

The girl who had carried the weight of that night for far too long.

She wasn't reckless.

She wasn't fragile.

She was fierce.

A force with one mission.

See it through.

It was about a thirty-minute drive to his old house. I say, his old house, because I don't actually know if he still lives there. That didn't matter. I wasn't planning to stop. I wasn't planning to knock. I just needed to see it. To face it.

Thirty-eight-year-old Jody sat behind the wheel, but teenage Jody held the reins. I was her shadow. Her driver. Her chauffeur.

Every nerve in my body screamed, turn around. But outwardly, I was calm, too calm, like a presence inside my own skin.

My knuckles whitened around the steering wheel. I told myself... You can do hard things. You can do this.

Each red light became a silent prayer. Let something stop me. Give me a sign.

But the lights kept turning green.

Closer.

And closer.

The air in the car thickened, pressing down on me. My heart pounded like it was trying to escape my chest. Yet still, I drove.

Then, as I neared the neighborhood, the past began to stir. The street signs. The small businesses. The old gas station on the corner. Each landmark unearthed something I had buried, fragments of a life I had deliberately locked away.

I hadn't just repressed the assault. I had erased this entire neighborhood from my memory. I made it disappear. Convinced myself it never existed.

But it was real.

It had always been real.

I turned a corner. Then another. And suddenly... I was there.

I pulled up to the street and froze.

My breath caught in my throat. My eyes locked on the street sign like it held a dark magnetic power.

I couldn't move.

Not yet.

Time stretched, elastic and unbearable.

Then, a car appeared behind me, snapping me back into the now. I had to move.

Left?

Right?

I sat at the intersection of fear and memory, paralyzed by a simple truth. I couldn't remember which way to go. I should have. But just like so much of that experience, the memory was still foggy. Fragmented. Hiding its secrets behind layers of denial.

I turned right, creeping down the street, eyes scanning every house. Each one blurred into the next, unfamiliar and indistinguishable.

My heartbeat thundered in my ears, drowning out logic.

I reached the end. Nothing. I had gone the wrong way.

I pulled over, hands aching from the grip on the wheel. I closed my eyes.

This is my sign, I told myself.

The perfect out; a reason to leave. To try again another day. To protect the fragile threads of control I still had.

It would've been the safe choice.

But something deeper whispered:

No.

This wasn't meant to be easy.

This moment was meant for more.

So, I turned around.

Back down the street I went, breath shallow, limbs heavy.

Then, I saw it.

A small white building on the corner. Recognition hit like a punch to the gut. I knew where I was, and I knew what was coming next.

A few more houses.

A few more seconds.

And then…

There it was.

I wasn't sure if I would recognize it.

Told myself maybe time had changed it.

But I did.

Oh, did I ever.

The narrow, cracked walkway.

The weathered wooden gate.

The shortcut to the side door.

The door.

The one that led straight downstairs.

To the basement.

The basement that changed my life.

The basement that stole a part of me.

The basement that still haunts me.

At first, I drove by.

Okay, I told myself. I did it. I saw it. Good enough. Now get the hell out of here.

But realistically, a quick glance wasn't enough. A drive-by didn't give me what I needed. I needed to really see it. To sit with it. To take it all in. I'd already come this far. I wasn't stopping now.

So, I turned around, again. My hands were steady on the wheel, but my body trembled. I pulled onto a side street, parking directly across from the house.

I sat there.

Breath shallow.

Pulse erratic.

Chest tight.

The longer I stared, the more it came rushing back.

Not just the memories I had already unveiled, but more. So much more. Memories I hadn't expected. Memories I didn't want.

Details I thought were lost suddenly became vivid, sharp, and uninvited.

And in that moment, I felt it.

The house wasn't just wood and brick.

It was alive, with echoes, with shadows, with silence that screamed.

And I remembered.

More than I ever wanted to.

More than I thought I could.

I felt myself back in that basement.

The memories surged sharper now, more vivid than ever. The room reeked of stale ashtrays and sweat, the air thick and suffocating. Music played low in the background. Not a comfort or a distraction, just a dull, lifeless hum, masking the rot in the room.

Not loud enough to drown anything out, but steady enough to mute the tension. As if pretending nothing was wrong while everything was.

His touch at first was warm, flirtatious, and calculated. His voice, smooth and practiced, like he'd said the same lines before.

And then that look. The one that pins me in my sleep.

The moment his cold eyes locked in, vacant and predatory. The second I stopped being a person and became something to take, like an object, a target, or a body to conquer.

He didn't just steal a night. He took pieces of me I didn't know were breakable.

My confidence.

My dignity.

My sense of control.

And most devastating of all...

My self-worth.

He damaged me with his eyes before he ever touched my body.

I remember standing in that narrow, dim-lit bathroom afterward, fluorescent light flickering above, casting fractured shadows across the sink.

I was staring at myself in the mirror, but all I saw was a stranger staring back.

My body didn't feel like mine anymore.

It felt tainted.

Disgusting.

Foreign.

Disposable.

The fear I felt towards him cast a spell over me. A heavy, suffocating silence, an invisible muzzle, had sealed itself over my mouth, preventing me from ever telling my side of the story.

I was terrified.

Terrified of what he might do if I told anyone, or what they might think.

Would they see me the way I now saw myself?

Damaged.

That was the moment I began to hate myself.

The moment shame wrapped itself around my body like a second skin, telling its lies:

"This was your fault."

"You asked for this."

"You're broken now."

That was the moment everything changed. The moment that would alter the course of my life, and there was nothing I could've done.

I sat in my car, gripping the wheel, still feeling that familiar layer of guilt and self-hate as I stared at the house that had stolen a part of me.

I wasn't that girl in the mirror anymore. Yet, twenty-three years later, the pain was still fresh. Etched into my bones and woven into the fabric of who I became.

As I stared at that house, the weight of shame settled over me like a fog. Not rage, not anger, just shame. The kind I've carried for decades. The kind that dictated my worth. Feeding my mind with quiet poison…

You're not good enough.

You'll never be good enough.

The shame that kept me small.

Dimming my confidence, my voice, my ability to love myself.

Convincing me I was unlovable and unworthy.

As I sat in that vehicle, parked across from the house that haunted my soul, I didn't just feel it, I drowned in it.

Minutes passed.

Then nearly an hour.

And then…

I heard a voice.

Not the wounded teenager.

Not the weathered, thirty-eight-year-old survivor.

But her.

The deepest part of me.

The truest version of who I am beneath it all.

She rose up from the depths, steady, quiet, and unshaken.

Not screaming. Not sobbing. Just, knowing.

She took the reins.
She didn't beg.
She didn't plead.
She simply placed the blame back where it belonged.
Back in that house.
Back in that basement.
Back in that bathroom.
Back on him.
And then, I opened my mouth.
And the words came out firm, steady, and undeniable.
"This is your fault. Not mine."
"This is your guilt. Not mine."
"This is your shame. Not mine."
I said it again.
And again.
Until the words weren't just sounds.
They were truth.
And for the first time, I believed them.
With each repetition, I felt lighter.
Like layers of self-hate were peeling from my skin.
Like the weight of two decades was slowly lifting from my shoulders.
I had been a caged bird with broken wings, trapped in a prison built from shame. A cage I didn't build, but one I believed I deserved.
Then, in that moment…
I felt something I hadn't felt in twenty-three years.
Freedom.
My soul was coming back to life.
Piece by piece.
Layer by layer.
Truth by truth.
And maybe, just maybe.
I'm finally ready to fly.

Why do we, the victims, carry the shame when it was never ours to carry in the first place?

For years, I let it weigh me down. I let it shape my self-worth, my choices, the way I saw myself in the mirror. I let it convince me that I was the one who had something to hide.

But that morning, sitting outside his house, I gave it back.

I put the shame where it belonged.

Enough was enough.

I had carried it for far too long. And as I drove away, something was different. I felt stronger, not just on the outside, but deep in my core.

For the first time in decades, I felt connected to me, the real me. The version of myself that had been buried beneath layers of self-doubt, guilt, and grief.

That morning, I took one of the biggest steps yet on my healing journey. A step toward discovering who I truly am, without the weight of his actions on my back, and it was liberating.

I know there are still many steps ahead. I know healing isn't linear. But I'm on my way.

And the very next day, for the first time in a long time, I actually wanted to get out of bed.

The smile on my face?

It wasn't something I forced for my children.

It was real.

I was real.

If you are a survivor of sexual assault, hear me when I say this:

This is NOT your shame to carry.

This is NOT your fault.

You never asked for this.

You did nothing to deserve this.

You are not damaged.

You are not worthless.

You deserve the chance to rebuild what was broken.

To see yourself as enough.

To see yourself as beautiful.

As strong.

As capable.

To see yourself as unstoppable.

I see you.

I understand you.

I believe in you.

Because I am you.

You are never alone.

And together, we are stronger.

Together, we are a force.

It's time to put the shame back where it belongs. To release the darkness that was never yours to carry. To free yourself from the weight that was forced upon you.

I know, it's easier said than done. Especially if you've buried it as deep as I have. I know what I'm asking.

And I know... it's a lot.

You don't have to jump in your vehicle and drive to the place where it happened. That's what I needed.

But your healing?

It's yours.

Your journey is yours.

So, ask yourself:

What do I need to face the inner darkness?

What do I need to finally let it go?

Whatever that answer is, honor it.

Because this shame?

This pain?

This weight you've been carrying?

It was never yours to hold.

Strip it from your body.

Because your body is yours.

And no one else's.

If you're not ready yet, that's okay too. I know the grip it has. The suffocating hold. The way it wraps around you like chains, convincing you that you'll never break free.

But hear me when I say…
You deserve to heal.
You deserve to feel whole again.
I'm tired of feeling broken.
I'm rebuilding myself as a warrior.
I'm done watching abusers walk free.
Done watching survivors stay silent, because we know that speaking up rarely brings justice.
Because we know the consequences never match the crime.
But I refuse to stay silent any longer.

My voice is ready.
And I'm going to use it.
LOUD and PROUD.
For all of us.
For every survivor who's been silenced.
For every soul still drowning in shame that was never theirs.
For every person still fighting to reclaim their power.
Enough is enough.

We are not damaged.
We are not weak.
We are WARRIORS.

Our voices will be heard.

THIS IS NOT MY SHAME.
THIS IS NOT OUR SHAME.

CHAPTER 25

Becoming Whole: My Healing Journey

"I am not what happened to me. I am what I choose to become."
— *Carl Jung*

Just like that…
I resurrected the darkness.
Dug it up from the depths where I thought I had buried it for good.
And in doing so, I stumbled my way back into a second rock bottom, a place I swore I'd never return to.
But this time something was different.
This time, I didn't unpack.
I didn't settle in.
I stood in the wreckage, looked around, and chose to climb.
There was no ladder waiting for me. Slowly, I had to build it, one painful rung at a time.
I put in the work to climb out, and now I am climbing further with each intentional step.
Because healing isn't a destination. It's a journey.
Recovering from trauma doesn't happen overnight.
It's not a straight line. It's disorganized. It's exhausting.

It's full of setbacks and moments where you wonder if you'll ever feel whole again.

But even in the mess, there's progress.

Even in the darkness, there's light… if you keep going.

Healing, I've learned, is like playing a game of Jenga to become whole again. You can't just stack new pieces and hope for stability. You have to pull out the missing ones. Examine them. Understand them. Accept them. Then carefully and intentionally rebuild.

It's about balance. Structure. Learning how to stand tall even when life feels shaky. Rebuilding, one piece at a time. And when the tower crumbles, and it will, you rise from the ashes. You rebuild again. And every time you rebuild, you're that much stronger.

The game doesn't end with a setback. You keep playing. You adapt. You refine your strategy. You get better. Then one day, without even realizing it, you become a force. A legendary opponent that no one dares underestimate.

Because you've learned how to rise.

Rise faster and stronger.

Every.

Damn.

Time.

As challenging as this journey is, I've discovered…

There is a way to live in the light again.

To feel warmth where there was once only shadow.

And I'm finally on my way.

With each therapy session and time away from my typical life, I started to see teenage Jody more clearly. Not just as a version of myself from the past, but as someone truly remarkable.

I dug up an old photo of her and stuck it on my fridge. Every time I look at her, I feel something new.

She looks happy on the outside. But I know better. I know the weight she carried. I know the storm she endured.

Her eyes smiled for the camera, but I could see through them. I could see the ache behind the grin.

The silent scream no one ever heard.

That one day, that experience changed everything.

It flipped her world upside down.

So, she built walls. Thick, unbreakable ones.

A fortress designed to keep pain out, and herself safe.

Chin up. Eyes forward. Heart shielded.

I can't believe how strong she was.

Strong enough to repress something so dark.

Strong enough to pretend it never happened.

To push it so far down that she even started to believe it wasn't real.

How does someone bury something so painful for so long?

She felt damaged.

She felt unlovable.

And somewhere along the way, she started to hate herself.

And that?

That wasn't fair.

She was just a girl.

A girl trying to survive.

A girl who grew up too fast.

A girl who lived in fear for far too long.

But she was resilient.

And I am so proud of her.

She made us who we are today.

And I'm so damn grateful that she never gave up.

As part of my healing journey, I wrote her a letter.

At first I felt silly, pen in hand, staring at a faded photo of my fifteen-year-old self.

I didn't know where to begin.

How do you speak to a version of yourself who was both a child and a warrior?

But the longer I looked at her, really looked, the noise around me faded. The world went quiet, and the words poured out like a dam finally giving way.

What began as hesitation turned into release.

Each sentence chipped away at years of silence.

I told her I was sorry.

I told her I believed her.

That she didn't deserve any of it.

That she was brave.

That she mattered.

That I loved her.

To my surprise, writing that letter became one of the most freeing experiences I've ever had. It felt like breathing for the first time in years.

If you're navigating past trauma, I can't recommend this enough. There's something sacred about acknowledging the version of yourself who carried the weight. The one who walked through fire without ever being handed a map. The one who kept going, even when no one saw the pain.

I'm not out of the woods yet.

Healing takes time, and I know there's still work ahead. But for the first time in a long time, I feel in tune with my body, my mind, and my soul.

For once, I'm sleeping better.

I used to spend countless nights replaying every moment of my day, overanalyzing every move, every word, every breath.

I never felt like I measured up.

Never felt good enough.

Never felt deserving of more.

Sleep became my escape. A doorway into a dream world where everything made sense. Where I was happy. Where I loved myself.

That utopia doesn't exist. It never did. But for the first time... I don't need it. Because in the real world, the one I wake up to every morning, I feel something I haven't felt in years:

Hope.

I feel more love, more acceptance of myself and I feel more worthy of chasing my dreams.

More capable of becoming the person I was always meant to be.

As time passes, something amazing is happening.

I have more energy.

And most importantly...

I'm less angry.

I'm not carrying the same resentment, the same suffocating weight.

I'm finally letting go, and it feels like breathing fresh air after living underground for far too long.

I've always known I have a temper.

I'm emotional.

I never realized how much of my irritability was fueled by unspoken pain, by darkness I didn't even know I was carrying.

I like to think of myself as a patient person, but too often I react in a fury of frustration before thinking.

Especially as a mother.

Why is Mommy like a yo-yo with her emotions?

Cheerful and bright one moment, then short-tempered the next?

I've been holding onto so much rage, so much unprocessed emotion, for so long, I didn't realize how deeply it was shaping me.

Affecting my energy.

My presence.

My ability to fully show up.

But the moment I started facing my trauma, something changed.

I felt more at ease, less reactive, and less irritable.

In turn, I found more patience.

With the darkness exposed, there was finally room for love.

I'm not saying I've become Little Miss Daisy.

I still have my moments.

I'm still human.

Still imperfect, but now I finally have the ability to pause.

To breathe.

To think.

To respond with intention instead of instinct.

Before, it felt like my reactions were stuck on autopilot. No matter what I tried, I always ended up snapping. Always felt like I was falling short.

But now?

Now I feel like I have a choice, and that changes everything. For the first time in years, I can see real change on the horizon.

And more importantly, I believe it's possible.

I believe my efforts will pay off.

And that belief?

It's everything.

I can't quite explain it, but the heaviness I used to carry feels a little lighter. The things that once felt impossible are now starting to feel manageable, doable, and hopeful. Now for the first time, I'm not just wishing for change, I believe in it.

I believe in me.

I'm no longer haunted by what was buried so deep inside.

Yes, I'm still dealing with it.

Some days are harder than others.

But it's no longer consuming me.

No longer shaping my identity.

No longer defining who I am in this world.

I never would have found this new path, this new version of myself, if I hadn't brought my trauma into the light.

And now, as I begin to release that weight... I'm finally making space for something else:

A fuller life.

My eyes are open now.

I see the world differently.

I see myself differently, too.

A better version of me is in the making and I'm welcoming her in with open arms. With growth comes clarity.

And here's something else I've noticed about myself lately...

I flinch.

When a man reaches out to touch me, even in the most innocent and loving way, I flinch. It's just a second, a flicker. But it's there, every time.

Even with Kris, my husband, a man I trust, and a man I love.

Yet still... I flinch.

It's like I've been living in a constant state of fight or flight response, and I didn't even realize it.

Until now.

Now, it makes sense.

It's my body's automatic response.

A reflex born from fear.

A side effect of being assaulted that I never named, never questioned, never acknowledged.

Until this moment.

Now that I've made that connection, I find myself wondering…

Can I learn how to soften?

Can I lean into affection?

Can I fully surrender to love, even knowing that's where I'm most vulnerable?

Can I rebuild the part of me that was stolen?

Can I reach a place where I no longer feel broken?

Can I make peace with myself?

Can I love and accept more than I ever have before?

I don't know all the answers yet.

But for the first time in my life, I'm ready to start asking the questions.

I never got the chance to experience a real relationship before I was assaulted. I never got to discover who I could be, in love.

How I'd naturally show up, how I'd allow myself to trust, to be seen, to be loved... without fear.

That experience was stolen from me.

Now, looking back, I realize just how much it's shaped the way I perceive relationships. The way I exist within them.

Maybe that's why I was always terrified of being caught.

Why I ran.

Maybe it's the reason my guard has always been up. Even in my safest moments, it's never fully come down.

Yes, I've let my walls drop before, but never completely.

Even now, I'm in love, I'm happy, I trust Kris with my whole heart.

I know he'd never hurt me.

I know I'm safe.

But still…

Something inside me holds back.

And I wonder, is this why?

Is this the final piece of the puzzle?

The lingering wound I never realized was still festering?

I don't want to be guarded forever.

I don't want to hold onto fear when all I crave is freedom.

So, I'm hoping that the more I heal, the more I release this experience, the more I can free myself. The more I can truly open my heart to a deeper love. To finally know what it feels like to let my guard all the way down.

Wish me luck.

Because I'm only just beginning this part of the journey.

My assault has always felt like an open wound, but now, it's slowly transforming into a scar.

Because wounds?

They still sting.

They're raw, tender, pulsing with buried pain.

You can cover them with a Band-Aid, try to ignore them, pretend they don't exist…

But wounds don't heal in the dark.

They need air.

They need light.

They need to breathe.

Scars, though?

Scars have weathered the storm.

They've closed.

They've hardened.
They've transformed.
They're proof of survival.
And because of that, they're stronger.
I'm not quite there yet.
This wound still aches.
But I'm closer than I've ever been.

Some days, I wake up feeling light, free, unburdened, and whole.
Other days, memories creep in like shadows slipping under the door. A flash, a slither, a flicker of the past I thought I had buried.
Sometimes, I go days, even weeks, without thinking about it. And in those moments, I feel normal. Like maybe I've finally turned the corner.
Then it hits.
Out of nowhere.
A memory rises from the depths and refuses to stay quiet.
On those days, I find myself pulled to the shower.
Just like the day I woke the beast and cleansed my body in the lake.
That was a pivotal moment in my life.
For the first time, I truly began to let go of his control.
The control he had over me.
Over my body.
There's something about the water, the way it pounds against my skin, steady and powerful.
It feels like ritual.
Like rebirth.
It's where I wash away the heaviness.
Where I reclaim my body.
Where I breathe.
Where I begin again.
It may look ordinary.

But for me, it's sacred. A strategy, a sanctuary, a place where peace finds me.

Do I wish I didn't feel the need to cleanse my body every time I'm triggered?

Hell yes.

Of course I do.

I believe I'll get there.

I'm just not there yet and that's okay, because I'm okay.

Still learning, still rising, still becoming.

That's what life is, isn't it?

A constant unfolding.

We uncover truths, stumble into awakenings, and revisit pain we thought we'd left behind. And somehow, through it all, we adapt. We survive. We ascend.

Now, I'm ready.

Ready to rebuild what he took.

Ready to reclaim what was always mine.

Most importantly…

My body is mine.

It doesn't matter what happened to it in the past.

This body is mine again.

I am not a prize.

Not something to be claimed.

I choose what I do with my body.

I choose who touches it.

There's a beautiful power in this reconnection.

I'm beginning to love this body more than ever.

To honor it for what it truly is.

Resilient, powerful, sacred.

Not broken.

Not damaged.

Stronger than ever.

And finally, mine.

After writing this book, I uncovered something I never expected:

I'm not just a voice for those battling eating disorders.

I've become a voice for those of us who've been sexually assaulted, too.

So, to those who have buried it deep…

Who can't speak it out loud…

Who push it down just to get through the day…

I don't blame you.

Not for a second.

That silence?

It's a shield.

I wore it for most of my life.

Because naming it hurts like hell.

I'm so sorry you're in this "clubhouse," this place none of us ever asked to be.

None of us chose this.

None of us asked for this to be part of our story.

And yet, here we are, members of a club no one wants to join.

No invitation.

No tryouts.

No warning.

Just pain.

Still, we sit together in this invisible club.

Some of us trapped in the wickedness.

Some of us rising to face it.

All of us fighting.

Fighting to breathe.

To function.

To heal.

This battle is ugly.

It's exhausting.

It's demanding.

But as much as it hurts, as impossible as it feels on the darkest days, I know this now…

You are not alone.
We are not alone.

There are many of us here, far too many.
But we see you.
We know you.
And while I wish, with every piece of me, that you didn't have to carry this…
We will carry it with you.
We will stand beside you.
Always.
This clubhouse is made of warriors.
People who've walked through fire and made it out, even if scorched.
We carry scars, some visible, many hidden.
But still, we stand.
We stand shoulder to shoulder, arms outstretched, ready to catch you when you fall.
Because we've fallen, too.
We know that weight.
You don't have to hold it alone anymore.
There is quiet strength in shared survival.
In walking the path together, even when it winds through darkness.
We can't rewrite the past.
But together, we can reclaim the future.
We are here for you.
Always.

More than anything, I want you to know this…
I'm learning how to feel free again.
I believe, deep in my bones, that healing is possible.
That doesn't mean I don't still feel rage, that I don't grieve, that I don't ache from what was taken. But now, I feel something else too… Control.

I'm no longer paralyzed by fear. That stolen piece of me, that sacred part, it's still gone. And no, I'll never get it back.
But I don't want it back.
It's been tainted.
So instead, I'm creating something new.
Something stronger.
Something mine.
I'm filling that hollow space with power, not pain.
With truth, not silence.
With light, not shame.
And it's my hope you can, too.

If you'd asked me before I started this book whether I could ever feel whole again, I would've told you no.
I thought I'd carry that pain forever.
That I'd always be fractured.
But here I am.
Reclaiming control.
Stitching myself back together.
Healing in real time.
And for the first time in decades…
I believe I'm going to be okay.

Your journey may not look like mine.
There's no map.
No checklist.
No perfect path.
But I can tell you from my own journey I've discovered…
Facing the darkness is life changing.

Because on the other side?
The light is brighter than ever.
And every single day…
I'm getting closer to it.

CHAPTER 26

Perfectly Imperfect

"You are not a problem to be fixed. You are a story unfolding."
— *Brianna Wiest*

Perfection doesn't exist.
And accepting that?
It shattered something in me.
It was one of the hardest lessons I've ever had to learn.
Harder than recovery with an eating disorder.
Harder than silencing the voice of body dysmorphia.
Harder than facing the ghosts of my past, head-on.
Because buried beneath it all was a belief so deep, so consuming, it wrapped itself around my worth like ivy.
The belief that I was never good enough.
Not unless I was flawless.
Not unless I was perfect.

Perfection is an illusion.
A lie dressed in gold.
And still, I clung to it like a lifeline.
Afraid that if I let go, I would unravel completely.

For almost 40 years, I held it close, like gospel.
And where did it get me?
Sure, it made me ambitious. Driven and accomplished, even.
But did it bring me peace?
Did it teach me how to love myself?
Hell no.

Perfection is not sustainable. It's not constant. It's not real. It's a mirage on the horizon, you keep walking toward it, but it never lets you arrive. The more you chase it, the further you drift from your true self.
Perfection doesn't love you back.
It doesn't hold your hand on the hard days.
It doesn't whisper, "You're enough" when you're falling apart.
It just keeps moving the goalpost. Again, and again.
I'm not perfect.
Far from it.
And if I'm going to write my story, I have to write it honestly, the good, the bad, and everything in between.
I'm human.
I mess up.
I fall short.
And that's okay.
I see it clearly now.
The goal was never perfection.
It was growth.
It was grace.
It was learning to stand before the mirror, even on the heavy days, and say:
I see you.
You're still standing.
You've got this.
That is what matters.
It took years to believe it.

To stop sprinting from my flaws and start listening to what they came to teach me.

So, if you're still out there, chasing that illusion of perfection.

Stop.

Right here.

Right now.

Pause.

Breathe.

Perfection isn't real.

It never was.

And the moment you stop grasping for it is the moment you set yourself free.

Even the best athlete misses some shots.

Even the most gifted musician can play off-key.

And you?

You won't be flawless every day.

But you'll be real.

You'll be growing.

And that is more than enough.

Now imperfection?

That's where the magic lives.

That's where we grow.

That's where we become.

Life won't stop changing.

It won't stop teaching you.

It won't stop testing your strength.

Your job isn't to be perfect, it's to keep going.

To evolve, to feel, and to live.

Because something powerful happens when you stop trying to be polished and start simply being real.

That's when the light switches on.

Not the kind you chase, the kind that comes from within.

When you stop trying to be the light for everyone else, you realize you are the light.

So do me a favor.

Let go of perfection.

Loosen your grip.

Even just a little.

Because every step you take toward self-acceptance is a step toward freedom.

When I finally started to let go of perfection, it felt like a weight lifted off my chest. The pressure, the shame, the impossible standards, they didn't disappear overnight.

But they started to loosen.

And I started to breathe.

I'm finally learning to believe I am good enough just as I am.

I've learned how to slow down and to let go of the endless to-do lists. To leave the dishes in the sink and catch a sunset instead.

Life doesn't happen in checkboxes.

It happens in moments.

If you're always chasing perfection, you'll miss them.

You'll miss the sunrise.

The belly laughs.

The quiet magic of being present.

Trust me…

Pause what you're doing.

Pull over.

Watch the beautiful sunrise.

The laundry can wait.

The world won't fall apart.

But that moment will pass if you don't catch it.

Chasing perfection is like living in a dungeon. Chains around your wrists, not tight enough to cut off your circulation, but just tight enough to remind you that you're not free. And outside that barred window, there's a dragon. You think if you can just be flawless enough to please the dragon, then maybe, just maybe you'll earn your freedom.

But the dragon's job is to breathe fire, to conquer, to keep you caged. Just like perfection, it doesn't want you free. Because if you were free, you'd stop chasing.

Here's the secret.

You've always had the key.

You don't earn freedom by being perfect.

You create it by giving yourself permission.

Permission to slow down.

To rest.

To be messy.

To be human.

And now, standing here on the other side of all that striving?

I can say this with certainty. The grass really is greener on this side. Because for the first time in my life I'm not pursuing perfection anymore.

I'm pursuing presence.

Joy.

Truth.

Love.

And let me tell you… It's beautiful here.

I wrote this book with a clear intention.

To reach anyone struggling with an eating disorder.

Whether you're deep in it, clawing your way out, or learning how to exist in recovery.

This is for you.

There's more awareness and support for those in the active stages of ED.

But what about the rest of us?

The ones who've lived with it for years, maybe even decades, no longer in crisis, yet still silently fighting.

What about those of us who aren't actively purging, restricting, or obsessing… But still feel body dysmorphia lurking behind our reflection?

Still find ourselves second-guessing what to wear.

Still feel self-conscious about how we walk into a room.

Still navigate the world with a hyper-awareness of our bodies.
What about the ones who look high functioning?
Who show up, go to work, raise children, and laugh with friends.
Who live full, beautiful lives…
While ED's voice still whispers quietly in the background?
The ones who fight silent battles.
Who make conscious choices, every single day, to silence the noise.
To pause the tape recorder that's been playing on loop for years.
This book is for you.
For us.

Recovery isn't black and white.
It's complicated.
It's layered.
It's complex.
And just because you're not in crisis, doesn't mean you're not still healing.
For those who know what it's like to live with an invisible battle,
I want to be a voice for this stage.
The in-between.
The not-sick-but-not-healed.
The high-functioning-but-still-struggling.
Let me remind you:
It's okay to not be okay.
It's okay to have good days and bad ones.
It's okay to still endure hardships, even in recovery.
And most importantly…
You are not alone.
You are doing the best you can, and we are in this together.
We are survivors.
And we are stronger than we think.

Have I purged in recovery?
Yes.

There were moments I felt overwhelmed, too full, too out of control, and I gave in. It didn't spiral, but it happened.

Have I restricted more than a "sprinkle?"

Absolutely.

Picked at food. Avoided "scary" meals. Said "all food is good food" while pushing carbs to the edge of my plate?

Yes.

More times than I want to admit.

These behaviors creep back in quietly, subtly, and justifiable in the moment.

For a long time, I minimized them. Told myself they were harmless.

But here's what matters most…

They didn't win.

I've slipped, many times, but I fought back harder before they took over. Before they stole my power.

That's the line between relapse and recovery.

Not the absence of disordered thoughts…

But the refusal to surrender to them.

Recovery isn't perfection.

It's persistence.

It's choosing to show up for yourself, again and again.

Especially on the hard days.

And writing this book?

It was hard.

There were moments when it triggered my ED brain.

Most days, that voice is quieter, mostly dormant. But revisiting my story meant revisiting my pain. Reopening wounds I worked hard to stitch closed.

But I did it.

For you.

For me.

For anyone who's ever felt unseen in their recovery.

I remember one evening, deep in the thick of writing, when I found myself spiraling again. I was counting, questioning, and calculating.

The old voice crept in like an echo from a darker time:

"You don't need that. You've been sitting all day. Pick something safe. Clean. Earned."

I was hungry.

I craved something sweet, something satisfying.

But instead, I reached for something "safe."

Because in that moment, I felt lazy. Undeserving and afraid that food would change how I looked, how I felt.

But here's the difference now:

I caught it.

I recognized it for what it was.

Not truth.

A trigger.

A pattern.

And one of the strongest tools I've learned…

Speaking it out loud.

To Kris. To a friend. To anyone who'll listen in that moment. Because when I give the thoughts a voice, I strip them of their power. I hold myself accountable. I interrupt the spiral. I silence the tape recorder.

When we keep it locked inside, it festers.

But when we speak out, it loses its grip.

That evening, I still initially played it safe. I picked the "approved" snack, the one ED would nod at.

I ate it. And I enjoyed it.

But almost instantly, the guilt crept in. My inner voice saying: "You gave in. You let ED win."

I could see it, ED puffing up its chest, smug and self-satisfied. Acting like the alpha because it had won this round.

So, what did I do?

I leaned into my strategy; I said it out loud. I grabbed my phone. Called myself out. Held myself accountable. I shared the moment publicly on social media. Raw, real, and unfiltered.

And the response stunned me.

Message after message poured in.

People who got it.

People who had been there.

People who were just like me.

I've always known I wasn't alone in this fight.

But every time I speak up, I'm reminded just how many of us are battling ED in silence.

Shortly after, I felt empowered.

I walked into the kitchen, reached for the sweet, salty, satisfying snack I'd actually been craving, and I ate it.

No hesitation.

No apology.

And let me tell you.

It felt incredible.

I said it out loud.

And I had an army behind me.

That day?

I squashed ED like a bug.

Writing this book came with its fair share of surprises.

But one of the most unexpected?

The deeper I dug into my story, the clearer it became... ED's grip on me hadn't disappeared in recovery.

I knew it was still there.

But it was stronger than I realized, stronger than I wanted it to be.

Not loud or obvious. Just subtle, quiet, woven deep into the fabric of my everyday life, disguised as discipline and control.

Writing forced me to zoom in like examining my disorder under a microscope.

Suddenly, I was face-to-face with the tiny rules I'd obeyed without question.

The rituals.

The patterns.

The shame still hiding in the shadows of my routine.

It was one of the most eye-opening revelations I've ever had.

Then with that clarity... came power.

For the purpose of this book, I gave ED an identity, a persona.
Because that's what it felt like.
Not just a disorder but a presence.
A shadow stitched into my every fiber.
And the more I separated myself from it, the more I saw me.
Giving ED its own identity started to give me back mine.
It created a space between who I am and what I've battled.
That shift, subtle but monumental, ripped away so much of the control it still had over me.
I can't fully explain it, but the more I wrote about ED as something separate, the more I could reclaim who I was beneath it.
Yes, I've been in recovery for a long time.
But I have never felt this recovered.
Never felt this strong.
For the first time, I'm living with less guilt.
Less insecurities.
Less fear around food, around rest, around simply being human.

If you're like me, living with an eating disorder, whether active or in recovery, please hear this…
You are not your eating disorder.
It does not define you.
It does not own you.
There's so much more to you beyond ED.
Your laughter.
Your resilience.
Your kindness.
Your spirit.
That's who you are.

This journey won't always be smooth.
There will be detours.
Roadblocks.
Fog.

You may never know why this disorder chose you.
But I do know this…
You are a fighter.
With more grit, more grace, and more light than you realize.
There's a spark in you that has never gone out.
That spark is your truth.
And it deserves to shine.
Not just today, but every single day.
You matter.
You are seen.
You are heard.
You are loved.
You are worthy.
Exactly as you are.
You were not placed on this earth by accident.
You are not a mistake.
You are not a fluke.
You are here for a reason.
Your existence sends ripples through this world.
Your impact reaches farther than you know.
You inspire, simply by being.
I love you for the strength you don't always see.
For the light you carry on your darkest days.
For the fire that still flickers inside you, even when the wind howls.
You have a purpose.
A mark to leave on this world.

Thank you for being here.
I'm with you.
I stand beside you.
You are not alone.
We are in this together.
And we are resilient.

So, take a moment.
Pause.
Breathe.
Reflect.
Let yourself grow.
Stretch beyond the limits of who you used to be.

And remember, perfection was never the goal.
We're meant to stumble.
To fall.
To crack open… and rise again.

Like a tree breaking through the cracks in concrete.
You are not defined by what tried to break you.
You are defined by the way you keep rising again and again.

CHAPTER 27

The Ending, That Feels Like the Beginning

"What if I fall?"
"Oh, but my darling, what if you fly?"
— *Erin Hanson*

There it is.

That's my life.

That's my story.

That's me.

When I think about the human existence, its inevitable changes, its relentless growth, the evolution shaped by pain and resilience, I always envision a tree coming to life.

From the roots to the crown, we transform.

The roots symbolize our beginning, that first breath we take as we enter the world.

With that inhale, we're launched into the unpredictable journey of life.

The trunk stands as our foundation. Our childhood, our core, the steady column that holds us upright and prepares us for what lies ahead.

And then come the branches. Each one, every twisting limb, delicate twig, and fluttering leaf, represents our experiences.

The heartbreaks, the triumphs, the moments that define us.

Some branches grow strong and wide, others snap under the weight of the storm.

Not every leaf bursts with color. Some fade and some fall, because life, in all its beauty, is not perfect.

But it's real.

And it's ours.

Life is a mix of enriching joys and catastrophic hardships.

Some branches stretch toward the sky, thriving in the warmth of the light. Others bear scars, never fully healing, but they remain.

Still part of the tree.

Still proof of growth.

Beyond its beauty, the most breathtaking thing about a tree is its resilience.

It weathers brutal storms, harsh winters, and fierce winds.

It bends.

It breaks.

It bears the evidence.

And still, it stands.

We, too, carry that resilience.

But we forget.

We underestimate the strength woven into our bones, the courage pulsing through our hearts.

It's a power we all hold.

And when we remember, when we lean into it, trust it, let it guide us, it carries us forward.

To heal.

To overcome.

To reach for the light, again and again.

Yes, trees, like humans, have an expiration date.

One day, they return to the earth, becoming one with the land that nurtured them.

That part is inevitable.

But until that final breath of oxygen, the world is what we make of it.

You are the protagonist of your story.

The narrator.

The voice that defines the plot, the pen that shapes each chapter.

No one else gets to write your story but you.

So… what do you want yours to say?

Because this… this life, this journey, this tree… is yours.

Every scar.

Every leaf.

Every branch.

No matter how the wind blows, it is still standing.

No, we can't control everything life throws at us.

Circumstances shift, external forces disrupt.

But there are some things we do control…

Our mindset and how we respond.

Whether we reach for the light or let the darkness swallow us.

That choice is ours.

And yes, I know mental illness can make that choice feel impossible.

I've lived that truth.

I know how it feels to fall so far you forget there's even a way back.

But I also know, there is.

Because once you start to reclaim your power, once you step back into the role of the narrator, you begin to truly live.

Not just survive…

But live.

To wake up and feel something.

To breathe in morning air and know you're still here.

To build a life in the light, even if shadows still linger.

The sun might not shine every day outside.

But your inner light?

It can.

It can burn bright, every single day, if you choose to let it.

When I first sat down to write this book, I braced myself for an emotional rollercoaster. One lined with sharp turns, steep drops, and unflinching truths.

I knew I'd be digging deep, facing old demons, and unearthing long-buried pain.

I expected it to be powerful.

Transformative, even.

I thought I was ready.

But the truth?

I had no idea just how life-altering it would be.

This journey peeled me open. Layer by layer, I uncovered parts of myself I didn't even know were hidden.

Forgotten truths rose to the surface like old photographs in a dusty attic, blurred at first, then suddenly vivid.

The growth has been undeniable.

It feels like I've shed an old skin and stepped into a new version of myself.

Wiser, softer, and stronger.

My entire perspective has shifted.

It's like someone cleaned the glass I've been peering through all these years.

Every morning on my drive to work, the world feels textured, alive in a way it never did before.

The same streets.

The same buildings.

The same faded billboards.

But now, they feel different, like they're humming with quiet wisdom I was too distracted to notice before.

I hear everything.

The rustling leaves.

The distant song playing from the car next to mine.

The cadence of my own breath.

The steady heartbeat of life moving forward.

Everything is crisper.

Sharper.

Brighter.

And maybe it's because, for the first time in a long time, I'm truly here.

Not just surviving, but feeling.

Present.

Grounded.

Awake.

I may still be Jody…

But I'm not the same.

I've unraveled and rebuilt.

Released what was never mine to carry.

I've grown in ways I never saw coming.

I feel rooted now.

Anchored.

Not unshakable, but steady.

I've gathered tools I never knew I needed, and they live in my back pocket. Ready when the storm hits.

Control used to be something I chased like a lifeline.

Something I gripped with white knuckles.

But now?

Now I hold it differently.

Not with desperation but with trust, and with open hands.

For the first time in my life, I can honestly say:

I have more control than I've ever known.

Not over the world.

Or other people.

Or outcomes.

But over me.

And damn…

That feels like freedom.

Whether this book reaches one person or a thousand, I will never regret writing it.

I will never regret choosing truth over silence.

Through this process, I've become more aligned with the woman I was always meant to be.

More grounded.

More whole.

More me.

Yes, I'm still battling my eating disorder.

It's part of me, and maybe it always will be.

But now, I face it with eyes wide open.

I understand it in ways I never did before.

I'm still learning how to love myself without conditions.

How to accept the parts of me that once felt unlovable.

And that?

That's a lifelong journey.

There are no shortcuts.

No final destination.

No finish line to cross.

But here's what I've realized…

Self-love isn't a place you arrive, it's a practice you return to.

It's fluid and evolving.

Some days, it pours in effortlessly.

Other days, it's a whisper you have to fight to hear.

But what matters is that I choose it.

That I keep showing up.

Keep doing the work.

Because I am worth the work.

And every time I catch even the faintest glimpse of that deeper love…

I know I'm headed in the right direction.

Step by step.

Breath by breath.

Toward healing.

Toward wholeness.

Toward the light.

Loving yourself is a commitment.

The most important one you'll ever make.

Because the longest relationship you'll ever have… is with you.
From your first breath to your last, you are your own companion.
No breakups.
No running away.
No "see you later."
This is a forever kind of love.
So, if you're willing to pour your energy, your care, your heart into others, ask yourself:
Why wouldn't you do the same for you?
You are worthy of the same love you so effortlessly give away.
You deserve softness, compassion, and joy.
You deserve to come home to yourself.
Now, knowing this relationship is lifelong, ask:
Am I treating myself the way I deserve?
Am I making myself happy?
Am I bringing me joy?
If the answer is no, that's okay.
Because it's never too late.
Never too late to try again.
To begin again.
To become again.
You are not behind.
You are not broken.
You are becoming.
And that… is more than enough.

So, what are my next steps?
I wish I could say there was a cure for it all.
That one day, the trauma… the eating disorder… would simply disappear like smoke dissolving into the air, leaving no trace behind. No ache, shadow, or scar.
But I can't promise that.
Because healing doesn't always mean forgetting.
Recovery isn't about erasing the past.

It's about learning to carry it differently.

To grow through it.

To rise above it.

To live with it without letting it define you.

It's not a clean break.

It's a constant unfolding.

And that...

That's where the strength lies.

What I can promise is this:

Every single day you chip away at the pain...

Every day you show up and do the work...

Your wings grow new feathers.

And with each feather, you fly a little freer than you ever thought possible.

So, I vow to keep moving forward. To keep choosing the yellow dress. To stop letting my insecurities win.

To challenge the cruel whispers that echo when I catch my reflection. And if that means standing in front of the mirror for hours, rewriting the story piece by piece, then so be it. I'll do it.

Because I'm done letting shame steal my moments.

I vow to become a louder, more present advocate for us survivors. To offer more of my time, my voice, my energy to awareness, to action, and to change.

That's why I created my company, Embrace Your Reflection.

I offer Beyond the Mirror – A Positive Body Image Workshop, Through Our Eyes – An Inside Perspective on Eating Disorders, and Reflection Coaching – One-on-One and Small Group Sessions.

The goal is simple, but powerful:

To flip the narrative.

To challenge the harmful beliefs we were conditioned to carry.

To rewire the thoughts that keep us feeling small, insecure, and unworthy.

These workshops and coaching sessions are rooted in compassion, truth, and quiet strength. They are spaces where we learn to see ourselves through softer eyes.

Where I share the tools, insights, and coping strategies I've gathered through years of lived experience. Each one forged in fire and carried in love.

Because healing doesn't bloom in silence. It takes root in connection. In truth. In conversation. In shared humanity.

It's a space to learn. To unlearn. To finally appreciate the beautiful body that has carried you through every chapter of your life.

Because when we begin to embrace our reflections, we start to see the truth.

We are beautiful, inside and out.

Exactly as we are.

I vow to keep showing up for myself in therapy. To keep doing the work. To stop saying "I'll get to it later."

Because in reality, we don't find the time.

We make it.

No more excuses.

No more putting myself last.

I vow to deepen the bond with my inner self. The version of me that exists beyond trauma. Beyond pain. Beyond the weight I've carried for far too long.

If I need a day off to heal, I'm going to take it. Without guilt. Without hesitation. Without apology. There's still so much stigma around mental health days. We convince ourselves we're being selfish. That we're letting others down.

So, we push through. Smile through. Work through. All while our bodies and minds beg for rest. But the more we ignore that need, the more it builds, until it breaks us.

I refuse to let that happen again. I matter. My well-being matters. And I will no longer abandon myself in the name of productivity.

I've taken a massive leap forward in my healing journey. Confronting the trauma I once buried. Reclaiming power from the grips of my eating disorder. And slowly breaking free from the need to please everyone but myself.

I'm learning to trust my own voice, to value my opinions, and to stop shrinking just to make others comfortable.

As amazing as this leap has been, this is only the beginning of my new journey.

It won't be easy.

There will be days I'll want to quit.

Days when the weight feels too heavy to carry.

But there's no turning back now.

I can feel her, the new me, calling me forward.

The version waiting on the other side.

She's stronger than the old me.

Stronger than the version I am today.

She is beautiful.

She is grounded.

She is who I was always meant to become.

And I'm ready for her.

Over the past decade, I've dreamed of becoming a motivational speaker. A way to help others by using my voice, by sharing my words. To live out the passion and purpose the little girl I once was felt so deeply, wanting to change the world.

I can close my eyes and see it so clearly.

I'm standing in front of an audience, wearing a bright, colorful blazer. My heart is racing. My palms are sweating. I take a deep breath. I'm terrified, yet equally as excited. Then I go for it.

Because this…

This is what I'm meant to do.

Whether the venue is packed with hundreds, or there are only two people in the seats. It's still two souls. Two hearts that showed up. Two people open to change.

Open to healing.

Open to hope.

And something deep inside me is whispering.

No… It's shouting.

This is your purpose.

This is why you're still alive.

And this new voice in my head?

It's ED's worst nightmare.

It's loud.

It's unstoppable.

And it's drowning out the old tape recorder more than ever before.

I'm ready to pursue my dream. To step into my light. To see where it takes me.

Because dreams don't chase you.

You have to chase them.

Whoever you are, if you're reading this…Thank you.

Thank you for walking beside me on this journey of self-discovery and growth.

Thank you for holding space for my expression, my unraveling, my mending.

Thank you for allowing me to bear my heart and soul without fear.

Thank you for simply being you.

And above all, I hope that somewhere in these pages, my voice helped you find yours.

Because your story matters.

Your truth matters.

You matter.

And the world deserves to hear you.

It only feels fitting to end this story where it all began…

Back on the bathroom floor.

Full circle.

But this time, it's not the same bathroom floor.

I'm no longer the girl at rock bottom, lying on cold tile, begging to disappear.

I'm the girl who survived.

And now…

I sit on my kids' bathroom floor.

The tile is warm beneath me.

I hear the pitter-patter of tiny feet, carefree giggles drifting down the hallway. They're probably wondering, "Why is Mommy sitting on the floor?"

And I smile…

Because they don't yet understand the weight this moment carries. They don't know how far their mommy has come.

But I do.

And now… so do you.

For so long, the bathroom was a place of pain. Of destruction. Of disappearance. A space where I came undone.

But today?

Today is different.

Today, I choose to rewrite the stars.

To redefine what a bathroom floor means to me.

To make it a place of peace.

Of joy.

Of reclamation.

I am the author of my story.

And in this narrative, I feel freer than ever before.

So here it is, my mic drop moment.

I chose life.

And I got up.

My heart is beating.

There's air in my lungs.

My body is functioning.

And most importantly…

My body is mine.

And that alone…

Is beautiful.

I'm not perfect, far from it.

And finally, I'm okay with that.

I'm no longer drowning in expectations or bending over backward to please everyone around me.

I'm learning to honor my own opinion of myself, because that's the one that matters most.

The girl I once was?
I'll never be her again.
She's a tale in my story.
But no longer holding the reins.
She got me here.
And I'm grateful for her.
For every step she took so I could stand where I am now.
I don't regret the path I walked.
That path led me here.
To this life I built.
This messy, beautiful, unpredictable, breathtaking life.
Because being alive means I still get to laugh.
I still get to cry.
I still get to feel.
It means I get to watch the sunrise after sleepless nights.
Dance barefoot in the kitchen.
Hold the people I love a little tighter.
And chase dreams I once thought were too far out of reach.
I get to be here.

Maybe my journey broke me.
But it also built me.
And for that?
I'm forever grateful.
Grateful for the strength the bathroom floor gave me.
Grateful for the chance to begin again.

The deeper the pain, the more fiercely we cherish life.
We stop taking it for granted.
We stop waiting for "someday" and start living in the now.

Because we never know what tomorrow will bring.
The greater the struggle, the deeper the growth.
And I truly believe I'm alive for a reason.

Deep down, I have a feeling…
The best is yet to come.

My wings?
They're no longer broken.
They're ready to fly.
And I…
I am ready to soar.

This is my story.
I am resilient.
I am a survivor.
And my voice?
Will never be silenced again.

Acknowledgments

To my husband, Kris. Thank you for being my rock, my safe place, and my most trusted sounding board and editor. Your unwavering support, love, and belief in me gave me the courage to bring this story to life. I couldn't have done it without you.

To my mom. My angel. Because of you, I'm still here to write this story. Your strength, love, and quiet bravery carried me through more than you'll ever know. This book holds pieces of both of us.

To Casey Lanxon-Whitford. My talented photographer, for capturing the heart of my vision and beautifully designing the cover that brought my story to life in every way.

To every survivor who picks up this book. This story may be mine, but it's written for you. For the ones still in the fight, for the ones learning to speak, and for the ones who've stayed silent for far too long. You are seen, you are strong, and you are never alone.

And to everyone who has walked beside me, believed in me, or shared even a small part of my story, thank you. This book is for you.

Resources & Support

Canada
Talk Suicide Canada
1-833-456-4566 (24/7)
www.talksuicide.ca
Text support: 4 p.m. – 12 a.m. EST

Kids Help Phone (All Ages)
1-800-668-6868 | Text: CONNECT to 686868
www.kidshelpphone.ca

National Eating Disorder Information Centre (NEDIC)
1-866-633-4220
www.nedic.ca

United States
National Suicide & Crisis Lifeline
Call or Text: 988 (24/7)
www.988lifeline.org

RAINN (Rape, Abuse & Incest National Network)
1-800-656-4673
www.rainn.org

NEDA (National Eating Disorders Association)
1-800-931-2237 | Text: NEDA to 741741
www.nationaleatingdisorders.org

The Trevor Project (Support for LGBTQ+ Youth)
1-866-488-7386 | Text: START to 678678
www.thetrevorproject.org

Therapist Directory (Canada & U.S.)
Psychology Today
Find a therapist near you
www.psychologytoday.com

In an Emergency
If you or someone you know is in immediate danger, please call 911 or go to the nearest emergency room.

About the Author

Jody Unrau is a survivor of both an eating disorder and sexual assault. Her voice, once shaped by silence and shame, now speaks with purpose. She is committed to raising awareness, dismantling stigma, and reminding others that recovery is possible.

As a mental health advocate, public speaker, and workshop facilitator, she is deeply devoted to helping others feel seen, supported, and empowered in their healing.

She is also a writer, educator, coach, and certified fitness instructor. Jody spent over a decade working with youth, including those facing trauma, marginalization, and adversity. Her time in alternative education and youth justice shaped her deep understanding of resilience, empathy, and the transformative power of being seen.

Today, she is the founder of Embrace Your Reflection, a heart-led initiative rooted in lived experience, radical self-acceptance, and body-positive healing. With twenty years in recovery from an eating disorder and body dysmorphia, Jody offers more than insight; she offers compassion, connection, and hope. Her work centers on helping others navigate the complexities of recovery, reclaim self-worth, and rewrite the narratives they were once ashamed to speak aloud.

Through Embrace Your Reflection, Jody offers coaching, workshops, and speaking engagements designed to support healing from the inside out.

Reflections Coaching Sessions:

Available in one-on-one and small group formats, these sessions offer a safe, supportive space to explore body image, eating disorder recovery, and self-worth. Grounded in lived experience and delivered with empathy, each session blends mindset work, emotional support, and practical tools. Whether you're early in recovery or learning to reconnect with yourself, these sessions walk with you, not in front or behind, but beside you.

Signature Workshops:

Beyond the Mirror: A Positive Body Image Workshop
This interactive session challenges body dysmorphia and promotes self-acceptance. Through discussion, reflective exercises, and skill-building, participants learn to shift from self-criticism to self-compassion.

Through Our Eyes: An Inside Perspective on Eating Disorders
This workshop provides an unfiltered look into the mindset of someone living with an eating disorder. Through storytelling and education, participants gain insight, empathy, and tools to support themselves or others more meaningfully.

Jody believes that healing begins in truth, grows in community, and takes root in the courage to be seen. Her mission is simple: to help others embrace the reflection they've spent years running from and to remind them they are never alone.

She lives in Canada with her husband, Kris, and their two children, her greatest sources of love and inspiration. When she's not writing or coaching, you'll find her outdoors, teaching spin, or chasing moments of joy with the people who feel like home.

She's a Tale in My Story is Jody's debut memoir. It is a deeply personal journey of healing, identity, and the unrelenting pursuit of self-worth.

In telling the truth she once buried, she didn't just write her story. She stepped into it. She faced the silence, the trauma, and the parts of herself she once feared. Through that reckoning, she began the slow, courageous process of becoming whole again. It didn't happen all at once, and it's still not complete, but it was enough to begin believing that it's possible.

Connect with Jody

🌐 Website: www.embraceyourreflection.com

✉ Email: jody@embraceyourreflection.com

📷 Instagram: @jodyunrau | @embrace.your.reflection

A Note to You

Thank you for walking this journey with me.
For turning the pages.
For pausing to breathe, to cry, to feel.
Your presence made this possible.

This book holds more than memories.
It holds truth, ache, and the quiet strength it takes to stay.
It's a testament to the kind of resilience that isn't always chosen, but blossoms through lived experience. To the courage it takes to face the darkness, and the grace it takes to rise from it.

Healing is not a straight line.
It is messy. Relentless. Tender.
But from my own experience, I can tell you this:
It is possible.

Everyone's journey is different, but I've discovered something through mine.
The person I'm meant to be was waiting on the other side.
Braver. Softer. Wiser.
Beautiful and confident, not because I changed my appearance, but because I'm finally finding love and acceptance in who I am.
The new version of me is rebuilding.
Because I am not broken.
I am becoming whole again.

And every day, I feel freer.

That, in itself, is an incredible feeling.

I won't stop putting in the hard work to heal and love the life I deserve. I am replacing hate with love, and shame with joy.

If even one line reminded you that you are not alone, then this was worth every word.

Thank you for showing up.

For yourself.

For this story.

For the reminder that even when you feel lost, there is always a way back.

A way to be found.

And when you arrive, you won't just survive.

You'll be ready to fly.

Ready to soar.

With love and gratitude,

Jody

Manufactured by Amazon.ca
Acheson, AB